Praise for *The MoneySmart Family System*

"Every parent or parent-to-be should read this book! Steve and Annette Economides have given concrete steps to teach your children financial responsibility and independence, while making it fun as they learn. Adults can learn from this system too. A must-have for every family library shelf."

—Dr. Laura Schlessinger, *New York Times* best-selling author
and host of *The Dr. Laura Program* on SiriusXM

"Kudos, Steve and Annette, for another awesome winner! *The MoneySmart Family System* is the perfect guide for strategies to help raise financially responsible children with skills to successfully deal with the uncertainties of adult life. Sixty percent of today's parents are assisting their financially dependent kids, so this book could not be more timely. It's a must-read and a must-take-action tool."

—Glinda Bridgforth, financial coach for Oprah's Debt Diet and
best selling author of *Girl, Get Your Money Straight!*

"Foreign aid to poor countries and overly generous parents produce the same outcomes: initially, thankful responses; then in short order, increasing expectations; and not long after that, an attitude of entitlement. The best way I can think of to break the iron law of entitlement is through financial independence by becoming money smart. There is a saying that we should leave a better country to our children. But it's more important to leave better children to our country. *The MoneySmart Family System* does all of this."

—Dr. Barry Asmus, senior economist, National Center for Policy Analysis

"You've made a great choice! You can't go wrong by following in the footsteps of Steve and Annette as they walk you through a comprehensible, practical, and fail-safe way of getting your kids financially ready to stand on their own. Bottom line—your family's stock value will go way up by reading and applying this life-changing book."

—Dr. Tim and Darcy Kimmel, authors of *Grace Based
Parenting* and *Little House on the Freeway*

"Steve and Annette's tips, ideas, and how-tos are useful no matter what your income level. All kids need to learn to be independent financially and emotionally, and this book encourages you to be counter culture. Their proven methods give you hope that your kids can and will be financially stable adults. Thank you, Steve and Annette, for your insight, discernment, and desire to share such wisdom. We're anxious to get started with our own four kids!"

—Marci and Tim Salmon, retired MLB player for the Los Angeles Angels

"Once again Steve and Annette Economides have done it. They've taken a complicated (and sometimes terrifying) subject and turned it into something that's understandable for everyone. *The MoneySmart Family System* is truly a work of love. It's about family first and finances second. Unlike other books that rehash the common expert views, Steve and Annette's book provides logical, personal, and practical advice. Money dominates many family dynamics today, often with devastating results. If you want your family to have a healthy relationship toward money and personal finances, you'll want to use this book as your guide."

—Gary Foreman, publisher of TheDollarStretcher.com

"Regardless of the state of the economy or our bank account, we simply must be good stewards of our finances. Steve and Annette Economides have given every family in America a jump start toward that end. Read this book. Have your children read it. See your family budget and spending practices and savings account transformed. Our family has benefited from this valuable resource. So will yours!"

—Doug and Beall Phillips, founders of Vision Forum Ministries

"The money-saving power couple has done it again. In their new book, Steve and Annette Economides deliver must-have advice on raising MoneySmart kids. They share their experiences, parent to parent, about what works and what doesn't when trying to teach your children about finances. This book goes far beyond a discussion of chores and allowances. Steve and Annette offer their take on everything from kids' TV watching and video gaming to buying a first car and attending college. Give your kids the tools they need to earn, save, spend, and give their way to success. Start with buying this book."

—Gregory Karp, author of *Living Rich by Spending Smart* and *The 1-2-3 Money Plan*

"*The MoneySmart Family System* is just that—smart. Steve and Annette have been passing on financial principles to their children for years and now you can learn their secrets too. The next generation needs to know how to steward their money, time, and possessions in a way that makes God and their parents smile."

—Howard Dayton, founder of Compass—Finances God's Way
and author of *Your Money Counts*

"Intentional parenting! Two words that best describe this book. Why let the uninvited voices of the world determine how your children view money? This book is a foundational tool that will allow you to speak to the lives of your children in a positive way by enabling them to take control of their finances. This will give them a head start in life by teaching them principles that will stand the test of time regardless of the world's financial challenges."

—Jeff Jones, drummer for Big Daddy Weave and founder of Customstix.com

"This book is both insightful and right on the money! Excellent advice for families with kids of all ages."

— John Rosemond, author of *The Well-Behaved Child*

"Steve and Annette provide insightful and meaningful skills for parents as they instruct their children to not just be money conscious, but develop character that will push them toward success in their future. I look forward to sharing many of these life skills with my girls as they grow up!"

—JJ Heller, singer/songwriter

"Steve and Annette Economides are American parenting heroes! Their latest book, *The MoneySmart Family System*, is magnificent. It is a beacon of hope for families. In it, moms, dads, and educators will discover several proven strategies on how practicing great money habits can transform the lives of people of all ages, regardless of their income or social or ethnic stratum. It's a must-read."

—Sam X Renick, author of *It's a Habit, Sammy Rabbit* and founder of ItsAHabit.com

"For more then twenty years, my wife and I have seen how Steve and Annette Economides's down-to-earth, creative, fun, and brilliantly wise lessons on money have blessed their own family and helped hundreds of other families as well. At last, they've captured all those hard-earned nuggets and put them into a MoneySmart system that can help even the most out-of-balance parents finally know how to raise MoneySmart kids. You will love this book's authenticity, practicality, humor, and "Why didn't I think of that?" reality. Most of all, this book will make you a hero in your kids' eyes—particularly when they grow up being self-supportive, positive, happy adults who aren't afraid of a changing, challenging future. Buying, reading, and applying this book is that rare, incredible investment that can absolutely protect, encourage, and "bless" your child—and you."

—John Trent, PhD, author of the million-selling parenting book
The Blessing and president of StrongFamilies.com

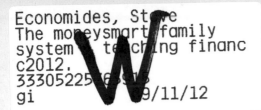

the
MoneySmart
family® system

Teaching Financial Independence to Children of Every Age

Steve and Annette Economides

THOMAS NELSON
Since 1798

NASHVILLE   DALLAS   MEXICO CITY   RIO DE JANEIRO

Published in Nashville, Tennessee, by Thomas Nelson. Thomas Nelson is a trademark of Thomas Nelson, Inc.

Thomas Nelson, Inc., titles may be purchased in bulk for educational, business, fund-raising, or sales promotional use. For information, please e-mail SpecialMarkets@ThomasNelson.com.

Library of Congress Control Number: 2012941594

ISBN 978-1-4002-0284-3

Printed in the United States of America

12 13 14 15 16 QG 6 5 4 3 2 1

We dedicate this book to our courageous kids, John, Becky, Roy, Joe, and Abbey, for being our "test market" and for showing the world that it is possible to raise MoneySmart kids! Your willingness to trust us and to trust yourselves to wait, save, and research has helped you stand as financially independent young adults. You inspire us!

Also, to all of the foster kids who have come in and out of our lives—April, Justin, Stephanie, Anthony, Sammy, Oscar, and many others. You've proven to us that children are truly a blessing and a precious treasure.

Contents

CHAPTER 1

The 5/50/500 Rule

No matter what age your children are, you will always have a financial connection with them. It starts before they are born and will continue after you die. That connection will be defined by how you view and handle money, and how you train your kids to view and handle money. The flow of cash from you to your children may be a trickle or it may be a torrent. The control of the spigot and the power of the flow should be determined by you, but in many cases, unfortunately, the child controls the tap.

This is a book for parents who have money—any amount of money, from a small amount to a small fortune.

This book is about how we, as parents, deal with our money and how we deal with our kids at every age and stage of life.

You will always be your child's parent. Sure, over time the relationship will change. The first change starts when the umbilical cord is cut. But one cord that will never be cut is the cord of money and possessions.

We really love our kids, and we know that most of you feel the same about your own children. The strategies and philosophies we espouse aren't anti-kid—they are pro-parent *and* pro-child. We want to equip parents (grandparents, aunts, uncles, and anyone who might regularly interact with children financially) with tools that will help them empower their children rather than enable them.

We are going to base what we write on a few assumptions:

1. All children and parents can learn.
2. All children and parents can learn to work.
3. All children and parents can learn to save.
4. All children and parents can learn to manage money.
5. All children and parents can learn to spend money responsibly.

What we have written is pro-parent, if you define successful parents as those who desire to raise their children to be independent, self-sufficient, and mature adults who can stand on their own two feet financially.

And what we have written is pro-child, if you define successful children as those who want to be independent and self-sufficient adults, able to stand on their own two feet and look back at their parents with a smile of gratitude for helping them to be autonomous.

Unfortunately, this rosy scene is becoming a rare occurrence as many parents are finding it more and more difficult to cut the cord of cash flow to their aging children. We're going to show you how we've carefully and progressively minimized the transfer of funds and how you can too!

Raising Kids Costs and Costs, and Costs Some More

If you've got kids, the experts say you're going to be spending money—and a lot of it. The "experts" at the USDA in their 2010 report "Expenditures on Children and Families" say that we should expect to spend about $261,000 to raise each child from birth through age seventeen ($14,500 per year). Do you think this is accurate? We don't! In 2009, according to the U.S. Census Bureau, the median annual household income fell to $49,777. Meaning that it could take more than five years and three months of your entire gross household income to get Junior through the formative years and ready for college. And if you have more than one child, the situation is even bleaker. Unless you have some sort of trust fund or rich uncle who has left an inheritance, the money you'll be spending on your kids today is probably the money you should be saving for tomorrow—for your retirement.

The Experts?

Throughout this book we'll refer to experts and their statistics. While we like to use these numbers as points of reference, we are very cautious about basing serious life decisions solely on their conclusions—particularly any survey telling us what it will cost us to raise a child for the first seventeen years of life. Here's why we're skeptical.

When we actually dissect their numbers, we have found that they are based on providing a prescribed number of square feet of living space per person, a certain number of cubic feet in a car, a certain amount of money spent at restaurants each month, and an average cost for clothing, food, and health care expenses. In short, the numbers might be accurate if you lived in a major city, paid retail for everything, never shopped sales or thrift stores, bought all designer clothes, and drove a late-model car.

Just calculate with us for a minute. If you're an average family with 1.8 children (according to USDA figures, this alone should cost you $26,100 per year), living in an average city, spending an average amount on food ($200 per month per person × 12 months = $9,120 per year) with an average yearly household income ($50,000 per year about $40,000 after taxes), you'd be left with $4,700 a year ($392 per month) to spend on cars, clothes, housing, debt, recreation, gifts, utilities, health care, cell phones, cable TV, medical bills, dental bills, and chewing gum. Something simply doesn't add up!

Do you think that the experts are right on the money when it comes to the cost of raising *your* children?

The Best Things in Life?

Most parents want to give their children the best things in life. But the truth is, if you give your children the best (whether you can afford it or not), they'll be very obliging and take it. It's human nature to receive when someone generously provides. And the more you give, the less incentive your kids will have to work and provide for themselves.

Even if you can afford the very best for your children (because you earn a higher income), what will the end result be, especially if your children never achieve your level of earning?

1. Will they shun your lifestyle for one they can afford?
2. Will they work two or three jobs so they can afford your lifestyle?
3. Will they look for alternate ways to get the things you earned?
4. Will they look to you to continue providing for them?

We've got to honestly ask ourselves: Will giving my child the best things in life truly create financial independence?

The questions we're posing aren't the result of mere speculation. They are based on our experience with our own kids, observations of other families, and from our time as volunteer budget coaches. For many years, before we started our writing and speaking career, we met with families to help them sort out their debt and spending. While reviewing their financial habits, we regularly discussed how much money they were giving to or spending on their children. Usually it was money they could ill afford. We often heard reasoning like, "My children shouldn't suffer and do without because I've made bad decisions," or "I need to give my children the same things that my parents gave me." Does this type of thinking actually help kids become financially responsible?

But we've gotten ahead of ourselves. Before we answer these questions, or get too deep into a subject we're obviously passionate about, we should give you a little background on how we became so zealous about parents needing to train their children to manage money.

How We Started

We are Steve and Annette Economides (Econo me dis), and are the parents of five children. Some of you will gasp and ask, "What were you thinking?" while others will say, "Only five?"

We have worked hard to help our kids grow into financially independent adults. We aren't accountants, stockbrokers, or financial gurus. We're just an everyday couple who found some great ways to transfer financial principles to our children.

We were married in May 1982. Eleven months later our first child, John, was born, and two years after that, Becky came along. Roy, Joe, and Abbey followed. In 1985, right before Becky was born, we put 15 percent down on our first home—a bank repo "fixer-upper." We weren't earning a lot of money at that time. Steve was working as a graphic designer and Annette stayed home with our kids. Laboring together, we were able to find plenty of ways to get the things we needed to transform that house into a home.

We were committed to living within our means, which meant that we'd only spend the money we had saved for specific purchases and wouldn't use credit cards. As our income increased, we continued to utilize our personalized budgeting system (detailed in our book *America's Cheapest Family Gets You Right on the Money*), which helped us manage *all* of our expenses and allowed us to pay off that first home in nine years, on an average income of only $35,000.

We looked pretty normal on the outside—a tidy little home with a one-car carport and two cars on the driveway. Steve would leave for work in the morning carrying a briefcase, and the kids would wave from the front window as he drove away. But the inner workings of our home were anything but normal. Because we were committed to living within our means and not using credit, we needed to communicate more with each other, shop differently, research better, and apply more patience than most families our size. Our frugal habits started out of necessity, but eventually turned into a game—a fun challenge where we looked at our lack of funds as a blessing and obtaining deals as the reward.

Some friends started asking us where they could find good deals, and others came to us looking for help in managing their finances. A few years later, in 1990, a man from our church asked us to be trained as personal budget coaches. We learned how to evaluate a family's financial situation, identify areas for improvement, and walk them through a process of paying off debt and right-siding their often upside-down financial condition.

The Pivotal Question

One evening after a coaching session with a couple in our home, our nine-year-old son, John, approached us and said, "When are you going to do financial coaching with me?" We both stood there dumbfounded. We'd never discussed the problems any family was experiencing with him. He'd usually spend his time in another room of the house, reading or playing with toys. We now realized that he'd been listening the whole time—listening and thinking about his own situation. He had seen some of these families go from tears to resolve, and from resolve to joy as they worked to restore their financial lives. He was keenly aware that there were misfortunes and miracles occurring in these families, and they all centered on how they handled money. He knew we cared about these families and that we wanted them to succeed. He wanted us to care about him in the same way.

As John grew from a toddler to a youth, he would help Steve with little projects around the house—building shelves, mowing the lawn, washing the car, and trimming trees (we wanted him to learn to be a working man). We also tried to teach him about money, as some showed up at Christmas and birthdays or when he earned some for doing special chores. We didn't have a plan, because our parents hadn't had a plan that they used with us. We were simply clueless about how to transfer our financial ideals to our children.

When it comes to the topic of preparing children to manage money, most parents don't know where to start. They barely feel competent to manage their own earnings, let alone pass on a "vast storehouse of knowledge" to their progeny. Failing to have financial limits and a plan for transferring financial literacy to their children *will* cause most parents to unwittingly siphon off much more money than they can afford. And in the end, the spending won't stop—especially if they have created financially dependent adults who will come back home to turn their "nest egg" into a "goose egg."

A System Is Born

After John asked us that question, Steve was motivated to find a way to logically and systematically teach our children to manage their own money. There would be several false starts, several books read or listened to, a few failed attempts, and finally the development of a system that we've used since 1995 with all of our children.

What we ended up developing and testing on our own kids is not only a method for teaching them to handle money, but it also teaches them to have a good attitude as they learn to work, earn, plan, budget, research, and spend wisely. As a result of this system (and our involvement), all of our children have accomplished things that most of their peers have never even attempted. Things like paying for their clothes, recreational activities, sports fees, Boy Scout camps, Boys State, 4-H leadership camps, Christmas presents, auto insurance, and cars (with cash).

We won't tell you that they are perfect in their management skills or in their planning and evaluating—neither are we, for that matter. But we *will* tell you that the "trophies" from their triumphs far outnumber the penalties for their problems.

As our children have grown older and left home, our front door has always been open to them to come and visit, but they've never used it as a revolving door—moving in after a financial upset. They've stood on their own two financial feet and have become more and more confident as time went on. We're proud of our children and what they have accomplished, and you can experience the same.

Like any well-honed skill, teaching our children to handle money was something that we learned slowly, made frequent mistakes with, fine-tuned, and eventually felt sure enough about that we began to share it with others.

A Message to the Nation

In 2003, after more than twenty years in the graphics and advertising business and several years of volunteer budget coaching with scores of families, we drew up plans to start our own business. We wanted to communicate in writing the many lessons we learned by living frugally and raising five MoneySmart kids. Steve wrote an article about our kids and money system, and it was published in a statewide journal, with very positive responses.

We started writing a frugal newsletter, which has since been retired (now all of those articles appear as part of a membership at AmericasCheapestFamily .com), and within three months we were interviewed by several local newspapers and even on local TV! One year later a producer from ABC's *Good Morning America* heard about our story, and the following week we found ourselves in New York City being interviewed by Charlie Gibson! Four of our kids were with us (John was working a full-time job and couldn't come), and they were able to tell a national audience about some of the things they had purchased with their own funds by shopping smart. The flood of e-mails and letters overwhelmed us. Our kids validated our lifestyle and proved to the nation that financial training at a young age could produce happy, well-adjusted, money-savvy children. (You can view that interview on our website by clicking the "In the News" tab.)

Since that first appearance on national TV, our children have continued to encourage their friends and millions of families at conventions, in newspapers and magazines, and on TV, radio, and the Internet.

No matter what age, or how many children you have, this book will arm you with information and tools to help you confidently lead them through the money jungle to the lost city of Self-Sufficiency.

Why This Book Is Important

Very few books have been written that *comprehensively* cover the topic of helping children of all ages to be financially independent. And when we say children, we mean your children or grandchildren from the ages of zero to fifty-five!

We can hear the resounding, "What! Fifty-five! You've got to be kidding!" You're right, we should have been more careful in what we wrote. We've seen cases where the financial dependents were well into their sixties, and their parents were still funding a "child's" habitual overspending. We are going to address every stage of life and how you can help your kids (no matter what age) spend their own money instead of your retirement reserve.

We believe that it is best to start teaching children about working, earning, saving, and spending their own money as young as possible. But if your children are older, don't despair, it's *never* too late to start—and we'll tell you how. However, you should be aware that any kind of delay might intensify the power of a menacing money rule we discovered.

What Is the 5/50/500 Money Rule?

Many years ago when Steve worked as a graphic designer, a printing company salesman taught him an important lesson about making type changes during the three-step printing process.

Step 1. Back then, a typesetter would print out text for an ad or brochure on photo paper; a paste-up artist would paste the type and any borders, headlines, and photos on an art board. The work would be proofed by someone else in the office and then sent off to the printer.

Step 2. The printer would put the art board on a reproduction camera and take a picture of it on negative film. That film would be "stripped" or taped to an orange carrier sheet or flat, a blue-line proof (like a blueprint) would be made from the negatives, and then a metal printing plate would be burned.

Step 3. Finally the plate would be put onto the printing press and the actual transfer of ink to paper would begin.

The print salesman told Steve to make sure he proofed the typeset copy very carefully, because catching an error during Step 1 would cost only $5 to fix. But a typo caught in Step 2 would cost $50 to fix, because new film would have to be imaged. The salesman paused, furrowed his brow, and said, "But if you find a mistake once the job is on the press [Step 3], the press will need to be stopped, the pressman will be standing around with nothing to do, the print shop schedule will be delayed, and that will cost you around $500 an hour. So be sure to proof your work."

That was when we discovered the 5/50/500 rule of life. Most of life's lessons have an escalating scale of cost. For instance, a toddler who throws a tantrum may need to be put in time-out for five minutes; a teen throwing a tantrum at school may receive fifty minutes of detention; but a young adult who loses his cool and starts a fight may get a criminal record and five hundred hours of community service. The cost of an unlearned lesson will always escalate with time.

The same is true with teaching kids about money. Unfortunately, the rising cost of funding this unlearned lesson is usually borne solely by the parents.

There are five stages to the 5/50/500 money rule:

The $5 stage: ages 0 to 5

The $50 stage: ages 6 to 11

The $500 stage: ages 12 to 17

The $5,000 stage: ages 18 to 23

The $50,000 stage: age 24 and beyond

In the $5 stage, each of your toddler's "wants" costs you five dollars. Repeatedly footing the bill for his whims reinforces the thinking, *Every time I want a toy, Mommy will buy it for me.* If you don't deal with that attitude now, you will enter the escalating cycle of the 5/50/500 money rule.

Not teaching your children to manage their own money when they're young—at the $5 stage—will ensure that the price tag keeps increasing. Some teens expect their parents to buy them $50 sneakers, pay for their $500 cell phone or portable computer, and replace their totaled cars. And how about the college freshman who calls home looking for a $5,000 credit card bailout, and Mom and Dad pay the bill? Some twenty- or thirty-somethings, boomerang kids, return home expecting their parents to pay for extravagant weddings, graduate school, or divorce-debt rescues. Unfortunately, these stories are becoming increasingly common. That's the $50,000 stage, and that's bad news.

Of course there are times when parents need to be a safety net for their adult children and grandchildren. And we'll talk about that in later chapters.

The good news about knowing the 5/50/500 money rule is that the sooner you start training your children to manage their own money, the smaller the price tag will be, and the sooner they'll proudly be seated upon their own nest egg.

Each chapter in this book tackles a specific area of a child's learning, working, or spending. We will describe what we've done with our kids during the various phases, what you can expect of your children, and what it could cost you if you fail to train them. If you start young, the price tag for failing is relatively small, but the longer you wait, the more expensive it becomes. When we address specifics about the older stages of the 5/50/500 rule—the $5,000 stage (18 to 23) and the $50,000 stage (24 and beyond)—we'll mainly be referring to situations where these adult children are single and living in your home. Once your kids leave home, financial training will usually stop, unless they come to you for advice or for a handout. In Chapter 19 we'll talk about dealing with requests for adult child bailouts.

You are a rare breed of parent. You want to support, love, and help your children. But you know that there is incredible value in the struggles, failures, and trials that life often sends their way. You want to protect them from harm, but you don't want to shield them from growing strong through the experiences that life's "vitamins" bring their way. Let's stand shoulder to shoulder, committed to raising a generation of strong, courageous, principled, and MoneySmart kids!

We created a thirteen-question interactive quiz to help you evaluate whether you're raising financially dependent or financially independent kids. Visit our Facebook Fan page at Facebook.com/AmericasCheapestFamily to take the MoneySmart Family quiz. After you've finished this book and started applying some of its principles, take the quiz again to see how you're doing.

CHAPTER 2

How We Raised Five MoneySmart Kids

When children ask you to teach them a new skill, you know that they are usually ready to learn. As we mentioned in the previous chapter, we were incredibly motivated when our son John asked us to start teaching him to manage money. After he posed that crucial question, we embarked on a journey to discover a way to intentionally transfer the money-management skills we possessed to our kids. We knew it would take some time to find a system that worked. But what we didn't know was that finding a system that taught financial discipline to our kids was of less importance than us being disciplined in administering that system.

In this chapter we'll walk you through how we set up and manage the MoneySmart Kids system we developed to maximize our kids' desire to manage their own money. We'll also share how we've adapted the original system for older kids heading off for college or to live on their own.

Allowances Don't Work

We don't believe in paying a child simply for being part of a family. We've seen too many grown kids who received paychecks from a family business, not because of their diligent efforts, but simply because of their relationship with the owner of the company. The result was overindulged, entitled kids who did little work and created great distraction and frustration for other employees. Entitlement "earnings," whether in a business, a government, or a family, have been proven over and over again to be detrimental to initiative, creativity, and productive labor. Basically, entitlements are a total failure.

An allowance is not a "real world" method for teaching kids to be responsible with money. Unfortunately, this left John with a very inconsistent source of income. The only money he would accumulate was from an occasional special chore he did, items he sold at our garage sales, or gifts from relatives on his birthday and Christmas.

Initially we had John put all of his money in a small piggy bank. But once we actively started searching for a system, we tried a couple of other things: three Styrofoam cups labeled Give, Save, and Spend; and multipart banks—similar to My Giving Bank, the ABC Learning Bank, or the Money Savvy Pig bank. All of these offer young children the ability to segment their money into multiple categories and are a wonderful way to take the first steps toward budgeting. John enjoyed using his My Giving Bank for about two years.

But as John grew older and accumulated more money, the bank became harder to use. It was difficult to get specific amounts of money out of it when we wanted to go shopping, and the bank became increasingly heavy. Plus, it was hard to calculate, on a regular basis, just how much money John had, or keep track of what he had spent on a particular purchase. In spite of a three-part bank's shortcomings, we still believe that it is valuable for teaching younger children basic money-management skills.

A System Discovered

About two years later, in 1995, Steve discovered several more components for our system from the book *Three Steps to a Strong Family* by Richard and Linda Eyre. The Eyres discussed Family Traditions (we had some), Family Laws (we had those also), and a Family Economy (that's what we were missing)!

In the Family Economy, their kids earned points each day for accomplishing four predetermined tasks or objectives. Once parental approval was received, the kids marked their accomplishments on a wooden peg board. Four points each day, six days per week, for a total of twenty-four points. The kids earned a set amount of money for each point based on their age, with a bonus if they reached a specific point threshold. Afterward, they were required to divide their earnings into predetermined budget categories.

Steve created a daily paper "time card," one for each kid to record daily points on. He printed sixteen time cards on a sheet of paper, in a word processing program, and then cut the sheet into smaller rectangles. Our older kids received one small time card each day (Abbey and Joe were too young). Every morning at breakfast, Steve would review the points on each time card and sign off on what they had earned. Since Steve was away from home most days, Annette was often called on to corroborate the points that were earned. The time cards were then put into a little wooden bank with a post-office-box lock on the front, giving the system an air of value and security.

Each Sunday we would pull out all of the small sheets of paper, organize them by day and child, and total the points.

The system was taking shape and the kids loved it, but there were still flaws. With three kids actively participating in the program, it was hard to keep track of eighteen little sheets of paper. Inevitably one of the kids would misplace a time card and we'd all try to either locate it or re-create it. Eventually Steve created a single-page time card for all of the kids to use each week. One large 8½ x 11–inch sheet of colored paper, with one column for each child, was much easier to keep track of. Each column consisted of six days—Monday through Saturday—and within each day there were lines for the daily points. A completed time card is shown in figure 2.1, and a blank time card that you can photocopy is shown in figure 2.2.

We started using the system in 1995 and have fine-tuned and utilized it for our kids from that day on. We'll give you a brief overview of how we ran the system and what we expected of our kids. In subsequent chapters we'll go into much greater detail and provide age-appropriate ideas for each point and each stage of life.

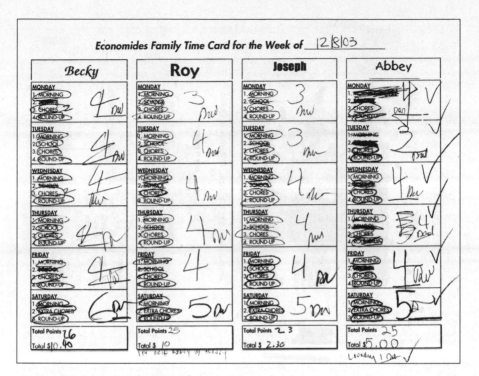

Figure 2.1 Completed MoneySmart Kids time card.

The Points

We now call our system MoneySmart Kids, but since 1995 our kids have just called it "payday." They earn four points each weekday, Monday through Friday, and three points on Saturday. We assigned tasks associated with each point based on behaviors we valued for our kids, but each family can modify the system based on their particular situation and desires.

The kids earn the points when they successfully complete tasks in four categories:

1. Morning point
2. School point
3. Chore point
4. Round-up point

Figure 2.2 Blank MoneySmart Kids time card.

MONEYSMART KIDS™

Family Time Card for the Week of

NAME

MONDAY
1. MORNING
2. SCHOOL _____ POINTS
3. CHORES
4. ROUND-UP _____ OK

TUESDAY
1. MORNING
2. SCHOOL _____ POINTS
3. CHORES
4. ROUND-UP _____ OK

WEDNESDAY
1. MORNING
2. SCHOOL _____ POINTS
3. CHORES
4. ROUND-UP _____ OK

THURSDAY
1. MORNING
2. SCHOOL _____ POINTS
3. CHORES
4. ROUND-UP _____ OK

FRIDAY
1. MORNING
2. SCHOOL _____ POINTS
3. CHORES
4. ROUND-UP _____ OK

SATURDAY
1. MORNING
2. SCHOOL _____ POINTS
3. ROUND-UP _____ OK

TOTAL POINTS:

TOTAL PAY:

NAME

MONDAY
1. MORNING
2. SCHOOL _____ POINTS
3. CHORES
4. ROUND-UP _____ OK

TUESDAY
1. MORNING
2. SCHOOL _____ POINTS
3. CHORES
4. ROUND-UP _____ OK

WEDNESDAY
1. MORNING
2. SCHOOL _____ POINTS
3. CHORES
4. ROUND-UP _____ OK

THURSDAY
1. MORNING
2. SCHOOL _____ POINTS
3. CHORES
4. ROUND-UP _____ OK

FRIDAY
1. MORNING
2. SCHOOL _____ POINTS
3. CHORES
4. ROUND-UP _____ OK

SATURDAY
1. MORNING
2. SCHOOL _____ POINTS
3. ROUND-UP _____ OK

TOTAL POINTS:

TOTAL PAY:

NAME

MONDAY
1. MORNING
2. SCHOOL _____ POINTS
3. CHORES
4. ROUND-UP _____ OK

TUESDAY
1. MORNING
2. SCHOOL _____ POINTS
3. CHORES
4. ROUND-UP _____ OK

WEDNESDAY
1. MORNING
2. SCHOOL _____ POINTS
3. CHORES
4. ROUND-UP _____ OK

THURSDAY
1. MORNING
2. SCHOOL _____ POINTS
3. CHORES
4. ROUND-UP _____ OK

FRIDAY
1. MORNING
2. SCHOOL _____ POINTS
3. CHORES
4. ROUND-UP _____ OK

SATURDAY
1. MORNING
2. SCHOOL _____ POINTS
3. ROUND-UP _____ OK

TOTAL POINTS:

TOTAL PAY:

NAME

MONDAY
1. MORNING
2. SCHOOL _____ POINTS
3. CHORES
4. ROUND-UP _____ OK

TUESDAY
1. MORNING
2. SCHOOL _____ POINTS
3. CHORES
4. ROUND-UP _____ OK

WEDNESDAY
1. MORNING
2. SCHOOL _____ POINTS
3. CHORES
4. ROUND-UP _____ OK

THURSDAY
1. MORNING
2. SCHOOL _____ POINTS
3. CHORES
4. ROUND-UP _____ OK

FRIDAY
1. MORNING
2. SCHOOL _____ POINTS
3. CHORES
4. ROUND-UP _____ OK

SATURDAY
1. MORNING
2. SCHOOL _____ POINTS
3. ROUND-UP _____ OK

TOTAL POINTS:

TOTAL PAY:

Successfully completing all of the required tasks would earn them twenty-three points. Sunday was our family day, so no chores were done and no points were given. We'll briefly describe what each point entails here and then discuss the points in more detail in the following chapters.

Morning Point

With five kids in the house, mornings could become a litany of complaining about what was on the breakfast menu or constant prodding by Mom for them to get dressed and have their beds made. If our kids wanted to earn a morning point, they had to eat breakfast and get ready for the day without complaining or procrastinating.

School Point

We created the school point to encourage our kids to do their schoolwork well, to follow the full instructions they were given from their teachers or us, and to do it on time, all with a good attitude. This point could also be applied to homework or other worthwhile activities that help your child's personal development. If our kids completed all of their assignments with a good attitude, point number two was earned.

Chore Point

Chores are the gateway to a productive life. From a young age (around three years old) each child in our house had some daily age- and ability-appropriate chores. Do your chores well and you've just earned your third point of the day.

Round-Up Point

We live in the state of Arizona, with town names like Tombstone, Boneyard, and Two Guns. We gave the final point a western flair by calling it "round-up." It's the time when kids *and parents* need to round-up all of the things they left out during the day.

Initiative Earns Extra Points

With the establishment of the four daily points (three on Saturday because normally no schoolwork is done), we had successfully tackled several areas of attitude and performance in our home. But we soon discovered that while simply doing what was requested of you was okay, it lacked one small real-world detail—self-initiative.

Cyrus Curtis, the founder of the *Ladies' Home Journal* and the *Saturday Evening Post*, said, "There are two kinds of people who never amount to much: those who cannot do what they're told, and those who can do nothing else."

If an employee sees a need at work and of his own volition steps up to solve a problem or help a team member (while still doing all of his other required tasks), wouldn't that person be rewarded? You bet he would! We wanted to reward initiative and selfless service. So, if our kids saw a job to do or saw a mess to clean up and did it without being asked, they would receive an extra point. If they earned two extra points during the week, in addition to all of their other points, they would earn a bonus—*double pay!* This additional point value definitely cost us more money, but it paid for itself by producing thoughtful, hardworking kids.

How Much to Pay?

Paying kids a fair amount for a job well done is important, but more important is being able to afford to pay them consistently. Pay them too much, and *you'll* go broke and stop training them. Plus, if you overpay for daily chores like taking out the trash, you could cause them to have an inflated view of their worth in the real job market. Pay them too little and you'll kill their incentive to do a job well.

We paid our younger kids (between three and five years old) five cents for every point they earned. They deposited their money into the three-part bank we described earlier. Sometime between the ages of six and eight, when their math and writing skills developed, we increased their pay to ten cents per point and they started using a cash envelope system we'll describe later. Sometime between eleven and thirteen years old, their pay increased to twenty cents per point, but we also required them to take on more financial responsibilities. And once they got their first part-time job, *we* stopped paying them at home and they enjoyed managing their new paycheck.

Basically we start our kids out managing a very small amount of money. As their ability and responsibility increase, so does their pay. Pay what you can afford, but leave room for raises as your child's skills improve.

Funding Your System

Most likely you're already giving your kid spending money and paying for their clothes and recreational activities. If you want to turn this money from an expense into an investment, simply calculate what you've been giving them over the past few months and use that money to fund your payday system. By allowing your kids to learn to manage this money, you'll start to train financially independent children.

If you truly don't have the money for this, then you'll have to be creative. One family we know started a small home-based business making and selling soft pretzels to family friends each week. The kids earned spending money and learned important lessons about running a business. If you need more ideas, read *Minding Your Own Business* by Raymond and Dorothy Moore or *Homemade Business* by Donna Partow.

If you want to know what the MoneySmart Kids system will cost you, review figure 2.3. It shows a breakdown of the points earned, the pay our kids received (by age), and the categories the money is divided into.

Knowing the potential costs is an important part of instituting a payday system. Steve started out paying too much per point and had to back off a little to keep the system sustainable and affordable. Spending between $100 and $500 per year on your kids may seem like a lot of money, but remember that this is a training system that will have a long-term positive impact on their lives and your bank account. Also remember that you probably spend that amount (or more) on them already. You're simply investing in your children's future and virtually guaranteeing a positive return as they grow into financially responsible adults.

Figure 2.3 MoneySmart Kids Costs and Categories					
AGE →	3 to 5 years old	6 to 8 years old	9 to 11 years old	12 to 16 years old	16 years old and older
COST VARIABLE ↓					
Pay earned per point	5 cents	10 cents	15 cents	20 cents	$0 (They get a part-time job.)
Cost at 23 points per week	$1.15	$2.30	$3.45	$4.60	
Cost at 25 points (double pay) per week	$2.50	$5.00	$7.50	$10	
Total cost per year (52 weeks at double pay)	$130	$260	$390	$520	
Type of money container	3-part bank	3-part bank or envelopes	Envelopes	Envelopes	Envelopes or bank account with debit card
Categories	1. Give	1. Give	1. Give	1. Give	1. Give
	2. Save	2. Save	2. Save	2. Save	2. Save
	3. Spend	3. Spend	3. Spend	3. Spend	3. Spend
			4. Clothes	4. Clothes	4. Clothes
				5. Gifts	5. Gifts
				6. Camps	6. Camps
					7. Auto insurance
					8. Sports fees
					9. Save for a car
					10. Save for college

Reality Spending

What do the kids do with their money? Our kids initially divide their money into three categories: Give, Save, and Spend. Then as they get older they add

Clothes, Gifts, Camps, and any number of other categories, including Auto Insurance, Sports, Car, and College.

Initially we set the percentages for each envelope: Give, 10 percent; Save, 20 percent; and Spend, 70 percent. In addition to practical math skills, we're teaching them a basic form of goal setting, delayed gratification, and patience—some of the best tools we can equip them with for adult life.

It's amazing to watch youngsters deny themselves a toy or candy purchase because they're saving for a bicycle or doll. And as they get older and the items on their wish list become more expensive, their confidence and determination increase as well. Our kids have paid for their own radio-controlled planes, iPods, expensive camp tuition, and cars. We provide the coaching, system, and encouragement, and they provide the discipline, patience, and money.

Sometime between the ages of nine and eleven, they're prepared for a larger dose of reality. We increase their pay a little and require them to start purchasing their own clothes. The percentages change to: Give, 10 percent; Save, 20 percent; Clothes, 40 percent; Spend, 30 percent. They keep putting money into Clothes until they've accumulated $100 in that envelope. Once that goal is reached, they can stop making deposits into Clothes until it dips below $100.

We've taught our kids the value of finding quality clothing at reduced prices from thrift and consignment stores. In reality, their "earnings" don't allow them to purchase all that they need by shopping at the mall and paying retail. But they'll tell you that they dress as well or better than their peers and love the great deals they've hunted down during their thrift store safaris (more on this in Chapter 9).

If for some reason (usually a growth spurt) they have unforeseen clothing needs, like underwear or shoes, and they don't have the full amount available, we'll help out. But, honestly, in more than fifteen years with five kids, that situation has only occurred two or three times. The training really does work.

The Envelopes

We started the older kids using paper 6 by 9-inch envelopes that we had lying around the house. We soon discovered that the envelope bottoms couldn't withstand the constant jingling of coins. Holes would develop and the coins would fall out. Eventually we converted to stronger envelopes that are basically indestructible. Inside the larger envelopes we put a couple of smaller bank, cash envelopes (dollar-bill sized)—one for the money and a second for any receipts that might be collected. You can purchase sets of these preprinted envelopes at AmericasCheapestFamily.com.

We printed the columns and rows (a ledger) on the envelopes, and once the printed ledger is filled up, we simply tape a new paper ledger on the opposite side of the envelope and continue using it (see figure 2.4, Abbey's Spend and Clothes envelopes, and figure 2.5, a version you can photocopy and use). Over time they do get a little ratty looking, but the kids decorate them and carry them with pride when they are shopping.

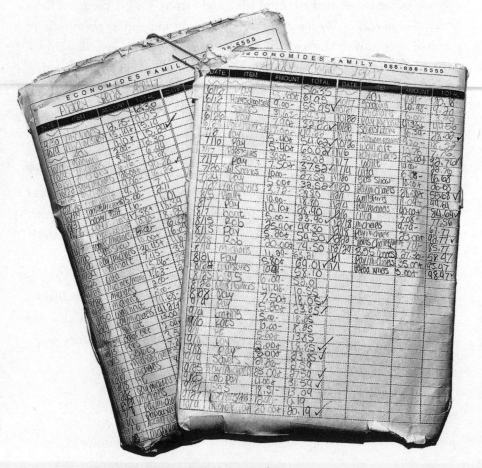

Figure 2.4 Abbey's Spend and Clothes envelopes

MONEYSMART KIDS

NAME _____ PHONE _____

ACCOUNT NAME _____

DATE	ITEM	AMOUNT	TOTAL	DATE	ITEM	AMOUNT	TOTAL

Figure 2.5 Envelope ledger.

It's amazing to watch a cashier's eyes flit from parent to child as a nine-year-old kid comes to the checkout counter to complete a purchase. We usually stand nearby to supervise, and redirect the cashier to our child to complete the transaction.

We have a spot on the top of each envelope for the kids to write their name and we also include our phone number. There have been a couple of times when an envelope full of cash has been left at the store and we've received a phone call. The caller usually says something like, "I think we have a money envelope that belongs to a child and we want to make sure they get their money back." Nothing has ever been taken out of their envelopes!

Accountability

Payday occurred every Sunday night. The kids would pull out their envelopes, Steve would review their time cards for the week, the points would be added up, and pay would be distributed. The kids were responsible for calculating the proper percentages for their envelopes and then would tell us how much money they were putting in each envelope. If we thought that they needed more money in Clothes or some other envelope, adjustments were made. Once the money was distributed and recorded on each envelope, we would check their math and count the money. If the written total and the cash in the envelope balanced, we put a red check next to the total on the envelope.

Accountability is crucial to teaching kids to record every expense, add carefully, and keep their envelopes neat. It's also a good time to praise them for doing an excellent job and talk about their plans for the money they have in each envelope.

Payday for the Young Adult

Somewhere between the ages of sixteen and twenty-three years old, depending on our son's or daughter's financial maturity and plans for their college years, we transition them from the cash envelope system to a checking account and debit card budgeting system that we've used as adults for more than thirty years.

Ready to Go Cashless?

About the time they get their first job you should start talking to them about transitioning to a noncash system. The age you convert from cash to a checking account or debit card and begin using the individual account sheets system will be determined by your child's ability to manage his or her cash. Some kids simply need the physical presence of cash to stay on track. Others can handle the abstract idea that their money is kept in a bank account while being divided into virtual envelopes and tracked on a piece of paper. Spending decisions are based on what they have recorded on their individual account pages.

Our daughter Becky managed the transition well. We deposited all of her various envelopes of cash into a checking account. She had Give, Save, Spend, Gift, Horse (at the time she was saving to buy a four-legged critter), Auto Insurance, and Car Savings envelopes. We created individual account sheets of the same names. Basically, each account sheet is used exactly the same as a cash envelope. Every expense was recorded in her checkbook at the time of purchase. Then once every week or two, she recorded each expense on the proper individual account sheet and put a check mark next to the expense in her checkbook, as an indication that it has been recorded in her budget. When she added all seven of her Individual Account Sheet totals together, it equaled the total in her checkbook. In our first book, *America's Cheapest Family Gets You Right on the Money*, we go into great detail about how to set up and manage this type of budgeting system.

The Payday Payoff

Payday has become an integral part of our family life. Not only does it teach excellent money-handling skills, but it also teaches planning, goal setting, delayed gratification, discipline, and math skills like addition, subtraction, decimals, and percentages. It took us years to perfect the system, and it did cost us some money, but the payoff in the confidence, stability, and maturity that it produced in our kids is so worth the time and expense.

Throughout this book, we are going to share very practical ways that you can impart financial values to your kids in virtually every spending category possible and at every age from birth through their fifties. We'll give you plenty of examples and tell stories of how we triumphed and failed in the pursuit to immunize our family from the 5/50/500 rule. So we ask you, like our son John asked us, when are you going to do financial coaching with your kids? Hurry before the 5/50/500 rule increases the price. There's no time like now!

CHAPTER 3

Morning: First Things First

When we developed our MoneySmart Kids system in 1995, we had five kids ranging in age from eleven months (Abbey) up to twelve years old (John). Annette was usually tired in the morning, and Steve left for work soon after everyone was awake. We realized that we needed a more disciplined morning routine to help the kids be a more productive part of our family team. Plus, we know that kids need to learn that there are certain things that they must do to get their day started right. As we established a predictable morning ritual, we went from having a sluggish start each morning to firing on all cylinders like a well-oiled machine. We call it doing your "first things first."

We made a list of our requirements to earn a morning point and started educating the kids about what we expected. With the morning point in place, there was less arguing about:

- What to wear: "You can't wear shorts and a tank top in the winter!"
- What to eat: "I don't like eggs. Can't we have cold cereal again?"
- What hairstyles were acceptable: the bed-head was not.
- What a properly made bed looked like: bedcovers "sculpted" into a Mount Vesuvius replica was unsatisfactory.

The changes took some time to implement, but eventually gaining points became so motivating that the kids willingly cooperated.

Our four morning point requirements are described below. Later in the chapter, we'll give you more ideas on what you can expect of your kids during various stages.

Getting Up

When you're trying to run an efficient household, get breakfast served, and get kids off to school or other activities, you've got to set a standard. When our kids were between the ages of two and five, they'd usually be jumping in our bed, waking us up. Between the ages of six and eleven, we sometimes needed to wake them up in the morning. Then between the ages of twelve and seventeen, they were encouraged to use their own alarm clock. Of course there is a learning curve, so initially we'd check on them and wake them if they'd overslept or set their clock for the wrong time. Over time, we expected them to become self-sufficient. Once we set a wake-up time, we'd count on their compliance so we could move on to other aspects of the morning point.

Getting Dressed

Some children view getting dressed in the morning as the ultimate expression of who they are, while others view it as a complete interruption of their day. Wanting to streamline our mornings and avoid emotional meltdowns, we instituted a few tactics to minimize wardrobe wars.

On days when we were planning on leaving the house early for a field trip, special event, doctor's appointment, or church, clothes would be selected the night before. Selecting the outfits ahead of time eliminated morning arguments and stress. As the kids grew older, they were given more control over their selections.

Ages 0 to 5: At this stage Annette would pick out the clothes and help the little ones get dressed. By the time they are four or five years old, kids are expected to dress themselves, with occasional help for buttons, zippers, or shoes.

Ages 6 to 11: Annette would pick out two or three outfits and let the kids choose one. As they near the upper register of this phase, they are given more control. Mom or Dad can say, "Pick out two outfits you'd like to wear and bring them to me for approval."

Ages 12 to 17: In this stage parents reserve veto power, but for the most part kids will select their clothes for the day. Communicating the night before about special activities or expectations is an important way to help them think ahead and avoid embarrassing wardrobe choices—or conflicts.

Getting Presentable

Learning to have good hygiene is an important skill and so is paying attention to your bed and your appearance. We wanted our kids to start their day off with getting their bathroom needs taken care of quickly and thoroughly: teeth brushed, face washed, hair brushed, and deodorant on (when they reached that age). And finally, we wanted their bedroom duties finished: pj's put away and bed made. Of course our expectations increased as they grew older.

Ages 0 to 5: Mom or Dad help them through this part of the morning, brushing their teeth and hair and helping them make their bed. They'll also need to be taught how to use the toilet properly. We realized we needed to do a little extra training when we discovered a tiny "lake" on the bathroom floor at the base of the toilet because one of our sons (who shall remain nameless) made a habit of looking around the bathroom while "weeing." Nana came up with a brilliant solution—target practice with a piece of toilet paper floating in the toilet. No more lakes.

Ages 6 to 11: They're pretty much on their own at this stage, but you should monitor that beds are made and teeth and hair are brushed (our sons seemed to have an aversion to hairbrushes).

Ages 12 to 17: During this stage kids tend to be busier and, as a result, more tired in the morning and often slog bleary-eyed through their morning duties. The goal is to get them up and headed toward the breakfast table as quickly as possible.

Eating and Cleaning Up Breakfast

When the kids were young, Annette would prepare a breakfast for everyone to eat together. As the kids got older and they became more capable of feeding themselves, Annette posted a breakfast menu on the door of the refrigerator for reference.

Whether Annette was there or not, the morning point was also based on eating what we prescribed and cleaning up afterward. If you left your bowl or dish on the table, no point; if you complained about what was on the menu, no point. If you helped to clean up someone else's mess or did extra breakfast preparation, we'd award an extra point. Once again our expectations changed as our kids became more capable.

Ages 0 to 5: Mom or Dad prepare breakfast and supervise how much is eaten and to which part of the body, *or the floor*, the food is applied. As they reach the ages of three through five, they participate in carrying safe things to the table: napkins, boxes of cereal, and fruit.

Ages 6 to 11: Kids can help in the preparation of the food: measuring the ingredients for oatmeal or starting the milk or water boiling, helping butter parent-sliced bagels, getting the cold cereal and milk out, setting the table.

Ages 12 to 17: We love this stage for breakfast; they are basically on autopilot, following the menu flawlessly and making breakfast for themselves and anyone else. The major focus at this stage is to supervise the cleanup in an effort to keep the kitchen and dining room neater.

No Complaining

One thing we factored into all of the points was attitude. Doing what you're asked with a good attitude can affect everything from how you greet the day to how you manage your money and how far you advance in your career.

Begin your day right by doing "first things first"—get up, get dressed, and get fed, all with a good attitude—and you're off to a great start. And you'll be one point richer too!

Dealing with Mornings at Different Stages

$5 Stage: Ages 0 to 5

Being involved with your kids and teaching them how you expect them to start their day is critical. Patience and consistency as you teach them to get up, get dressed, and get fed will pay huge dividends later in life.

$50 Stage: Ages 6 to 11

Clear communication with consistent training and accountability in this stage will guarantee that mornings go smoothly.

$500 Stage: Ages 12 to 17

If you're just starting at this stage to train your kids, be patient but firm in the communication of your expectations. Given the appropriate incentive or double pay, teens can exceed your expectations and soar.

$5,000 Stage: Ages 18 to 23

If you have college-aged kids living at home, you can still set a standard for them to adhere to. Read the next stage for more ideas.

$50,000 Stage: Ages 24 and Beyond

With the tendency for boomerang kids to return home after college or later in life, we need to address a few issues, especially when there are younger children in the home. If you choose to allow adult children to live at home, put your expectations in writing. You'll need to think through issues ranging from clothing styles, personal hygiene, and food consumption. Here are a few suggestions.

If there is a vast difference between the requirements you have for your other children and how your adult child dresses, you'll need to work toward an agreeable standard. Consider sharing the book *Dress for Success* by John Malloy to help them discover their own professional and casual dress code. However, if the difference is simply stylistic, you might want to let this issue go.

Poor personal hygiene and unkempt appearances can become offensive to parents and a bad influence to younger children. This type of lifestyle choice is easy to recognize and should be discussed before you allow your adult child to move back home. If he is willing to change, invite him home; if not, encourage him to live elsewhere.

Sharing meals together is an important dynamic of family life. Communicating about which foods are available for their consumption and posting a menu will prevent unexpected shortages. You might also provide a personal storage space for their own snack foods.

We'll address other issues that accompany adult children moving back home in Chapter 19.

CHAPTER 4

School: More Than Book Smart

S mart kids are more likely to make smart money decisions!

Instilling in our children a passion for education is the greatest gift we can give them. Toys will break, clothes will wear out, school days will fade into the past, but people who are willing to learn—to dig, seek, and see life as the consummate classroom—will be able to handle most anything that comes their way.

By high school graduation our kids will have spent more than 13,500 hours in school. That's the equivalent of 6.8 years of working a full-time job! With this amount of time devoted to education, we wanted to help them get the best education for the time they spent in and out of school. Making the school point one of the four daily points in our MoneySmart Kids system allowed us to encourage our kids to not merely endure school but to excel in their academics and to embrace learning—even if it was a struggle.

A Home Dedicated to Learning

As children entered our lives, we wanted to instill the desire to learn, so we read to them from infancy and never stopped. We searched for books with good messages at libraries, garage sales, and thrift stores. When we came across a real gem and couldn't find it discounted, we *did* pay retail, knowing that its value would far outweigh the initial cost.

Reading together is wonderful not only for transferring information, but for the bonding that occurs when parent and child sit next to each other for an extended time sharing a book. Teaching our kids to sit through the reading of a longer story was the precursor to sitting through their longer classes at school. But more than that, it taught them that books contained adventures, answers, and amusement. We determined that our home would become a place of endless education.

For our family, learning started at home at the earliest ages. But when it came to actual school attendance options, we weighed not only the educational value and financial costs but also the unique needs of each child.

School Choices

We live in an awesome time where there are numerous choices for educating our kids. In our area, we have great public schools, excellent private schools, a diverse set of charter schools, the freedom to homeschool, and numerous tutoring options. Finding the right situation, tailored to your child's learning style and your family's finances, is well worth the effort.

Let Your Finances Be Your Guide

Years ago Steve worked for a small advertising agency that eventually went out of business. By all appearances the owner was doing well financially—he drove a Porsche, lived in a nice home, and his kids attended private school and an extremely prestigious dance school. Over time we learned the true state of Keith and Gracie's (not their real names) finances and actually ended up financially coaching them. Amazingly, as we revealed their inability to afford their grand lifestyle, they simply couldn't or wouldn't let go of many of the trappings they loved. Eventually their home was taken from them, the Porsche was returned, but the tuition payments and dance lessons continued, even though their income was inadequate to fund either. They struggle to this day.

Another family we know of found themselves in a similar situation— reduced income and excessive private school tuition costs. But they made a very different choice. They, too, wanted an excellent education for their children. But realizing their income restrictions, they decided to research the public schools in their area, sell their home, and move to one of the best nearby public school districts. The parents volunteered at the school and helped their kids with homework. All of their kids did extremely well and graduated successfully.

Many states allow students to attend the school of their choice through open enrollment programs. This may be a less expensive option than selling your home and moving, but you should also consider drive time and gas prices when weighing this type of decision.

If your budget can't afford an expensive education option, don't teach your kids that debt is the solution. Research the best options you can afford and teach your kids that creativity and commitment provide the best education.

Materialism and Peer Pressure

If you're going to raise MoneySmart kids, you're going to have to prepare them to stand against the affluence or indulgence they'll encounter at school. Even if you don't live in an affluent area, there will always be other kids in your children's life that have the most desirable new "thingamabob," and it will have a costly influence on them—and you. Your kids have to be okay with where they are financially, which means that you've got to be okay with it too. Living in swanky Scottsdale, Arizona, we are well aware that it's not easy to live or go to school amidst affluence. We have taught our kids that all of the outward trappings they see are not necessarily a true indication of the financial health or happiness of their friends. Preparing our kids to be okay with who they are financially can have a huge impact on their future.

Joe wrestled through this issue when he was a college freshman. Between his academic and sports schedule he was only able to work his part-time job for a few hours each week. At baseball practice his coach encouraged the players to get psyched up during warm-ups by listening to their iPods. Joe didn't own an iPod and at that point in time, couldn't afford one. He struggled with not having something that everyone else had, but knew that he needed to be patient until the situation resolved itself. It wasn't easy for him.

Joe's birthday came at the beginning of the spring semester. His older brother gave him a gift card, and Joe used that, along with some other birthday money he received, to purchase an iPod of his own.

Because he had been learning to save and wait from the time he was much younger, Joe was able to endure this trial with patience. When selecting school options for your children, you've got to be aware of the culture that you are immersing them in and prepare them to withstand the peer pressure they will encounter. If you realize that you haven't mastered this important skill as an adult, teach it to your kids as you're learning it.

Children Are Unique

Most schools are set up to educate a large number of students, with similar intelligence levels, in an efficient manner. If you have a child with special gifts or hindering deficits, you may need to think about education differently. Children who are extremely intelligent, hyperactive, have reading disorders, or suffer from learning disabilities may not thrive in a larger school setting. Getting our children into an environment where they can reach their potential and thrive may require extra time, money, and sacrifice on our part.

We didn't learn until Becky was struggling with reading that she had dyslexia; Steve also suffers from a mild form of it. Because of her dyslexia, Becky did not become a proficient reader until she was eleven years old. Once she learned to work with her challenge, reading finally clicked for her and she quickly caught up to her peers. Homeschooling was the right option for her because she learned at her own pace without being labeled. She went to college and graduated magna cum laude. It wasn't easy, but she did it and we cheered for her!

Knowing your child's abilities and "dis-abilities" will help you make better school choices for them (and you). If your children have any type of learning disability or delay and they are in a more traditional school, you've got to be involved and ensure that they get the help they need.

Evaluate Your School Options

Public and Private Schools

Most of you are aware of the public and private schools in your area. Be sure to research them thoroughly before sending your kids there. Be different—be proactive—and get into the school to meet with the administrators and teachers before your kids ever attend. We say "be different" because the majority of parents simply trust that professional educators will instinctively do what is best for their child. Most parents rarely research and interview (in a friendly manner) their child's potential teachers and administrators. We did—and we were told that we were the only ones to ever do it.

According to the U.S. Department of Education, in 2011 there were 49.4 million kids enrolled in public school and 5.9 million children enrolled in private or parochial schools (down from 6.1 million in 2000). Public and private school are the most common education choices today, but as you'll see below, there are other good options if you find that the public school in your area doesn't meet your family's needs or a private school's tuition doesn't fit your family's budget.

Don't think that just because a private school's tuition is expensive that you're guaranteed an excellent education or that all of the families will have your same values. Drug use, behavior problems, and other issues are not solely relegated to the public school domain.

Charter Schools

Charter schools are growing in popularity and as of this writing are permitted in forty states. Their uniqueness lies in the wide variety of educational options they offer and tuition is provided through tax dollars. Some of the schools in our area focus on equine studies, math, the arts, medicine, and technical training. Charter schools have grown to become a formidable education option, growing from 450,000 enrolled students in 2000 to more than 1.4 million in 2010.

If you have a child who doesn't fit into the public school mold, you may find a more customized environment in a charter school. We know several excellent teachers who work in charter schools, and they love the greater freedom they have. As with any educational option, there are good and bad schools, so take time to research the school's history and interview the staff and other parents before enrolling your child.

You can research charter schools in your state here: USCharterSchools.org.

Top-Notch Teachers

How many times have you heard of a teacher who literally changed a troubled child's life? Anne Sullivan, a loving but firm instructor, helped Helen Keller grow into a woman who changed the world. Miss Freida Riley was the tough but dynamic chemistry and physics teacher who inspired Homer Hickam to aim for the stars. She encouraged his rocketry science fair project that eventually allowed him to leave Coalwood, West Virginia, and achieve his dream of working for NASA. Great teachers can lead our kids to places they've only dreamed of and are worth their weight in gold.

Unfortunately, there are also teachers who can have the opposite effect—those who discourage and destroy our child's desire to learn. We are not quick to suggest moving a child because of a supposed personality conflict or disagreement with a teacher. Often, learning to work through these types of issues will help your child grow stronger. But if, after careful research and attempts to rectify a bad situation, you determine that your child is being needlessly discouraged or tormented by a teacher, make a move to get your child into a more positive environment. We view education as a service we're purchasing. If the supplier isn't doing the type of job we expect, we have a right to request a change or to make a move that better meets our family's goals.

When researching any school option, we recommend talking with parents and educators along with making use of RateMyTeachers.com, a site that allows students and parents to write reviews about their experiences with specific teachers from specific schools across the country. There are thousands of public, private, and charter schools listed, with tens of thousands of teachers rated. It's a great resource to use before enrolling each year.

Distance Learning / Online Schools

According to the National Center for Educational Statistics, distance learning is becoming a more widely used option for all types of educational pursuits from grade school to adult education. And a 2009 study showed that public schools expanded their distance learning programs to include more than one million students—a 47 percent increase over 2005.

As our kids have entered their college years, virtually every class they take necessitates some sort of Internet connection—whether it's for getting assignments, turning in assignments, doing homework, or having class online. Distance learning is helping our kids to save time and gas. Many schools provide distance-learning access at no cost to the student, but there are some online schools that charge for access. As with any school option, do your research and get any costs associated with the program in writing.

While this wouldn't be our first choice, we've seen numerous high school friends of ours utilize distance learning or online schools to complete their graduation requirements. If you're dealing with a traveling athlete, aspiring actor, teen pregnancy, an expelled child, or any other unique situation, this may be your best option to help your child finish his or her education. Be aware that there are some pitfalls to online education. It may be harder to interact with the instructor, and some kids simply learn better from a live and visible instructor. Plus there have been problems in some programs with unqualified instructors, high dropout rates, poor administration communication, technology issues, and students cheating on course work. Even in distance learning, parents need to be involved!

Online school shouldn't be the primary learning force in your child's life unless it's absolutely necessary.

Homeschool

We chose to start homeschooling in 1987, when the movement was relatively new, because it fit best with our family's educational philosophy. Please review this section if only to better understand those who do homeschool.

The U.S. Department of Education 2010 survey estimated that there are approximately 1.5 million children currently being homeschooled. This represents a 35 percent increase from 2000 figures. The survey cited three main reasons why parents chose to homeschool:

- Concern about the safety in schools (drugs, sexual harassment, bullying, and peer pressure)
- Desire to provide religious or moral instruction
- Dissatisfaction with the academic instruction available at other schools

We'll add to the preceding list the ability to build a more unified family and flexibility of schedule. We'd like to briefly share some of our thoughts about homeschooling.

Many schools have ratios of twenty-five students (or more) to one teacher. At best, these teachers aim for the average student, bolster underachievers, and hope the brighter students can be challenged. When a parent tutors a child one-on-one, she can tailor curriculum to a student's interests and aptitude. For example, if your son likes weapons, he can study the history of war and learn the engineering and science behind the creation of weapons. You could also incorporate the names of various weapons into spelling and vocabulary lessons. A smaller student-teacher ratio also allows more material to be covered in less time.

We're commonly asked about socialization. Our kids socialize easily with both adults and kids. With Boy Scouts, 4-H, sports teams, church involvement, volunteer work, and family activities, our kids have no lack of social opportunities.

There is a cost to homeschool your kids. Over the years we assembled our own curriculum using a respected program for math, and various reading, writing, science, and history textbooks along with classic literature. Most materials can be purchased used, so our total outlay over twenty-plus years of teaching our five kids didn't exceed $1,000. Don't be fooled, though; you can spend plenty of money on whole grade-level curriculum kits from many well-established companies. We looked at the money spent to educate our children as an investment in their future for college and beyond—and we haven't been disappointed.

To learn more about homeschooling, visit YouCanHomeSchool.org presented by the Home School Legal Defense Association.

The Bottom Line on School Choice

When it comes to educating our kids, there is no room to have a babysitting mentality—merely finding a place that will watch our kids while we work. If we want our kids to truly learn and become productive, self-sufficient adults, we need to determine what we can afford to spend on education and find the best environment with the best instructors, while staying within our budget. And we as parents need to stay involved.

Amy, a first-grade schoolteacher, shared with us her struggle to get parents to support her classroom efforts. She merely asked that they read to their children for thirty minutes each day. Many parents said that they didn't have time. But what Amy heard was, "You're responsible for teaching our kids, don't bother us!"

The kids who do the best have caring parents who make time to be involved in their education. We don't advocate nagging your children or doing their homework for them. But we do encourage you to create a positive and quiet environment where studying and learning can occur and to help them and teach them to organize their time. Because of our involvement in our kids' early education, as they've entered college, they've all allowed us to become their academic advisors and proofreaders. It's awesome to see them succeed in their college-level classes as they use the skills they've learned at home.

Is Paying Them for School Realistic?

We never paid our kids for annual performance at school giving them $50 for getting an A in a class. But because our goal was to encourage our kids to love learning, we decided to award them points in our MoneySmart Kids system for doing their schoolwork well, on time, and with a good attitude. It's more about discipline and attitude than it is performance. Awarding a school point for work that is done well helps them focus on a daily benchmark, which results in yearly progress. And with our kids, it earned them excellent grades through high school, which translated into scholarships and debt-free college educations.

Dealing with School at Different Stages

$5 Stage: Ages 0 to 5

Sitting our kids on our laps and reading several books to them each day was how we started. We'd initially buy sturdy hardboard books so they could enjoy turning the pages without worrying about tearing them. As their vocabulary and attention spans increased, so did the length of books: longer picture books, classic kids' short stories, and some beginner chapter books would complete this stage.

Since kids in this stage are too young to write or do math well, their financial education consisted of merely giving them a few coins each week during payday time and teaching them the names and values. The money would be put into a single-container bank and would be pulled out of the bank if we went to a garage sale or if they wanted to give some money at church.

We've posted reviews of many of our kids' favorites books (for all ages) at AmericasCheapestFamily.com/books.

$50 Stage: Ages 6 to 11

School becomes an important part of children's daily lives between the ages of six and eleven. Finding the best school environment, monitoring their progress, and motivating them to do well are critical. Keep the lines of communication open with their teachers, and if you have time, be a classroom or school aide.

You may need to carve out time from work or other activities to spend more time helping your kids do their best work and understand the areas where they need extra encouragement. Use the school point to encourage them to complete homework assignments or participate in other outside learning activities such as Scouts, 4-H, or music lessons. In addition to the daily school point, we've awarded extra points as we saw our kids working hard on a science or history project or completing a merit badge. We focus more on the effort they put forth than we do on the final grade.

As our kids grew older we used our family dinner hour to read longer books together—it was like a dessert for our minds, and occasionally we'd completely lose track of the time. Reading as a family is a great way to encourage learning habits.

$500 Stage: Ages 12 to 17

By this age, your kids should have established good learning habits. If your child is struggling in school with a subject or two, don't wait—get help. Talk with the teacher or a guidance counselor, get a tutor, change your schedule, or change schools. Time can fly quickly when you're busy and personality conflicts, comprehension issues, learning disabilities, or other problems can swiftly derail your child's education.

This stage of schooling is really all about finding out where your child's passions lie and finding opportunities to try and possibly fail at various activities, in the pursuit of a lifelong calling or career.

All of our kids started taking Advanced Placement classes at a local community college when they were fifteen or sixteen years old. Over time we have discovered some excellent science, communications, humanities, Spanish, English, and math teachers whom our kids have really enjoyed.

We hold a weekly family staff meeting on Sunday nights to discuss all of the activities, transportation needs, chores, and tasks or assignments we're each responsible for during the upcoming week. We include the kids in this meeting, knowing that it will help them learn to plan better and pace themselves as they manage long-term school projects.

By the later years in this phase, most kids want to exhibit their independence. You will shift from the parenting role to that of an advisor.

College Entrance Exams

Our kids have all taken the SAT test while in high school. Pumping up their scores has yielded thousands of dollars in additional scholarships. We've discovered three great free resources to aid in their preparation:

- Number2.com: This site provides practice tests and tips for SAT, ACT, and GRE.
- LearningExpressLibrary.com: We received access through our public library, but you may also get it through your school. They provide more extensive practice tests and study guides for PSAT, SAT, ACT, CLEP, and many others.
- CollegeBoard.com: The people who sponsor the SAT test can provide fee waivers to lower-income families and can also qualify you for waived college application fees. Visit http://professionals .collegeboard.com/testing/waivers/guidelines/sat for details.

Remind your child that good grades in high school and diligent study habits can be worth tens of thousands of dollars in college scholarships and contribute to a much brighter employment future.

$5,000 Stage: Ages 18 to 23

Our role as encourager and advisor to our young adult children continues at this stage. Remember that during the college / trade school years there are many enormous financial decisions being made. If we aren't available to help our children evaluate the costs, long-lasting financial commitments can be made that could destroy them and eventually affect your finances. Read more about how we deal with these decisions in Chapter 18.

$50,000 Stage: Ages 24 and Beyond

If your adult child wants to pursue an advanced degree, or reenter school after divorce or because he or she was laid off, you'll have to carefully evaluate your involvement. Initially, we'd encourage the child to search extensively for scholarship or grant opportunities. If the child has a proven track record of diligent work and careful planning, then you might consider investing in his future—as long as you are financially able, without going into debt. Paying for some of the educational costs or allowing him to move back home while he goes to school could be a great help.

If he has exhibited a less serious attitude about work or school, flitted from one job to another, or is pursuing an advanced degree to avoid getting a real job, let him shoulder the full cost of his pursuits.

If your adult children come to you asking for your input, give it whether or not you choose to invest money. Your role as counselor and encourager—a part of their lifetime advisory board—is a privilege, not to be taken lightly.

CHAPTER 5

Chores: The Gateway to Productive Work

We had a dream of a large house on a big property with room to grow a sizable garden and plenty of fruit trees: a place where our kids could run and play, and where we could impart the habits necessary to help them grow strong, healthy, smart, and independent. We wanted them to learn many things, but one of our highest priorities was to pass on to them the skills necessary to manage a home. We couldn't maintain our property without kids who were willing and able to help. And even though we didn't live on a farm with chickens or cows, a large family with a large property requires constant maintenance—accomplished through constant chores.

When we talk about chores, we mean tasks that go beyond personal care (brushing teeth and washing up) and personal space (their bedrooms)—we're talking about duties that benefit the entire household. No matter the age or ability of your children, there are things they can do, however small, to assist the family. We know that most kids may initially bristle at the idea of chores; however, learning to do productive work with and for people they love will set your children on a path toward stable and successful living.

Who's Doing Chores?

According to a recent *Highlights for Children* magazine survey of 845 kids ages five to twelve, chores were required in 72 percent of homes—conversely, nearly one-third of all kids said that they weren't required to lift a finger at home. But, despite what a complaining teen may say, if you do require your kids to do specific tasks around the house, you are in the majority. Interestingly, the survey showed a wide gap between girls and boys, with 65.3 percent of boys reporting that they did chores as compared to 73.3 percent of girls. Also, a larger percentage of older kids, ages nine to twelve, reported doing chores (74.7 percent) as opposed to 67.3 percent of those ages five to eight.

Unfortunately, the survey didn't define what tasks the kids considered chores, so it could have been anything from making a bed to baking a cake. We define a chore as any age-appropriate household task that benefits the entire household, not only the worker.

The Purpose of Chores

Learning to Manage a Household

While working under your supervision, your kids will learn what it takes to run a household, a critical component of becoming financially independent. Later in life, rather than spending a large portion of their income purchasing services for running and maintaining their homes, they'll be able to use that money for living life, investing, or helping others.

They'll learn from doing chores that they're a part of something bigger—a family, a team. And being part of a larger entity requires each member to contribute time, effort, and sometimes money to support the whole. If we don't teach our kids this critical lesson, they may learn that being a consumer, an observer, or a taker rather than a contributor is acceptable.

While assigning chores to our children is beneficial to their development, it's important to avoid the Cinderella syndrome, where a child is given an unending list of chores, with no time for rest or recreation. If we overwhelm our kids with responsibilities that are beyond their mental and physical abilities, we could discourage or embitter them. If we don't require all members of the family to participate as equally as possible and create a good balance between work and play, we'll breed favoritism and dissention.

When Steve was a kid, his parents introduced the concept of "Kitchen Duty" to their family of four boys. One of the kids was assigned to clean up the kitchen, slogging through a pile of dirty pots and pans each night after dinner for an entire week while the other members of the family went off to do their activities, homework, or relax. It was overwhelming and lonely. We swore that it would not be that way in our home. Washing dishes, like making a bed, is always easier when it is done with someone else. We like the team building and the cross training that working together provides.

Our focus, especially with younger kids, is that chores are a training tool for independence, not indentured servitude.

Learning to Work

We know that the first time we ask our kids to do a task, it will take twice as long as it would for us to do it. Forget about speed, and focus on training your kids to complete the assigned task: *as instructed, in a timely manner, and with a good attitude.* These three concepts are critical to becoming an adult who will become a conscientious homeowner and a valued employee.

Managing Chores

Chore Chart

Assigning daily chores each morning for our kids while trying to coordinate breakfast and lunch preparations and getting kids dressed can be a monumental task for any parent. To help us recall tasks that needed to be done on a regular basis, we created a chore chart. We listed over fifty different chores (these changed with time and the kids' ages). The list included some chores that all of the kids, no matter what age, could complete—like scooping doggie doo in the backyard or picking citrus or helping to stack firewood. Then there were more specialized, age-related chores listed for each child. A customized chore list really streamlines assigning and tracking chores.

Every morning Annette would give each child two or three chores to complete. For younger kids, things like emptying wastebaskets, dragging the laundry basket to the washer, setting the table, unloading part of the dishwasher, or folding rags would be assigned. The older kids performed duties such as changing lightbulbs, sweeping or vacuuming floors, taking out the trash, mowing the lawn, or helping with dinner preparation. Sometimes she would assign a special chore like baking a favorite dessert—that always earned extra points! Figure 5.1 is an example of a chore chart from several years ago, which you can use as a starting point for your own family.

Economides Family Chore List

CHORES FOR EVERYONE
Laundry
Scoop Doggie Doo
Pick Citrus
◄──────── Water Garden / Potted Plants / Front Plots ────────►
Wash / Dry Dishes
Stack Firewood
Clean House

John – 20	Becky – 18	Roy – 13	Joseph – 11	Abbey – 9
Mow Lawn	Dust Curio Cabinet	Spot Carpeting	Spot Carpeting	Spot Carpeting
Spray Weeds	Dust China Cabinet	Set Table	Set Table	Set Table
Inside Pest Control	Dust Mop Floors	Dust Mop Floors	Dust Mop Floors	Dust Mop Floors
Lightbulb Patrol	Brush Dogs	Dishwasher Job	Dishwasher Job	Dishwasher Job
Pick Up PO Box	Iron Shirts	Disinfect Doorknobs	Disinfect Doorknobs	Disinfect Doorknobs
Wash Doormats	Sinks and Toilets	Disinfect Light	Disinfect Light	Disinfect Light
Rake Front Yard	Oil Knife Handles	Switches	Switches	Switches
	Oil Cutting Boards	Clean Fireplace	Wastebaskets	Wastebaskets
	Oil Kitchen Island	Trash Out	Trash Out	Feed Turtles
	Sweep Roof	Clean Pool	Hamster Cages	Hamster Cages
	Feed Dogs	Sweep Roof	Vacuum under Beds	

Figure 5.1 Sample chore chart.

Dealing with Daily Tasks

Some tasks are simply part of family life. Things like helping to carry in items from the car, wiping up a spilled cup of water, sweeping up messes on the floor, washing dishes, or taking out the trash are done as needed, when needed.

Dealing with Monumental Projects

To deal with larger projects, we'll set aside a specific amount of time or an entire day for chores. This usually happens when we're preparing to host a large family gathering or when we've got a lot of yard work to do before our quarterly bulk trash pickup. We'll write up a list of things to be done, and each person will either be assigned specific tasks or volunteer to do certain chores. The kids love putting their name next to a task and then checking it off when it's done. Teens who have part-time jobs don't get paid for helping (it's like a rent deferment), but children still on the MoneySmart Kids system earn loads of extra points.

Inspection and Training

Parents need to *inspect* what they *expect*. The most important thing we learned about the chore point, and all of the other points too, was that we couldn't just assign the task and then forget about it. We needed to follow up, coach, encourage, instruct, and sometimes correct the work that was being done. It took time and effort to inspect what we expected the kids to do. But in the long run, teaching them to do chores, inspecting them, and praising them for a job well done really paid off as they grew older.

Sometimes the realization that a chore wasn't being done properly took time to recognize. For instance, one of our kids was regularly assigned the task of watering a particular garden bed with dill and flowers in it. Early in the spring the plants looked fine, but as the heat of the summer gradually increased, the plants showed definite signs of stress. We needed to teach that child about changing his watering technique as the summer got hotter. We gave him a timer with instructions to water that particular bed for a set amount of time. We would check his work by digging a small hole in the ground to show him how far his water had penetrated the soil. Eventually all of our children learned to do a thorough job, and they were encouraged by us and rewarded with delicious veggies from our garden.

Vacation Pay

If one of our kids went on an overnight visit to a friend's home or to Nana and Grandpa's, the "vacationing" child would be awarded daily points even when away from home. We called it "vacation pay" to simulate a real-world working environment. Daily chores were reassigned to other siblings who were awarded extra points. Important but less frequent chores were either rescheduled or done prior to leaving.

Extra Points

A kid can negotiate for extra points by seeing a job that needs to be done and completing it without being told. Or the child can consult the chore chart and get approval to do an extra chore listed there. For example, vacuuming the car is 3 points, brushing the dogs is 2 points, cleaning up a younger sibling's mess is 2 points. We wanted to encourage our kids to look around, see a need, and do something about it. Remember that we view chores as the training ground for self-sufficiency and independent living. When you are a homeowner you are responsible for determining what chores and repairs need to be done and when. Giving extra points rewards this type of initiative and self-responsibility—and most employers reward it too!

Things That Can Derail the Best Kids

There are three things that can discourage even the best kids when it comes to chores.

Paid Help

Years ago when Steve was working as an advertising account executive and our kids were much younger, we hired a cleaning service to come in and clean the main portion of our home every other week. The companies we had quote on the job were surprised by Annette's request that they not clean the kids' bedrooms.

Even though our kids were younger, they could, with supervision, dust and vacuum their own (shared) bedrooms. They could also take out their wastebasket and change their bedsheets. As the kids got older, the cleaning crew disappeared. We now clean our own house, with the kids' help, in about three hours.

If we had allowed the cleaning crew to do the kids' rooms, they would have learned that someone else would clean up their messes. Even though Mom and Dad could afford to pay for a service, they would assume that this was the type of lifestyle to which they were entitled. It is a disservice to our kids to raise them to expect and enjoy a lifestyle that they may never be able to afford.

Impatience

Believe us, we aren't perfect parents. We get angry, we miscommunicate, and we get impatient from time to time. It's so important when we're training our kids to do new tasks that we exhibit much patience and speak words of encouragement. We know we're going to have to correct, supervise, correct again, and retrain several times before a child finally "gets it." And once she does "get it," we're going to have to keep inspecting and "oohing" and "aahing" over a job well done.

Impatience or perfectionist expectations can quickly derail initiative and cause a kid to simply give up. It may have been a long time since we tried to learn something like sweeping a floor—a simple chore for an adult, but a totally new experience for a youngster. We've got to give our kids time to try, learn, and master each skill. Being patient and giving encouragement to our children as they try will be the very things that keep them working at the skill until they master it. Take it slowly with your kids—expect great things from them, but don't "lose it" when they do a less than perfect job. They, like all of us, are a work in progress.

Lack of Inspection

Inspecting their work is a great time to show appreciation and give fine-tuning tips. We need to focus on what they did right, lavishing positive words to encourage their hearts. Criticism and correction need to be done with gentleness. And we must always inspect their work, because a lack of follow-up will lead to carelessness and forgetfulness, and is extremely demotivating.

Let's Get Cracking with Chores

We started this chapter saying that chores are the gateway to productive work, but in truth, they're really a foundation for self-sufficient living. If we value our kids and want to teach them to be financially independent, then this area will become a priority in our daily schedule. Even the busiest families can carve out ten to fifteen minutes each day for everyone to pitch in and do some chores. We don't feel badly about requiring our kids to do chores. With a well-planned chore system in your home, your kids will learn important life skills, and like us, you'll enjoy watching them get their first job, receive promotions, and eventually launch on a great career path. Training your youngsters to do chores is truly giving them a gift of lifelong, productive work habits.

Dealing with Chores at Different Stages

$5 Stage: Ages 0 to 5

Even the youngest toddlers can be helpful—and the younger you get them started, the sooner they'll be productive, contributing members. Kids between the ages of three and five can help with many tasks. The key would be to have them do the chore with someone who is patient and capable of allowing them to do the job to *their best ability*, not necessarily perfectly. Make a list of things your toddler can do and regularly ask them to help.

Kitchen Chores

❍ Helping to set the table (we used unbreakable plates and cups, knowing that they would be dropped often)
❍ Helping to clear the table after a meal
❍ Helping to dry dishes
❍ Helping to put away groceries
❍ Helping to take care of pets with food, water, and cleaning up "messes"

Meal Preparation
(simpler tasks not requiring a sharp knife or hot stove)

❍ Rolling meatballs
❍ Icing cookies
❍ Husking corn
❍ Washing fruits and veggies

Household Chores

❍ Light cleaning duties like dusting
❍ Picking up toys
❍ Making their bed (four- and five-year-olds) with assistance
❍ Sorting laundry

❍ Matching socks
❍ Folding cloth napkins
❍ Putting away silverware from the dishwasher

Outdoor Chores

❍ Raking
❍ Scooping doggie doo with a kid-sized shovel
❍ Watering the garden or potted plants

$50 Stage: Ages 6 to 11

Capabilities vary greatly during this stage, so it is critical that you monitor your child's ability when you assign new tasks. Provide lots of time to master new tasks and offer loads of encouragement. Abbey was our little organizer, and between six and eleven years old, one of her favorite chores became organizing plastic storage containers in the kitchen "Tupperware" closet. As often as possible, we try to assign chores that fit each child's talents and abilities.

Kids at this stage can do the chores on the previous list plus learn to master these additional skills.

Kitchen Chores

❍ Setting the table (because we wanted more kids involved, we divided table setting into three areas: silverware, cups and napkins, and plates)
❍ Emptying the dishwasher (we divided this into three chores: top rack, bottom rack, and silverware)
❍ Washing, rinsing, or drying dishes—usually one person washes, one rinses, and two or three dry and put away
❍ Putting away groceries
❍ Labeling cereal boxes with month and year purchased
❍ Cutting softer veggies (celery, green pepper, garlic, and potatoes)
❍ Cutting harder veggies (older kids ages nine through eleven), including carrots and broccoli
❍ Measuring and mixing batter or dough
❍ Grinding beef
❍ Dicing cooked chicken, turkey, or ham

Housekeeping Chores

❍ Dusting a room
❍ Vacuuming a room
❍ Cleaning windows with help
❍ Sweeping or dust mopping the floor
❍ Emptying wastebaskets
❍ Taking out the trash or recycling bin
❍ Sorting, washing, folding, and putting away a load of laundry
❍ Ironing some basic clothing items (starting with Dad's polo shirts)
❍ Sewing on a button
❍ Spotting the carpet
❍ Stripping and remaking a bed
❍ Helping with painting walls
❍ Helping with repairing broken household items
❍ Having shared or full responsibility for a small pet (hamster, rabbit, lizard, or bird), depending on ability
❍ Disinfecting doorknobs, light switches, and telephones

Outdoor Chores

❍ Raking the yard (we usually do this with several people). One or two rake and one or two load large bags for the trash or wheelbarrows for the compost pile.
❍ Replacing burned-out lightbulbs
❍ Trimming small tree branches using hand clippers
❍ Pulling weeds
❍ Helping wash the car
❍ Helping in the garden—planting, weeding, watering, and harvesting

Schedules and Activities

We start including older kids in this stage (nine to eleven) in our weekly family staff meeting where they'll write down daily activities, chores, and other tasks to be completed. When we discuss prospective activities, we solicit their input about whether or not we should participate as a family.

It's awesome to watch kids grow and become more capable through this stage of life. Their strengths, abilities, and personal gifts become apparent, and their ability to help and serve others makes them a real blessing to a family.

$500 Stage: Ages 12 to 17

The teen years come quickly when you're raising kids. As they near the upper age range in this stage, we expect our kids to be productive young adults, able to work alongside of us for several hours or an entire day. They also have the ability to cook a complete meal or help plan a large family gathering complete with food and activities. Around the house, older teens are an incredible asset, as they can be relied on to carry out a series of tasks with little accountability. They can rival most adults with their work ethic and ability.

Even though they are completely capable, it is important to encourage and check their work. Once again, giving positive feedback is critical to keeping their motivation level high.

Even when kids are employed outside of the home (while attending school), they should still contribute to the family through weekly chores. Chores are discussed and assigned during weekly family staff meetings, and they are carried out on the assigned day.

Here are some of the things our kids do at this stage. These are basically the same as the $50 stage—ages six to eleven—but they handle more of the responsibility and can add their own flair to the tasks to be done.

Kitchen Chores

❏ Planning and preparing an entire meal—breakfast, lunch, or dinner
❏ Completely cleaning up after working in the kitchen
❏ Baking desserts—unsupervised

Housekeeping Chores

❏ Cleaning windows (inside and out)
❏ Cleaning the bathroom: sinks, toilet, and bathtub or shower
❏ Ironing all their own clothes
❏ Household mending using a sewing machine

❍ Repairing some of their own clothes—sewing seams and hems (yes, even boys can do this)

❍ Ironing all of the clothes in the "To Be Ironed" area (older ages)

❍ Being totally responsible for any pet (dog, cat, turtle, hamster, rabbit, lizard, or bird)

❍ Brushing the dogs

❍ Cleaning ashes from the fireplace

❍ Spraying pest control around the house and patio

Outdoor Chores

❍ Washing the car (unsupervised)

❍ Mowing the lawn

❍ Cleaning the pool

❍ Trimming small tree branches using a hatchet, lopper, or tree saw (with supervision)

❍ Repairing simple plumbing problems

❍ Checking the tire pressure on the family car (unsupervised)

❍ Helping with car repairs

❍ Learning to change a flat tire and check the oil on a car

Supervisory Chores

We anticipate that the training our kids receive as they grow will enable them to lead others. Consequently at this stage we expect that they will be able to guide younger siblings in the completion of a task or series of tasks.

❍ Babysitting and staying on a schedule set by Mom and Dad—a paid chore

❍ Leading one or more siblings to complete yard work

❍ Leading a crew in the cleaning of the kitchen

❍ Leading a crew in cleaning a room or two in the house

Schedules and Activities

At this age teens should be able to set their own schedule for projects at school and around the house. They are a vital part of our weekly family staff meeting, responsible for writing down daily activities, chores, and other tasks they'll need to complete. We love getting their input on activities, and they love taking on some of the planning duties. They're also responsible for telling us of any upcoming purchases they need to make so we can set a time to take them shopping (either online or to the store), eliminating the need for things like last-minute birthday present runs.

The help kids in the $500 stage can offer a family is phenomenal, provided they've received the training from the time they were young. If they haven't, start them now. Do chores with them and they'll quickly get the hang of it.

More than ever, kids in this stage need encouragement and positive feedback. Mistakes and problems will happen as they try to do the chores you assign. Patience and accountability are the key to keeping them going. We have to constantly remind ourselves to focus on the good that they can and have done—and instruct on those things that need improvement.

$5,000 Stage: Ages 18 to 23

Young adults in this stage should be well accomplished at doing all of the previous listed tasks, especially the ones you've modeled and taught. If they're living away from home, at a university or on their own, it's likely that you'll be called on to help them with maintenance issues or repairs on some of their possessions. If they're in college, but living at home and either working a part-time job or involved in sports or other extracurricular activities, their time available for helping around the house will be limited during the school year. We still expect our kids to help even when they're in college. But we try not to overwhelm them with a long list of things to do. We ask them to carve out about twenty minutes each day to help around the house. Clear communication and accountability are the keys to compliance.

Joe was a terrific help the summer after his first year in college. He was working three part-time jobs and still made time to help with several house projects. If you have children in this stage but they aren't cooperating with your requests, get some input from a religious leader or family counselor on how to best deal with the situation.

For adult children who aren't involved in higher education, completing daily chores should be expected. Everyone living at home should participate in keeping the household running.

$50,000 Stage: Ages 24 and Beyond

A child returning home in this stage is likely to have had some failure in life: financial trouble, divorce, job loss, failed education, addiction, or some other trauma. Expecting to come home for a time of security, safety, and healing is understandable. But even the most traumatized patients in a hospital intensive care unit will eventually be moved into recovery and then therapy. Doing some daily tasks that contribute to the well-being of others and feeling useful are critical components to recovery. We aren't psychologists, but we do know that people who feel needed and can be productive will improve.

The only exception to requiring participating in chores would be having a severely mentally or physically handicapped adult child in your care.

If your adult child is recovering from an addiction, besides requiring the child to attend recovery group or therapy sessions, he or she can and should be expected to participate as part of the household team.

CHAPTER 6

Round-Up: A Neat Way to End the Day

Benjamin Franklin must have been a neatnik. Why else would he have said, "A place for everything, everything in its place." While we agree with his thinking, getting there with five kids and two busy parents is no easy task. One night in 1995, after seeing toys and other things left all over the house, we got the kids together and did some math. We calculated that if all seven of us left three things lying around the house "to put away later," by the end of the day there would be twenty-one items to clean up. And if those items didn't get cleaned up each night, by the end of the week there would be 147 things strewn on the floor, chairs, tables, and probably from the ceiling fans too—not a pleasant sight!

This was the genesis of our round-up point. Before the kids get dessert, they hustle through the house and pick up anything they've left out during the day. The older kids were also tasked with helping the younger ones.

The issue of teaching our kids to be organized and orderly is another critical component of helping them to be financially and personally independent. A child who can't put his shoes away will probably find it difficult to file bank statements or consistently reconcile his cash envelopes. Helping our kids to learn the little tasks that keep their stuff neat will eventually translate into all areas of their lives.

What If I'm Not Organized?

We are not the most organized, super neatnik, "put everything away" type people. Steve is a right-brain creative, "make piles and keep working" type person, and Annette is a left-brain analytical worker, with an endless to-do list, her mind always moving to the next project before finishing the last. If we can come up with a system that works for us, you can certainly start and even do better. But you need to start where you are, and start simple. Start with one room or one rule, get the whole family on board, and then move to other areas.

We set some general rules for different rooms of the house:

THE KITCHEN Dirty dishes go in the dishwasher or on the counter to the left of the sink if the dishwasher is full.

THE FAMILY ROOM The TV remote always goes on top of the DVD player. Don't pull out toys and play with them in a doorway or walkway. When we're done playing a game, everyone helps to put it away.

THE DINING ROOM Carry your plate and silverware to the kitchen, help clear the table, and put leftovers away when the meal is over.

BEDROOMS Clothes must be put away in drawers neatly. Shoes have a home, not in the middle of the floor.

Of course, these are only a few of the standards we eventually established for our family, and over time, these simple behaviors became habits. But to make the rules work, you may need to invest in some tools to facilitate your efforts.

The Right Tools

These are a few of the things we did to help our kids be more organized.

CLEAR PLASTIC BINS We bought various-sized bins designed to fit on shelves, under tables, and in closets. We labeled each container so the kids knew what belonged inside. For kids who can't yet read, you could tape a photo or logo on the bin.

DRESSERS At one point we didn't have enough dresser space in the room Abbey shared with Becky, so some of her clothes were neatly folded on a shelf in the kids' bathroom linen closet. With Roy and Joe, we labeled their dresser drawers so they knew what belonged in each one and had weekly dresser inspections on Sunday nights before payday.

CLOSETS When they were younger, we installed double bars in our kids' closets, allowing them to hang shorter clothes on two levels. Steve also built shelves on each of the deep sides of the closets to add to storage space.

SHELVES Steve also built shelves out of oak, old waterbed frames, and used plywood. He's mounted them on walls and over doorways, and made some that stand on the floor. They look nice and maximize storage space.

Having the proper storage spaces and containers, and working with your kids to establish places for their things, will go a long way to bringing order to your home. Plus, your kids will develop a mind-set that everything has a home, and that will help keep track of things as they deal with larger school assignments, expensive sports equipment, and electronic gizmos.

Round-Up Pitfalls and Solutions

Our round-up system is not perfect. For instance, there was that time when a black sweatshirt was left on the family room sofa for a couple of days. No one claimed ownership—until Steve picked it up and recognized it as something he had left out. The kids didn't miss the opportunity to razz Dad. There are simply times that we don't see an item that has been left out. We don't impose fines; we simply deal with it and move on with life.

Team Round-Up

To counteract the "I didn't leave that out" issue, there were times when we instituted what we called "team round-up." The team can tackle a messy room and get it in order in a matter of minutes and as a bonus, build unity.

Zone Round-Up

Another family we know of assigns each person an area or zone of the house to keep tidy. Jordan is responsible for keeping the family room neat, Mandy is responsible for the front hall, and so on. This concept works if the rest of the family cooperates, but can be a real trial if people simply dump things into another's area. It's a good idea to rotate zones to keep things fair and provide cross training.

Round-Up Exceptions

The best rules always have exceptions and round-up is no exception. After a few months of implementing our system we discovered that there were some legitimate reasons to let the kids (and us) leave some things out, because some projects may take more time to complete. We modified our nightly round-up to occasionally allow some exclusions.

FORTS On rainy days we let our kids convert our living room into a massive fort built with the couches, extra cushions, blankets, clothespins, and a few other household items. They would work and play in the forts for hours and even coax us to join them "inside" for a story or picnic.

BUILDING We encouraged our kids to assemble collections of their favorite types of toys rather than having lots of different kinds of toys to play with. As a result, they had large collections of Duplos, Legos, K'NEX, trading cards, and army men. There were times when two or three of them would work together to construct a large building, tower, city, or landscape.

PROJECTS For about a year we had a four-story, wooden dollhouse on a card table in our family room. Steve and Becky bought it at a garage sale and worked for hours together on it. Other projects included paint-by-number kits, State Fair crafts, Abbey's Barbie displays, electric racecar tracks, and train sets. When the projects were finished or sold (in the case of the dollhouse), we took photos for our albums.

Bedtime

We tried to make our bedtime ritual fun, quieting, and consistent. It was a good bonding time; plus, moving away from electronic stimulation (TV or computer) helps to slow down the mind and prepare everyone for sleep. We'd snuggle on the couch and read some stories, even after the kids could read to themselves. Reading, playing a board game, or just talking always preceded getting into bed.

We tied getting ready for bed—putting on pj's, washing face, washing hands, brushing teeth, and going to sleep—with the round-up point. A child who doesn't do his or her full bedtime routine or violates lights-out by reading under the covers forfeits the round-up point.

Monitoring

The round-up portion of our MoneySmart Kids system is no different from the rest of it. To work well, parents must be the driving force behind it. We've got to monitor, correct, recheck, and be an example. There were times when our schedule was so hectic that we simply forgot to inspect their end-of-the-day routine. We couldn't dock their points for our failure to follow up. If you have older, responsible kids, you could involve them in checking the round-up of your younger kids.

Bedroom Battles

Get any two parents of teens together and the conversation will inevitably turn to the toxic condition of one particular bedroom in their home. They'll joke about the odor, the food found under a pile of papers, or needing to don a hazmat suit before entering. But in the back of their minds they're screaming for a magic potion that they can sprinkle unnoticed in the room and instantly their teen will become neat and conscientious.

Unfortunately, we haven't discovered the formula for pixie dust, or for getting a teen to be concerned about dust of any kind. But we have found a few things that worked in our house.

Schedule

A weekly family staff meeting is the perfect time to give your teen notice that the bedroom has gotten out of hand and needs to be cleaned. Providing a few days warning that "this Saturday, you'll have two or three hours to clean your room" is a great way to help your teen mentally prepare. Of course on Saturday, you'll probably have to remind your child.

Time Test

Get your kids to commit to a test for two weeks. The first week they live as they have, leaving messes in their room, but on Saturday they spend as much time as is necessary to completely clean up the room. Record how long it takes to complete the job.

The second week they are responsible for cleaning up their room each night before bed. This effort is also timed and recorded.

Most kids will see that the daily cleaning up takes much less time than a once-a-week disaster zone intervention.

We've discovered with a few of our teens that the reasons behind a messy room are many:

- They're too busy running from one activity to another.
- They'd rather go out with friends or play than take the time to put things away.
- They have too much stuff.
- Their rooms are still decorated in preteen décor and they take no pride in them.
- There is no accountability for keeping it clean.
- Their room doesn't have enough storage space and isn't well organized.

Helping our kids get their rooms organized and then regularly checking on their tidiness has helped minimize the bedroom battles.

If you're having other relational issues with your older kids, it might be better to work on rebuilding the bond and deal with the neatness issue later. We're not advocating giving up, but are encouraging a balanced view, understanding that your kids are much more important than the stuff on the floor.

Lost and Found

Jackets, baseball gloves, books, toys, baby bottles, diapers, Bibles, watches, eyeglasses, sleeping bags, and hundreds of other items filled the tables of the church Lost and Found display that Annette volunteered to set up. Most of the items were worth less than $10, but the cumulative retail total of all the items probably exceeded $2,000. As our kids get older and more autonomous, the prospect of losing items increases.

Even with careful training, we've had our share of lost items, so we continually work on this area, giving grace, of course. We have minimized our losses by practicing the following six habits.

1. Create a Home Base.

Are there certain things that your kids use each day? Items like school backpacks, jackets, water bottles, sunglasses, lunch boxes, iPods, and cell phones? We encourage our kids to create a specific resting spot for these items, a home base. When they leave the house they consolidate their items into a backpack, purse, or bag, reducing the likelihood of setting something down and forgetting it.

2. Do a Verbal Check.

When we're heading out and heading home, we do a verbal check: "I have three things: backpack, water bottle, and lunch box." Our goal is to audibly lock the items in our minds to help us remember everything, eliminating the need for a return trip to retrieve something.

3. Label It.

Our experience with the church Lost and Found taught us that most people don't label their things. We tag water bottles with address labels or masking tape and permanent marker. Tagging schoolbooks and portable electronic items is especially important—they are costly to replace. Using a permanent marker to label the inside of clothes (especially for camps or retreats) increases the chances that they will be returned to you.

4. Turn and Scan.

We taught our kids to turn and scan the area where they have been sitting before they leave. This is particularly useful in libraries, airports, buses, and other areas where recovering lost items can be nearly impossible.

5. Establish a Home Away from Home.

When we go to visit relatives or attend a party, we always pick one spot and put all of our belongings together—a home base. This almost guarantees that everything will make it back home.

6. Pay for Replacements.

Allowing our kids to pay for their own stuff minimizes their forgetfulness. If they do lose something that is not absolutely critical to their survival (schoolbooks and TI83 calculators are about all we can think of; iPods and cell phones don't count), allow them the opportunity to spend their money to replace it, even if it takes a while. Or wait until a special occasion like a birthday or Christmas to provide a replacement.

Taking these tips to heart can help you and your kids minimize the lost and maximize the found.

Round-Up Their Future

We've had scores of media people come through our home. While they don't see a sparsely decorated designer home, they do quickly notice that we have specific ways of doing things and lots of systems to keep our home running efficiently. Helping our kids learn a system for managing their possessions will free their minds and their time so they can spend more time improving their lives and the lives of others.

Because each of our kids has learned to organize their belongings, they have accomplished some incredible things. Each of our sons has organized several Boy Scout outings, events, and Eagle projects, which entailed organizing hundreds of people who donated thousands of hours of volunteer labor. Abbey has what we call a "Mary Poppins" purse—full of things we might need, whether it's a nail file, nail clippers, gum, hair tie, pen, deck of cards, pencil, or other stuff. She has a place for everything and is always prepared.

As our kids have headed to college, we've seen their skills blossom and produce great benefits—often completing projects early, doing extra-credit work, and because they're organized, having the time to tutor others in their classes.

Dealing with Round-Up at Different Stages

$5 Phase: Ages 0 to 5

As soon as they're able, have your toddlers help put away their toys. Make a game out of it. Be sure to have sturdy, safe containers and avoid using a "catch-all" toy bin where toys are just dumped. The more orderly you start, the easier it is for your kids to catch on. By ages four and five, your kids should be able to be given three or four things to successfully put away without supervision.

$50 Phase: Ages 6 to 11

As your kids head out to school, teaching them how to organize their backpack or tote bag is critical. This will require regular monitoring and guidance, but will truly help them succeed in school.

Doing round-up each evening will reinforce the concept of everything having a home and will help mold young minds to be aware of what they pull out each day. It will also minimize the loss of things and the time spent looking for them.

$500 Phase: Ages 12 to 17

Helping your kids to be organized is critical in this stage. They will be buying more expensive items and will be responsible for more complex school and, eventually, work projects. Resist the urge to bail them out if they lose something. If they constantly misplace keys or school items, you'll need to draw a line as to how much time you're willing to invest in searching.

Be sure that you've helped your teens assemble the right organizational tools. This is especially critical as they change their bedrooms from childhood to the young adult years. Investing a little money in bins, shelves, and other organizing décor will help them succeed. Remember that we're training them to live on their own or with a family of their own. Keeping their possessions orderly leads to orderly thinking and better management of their time and money.

$5,000 Phase: Ages 18 to 23

If your kids live at home during this phase, even if it's only during the summer or school breaks, they should respect your standards for household neatness. Remember that encouraging and helping them order their world will help them succeed.

If they want to live at home but won't adhere to your standards, it's helpful as a parent to get some perspective from a trusted friend, family counselor, or spiritual leader. Noncompliance can be an indication of more serious relational issues that should be addressed.

If you have younger children in the home and your standards are not being respected, you may need to ask your young adult to launch out on his own. We had to do this with one of our sons. Later he told us that it really helped him grow up.

$50,000 Phase: Ages 24 and Beyond

With the world economy in distress, your adult child may need or want to move back home. Clear communication of your expectations prior to moving in will help make the situation more workable. Combining two households and lifestyles can be messy. You may decide that an acceptable solution is to keep the common areas of the house neat, while leaving your child's bedroom to his or her discretion. We've reminded our kids as they've grown older that the single life is usually temporary—most people get married and end up sharing a bedroom with their spouse. Helping your child grow in organization skills is a great gift to give their future spouse.

CHAPTER 7

Giving and Sharing: The Blessings of Generosity

Giving to Be Full of Life

Generosity and charitable giving are often the subject of water cooler discussions whenever a lottery jackpot reaches newsworthy proportions. When large sums of money are imagined, many people talk about how generous they will be. The problem is that a lifestyle of generosity doesn't instantly sprout from the ground when riches increase. It is a habit that should be nurtured and practiced from the youngest ages and with the most meager incomes. In this chapter we'll share how we've taught and encouraged our kids to be generous with their time and their money. Being generous isn't merely a financial principle; it is a principal at work in nature and in all of life.

The Dead Sea is a perfect example of what happens when there isn't a natural flow of give-and-take in life. For thousands of years water has poured into this geological phenomenon from the Jordan River and several underground springs. But unlike other bodies of water, the Dead Sea keeps all of the inflow for itself—not one drop of water flows out. Due to its extremely low elevation—1,388 feet below sea level—the only thing that keeps it from continually rising is evaporation. As the water evaporates, its mineral content is left behind. Consequently, the Dead Sea is 8.3 times saltier than the oceans of the world, which means that while people can easily float in the water, fish and aquatic plants cannot survive. There is no life in it—it is truly a dead sea.

A body of water that is always taking in but never giving out does not produce life, and the same is true of people. We must help our children comprehend that the money they earn is not solely intended for their personal use or enjoyment—they have a responsibility to be a conduit of benefit to others. They also need our help in discovering that when they do give, they will receive more in return. We're not necessarily talking about money, but goodwill, love, and the knowledge that they have given someone else hope. By learning to give, they will be teeming with life!

Who's Giving?

According to a recent Harris poll, more than 80 percent of people are giving money or time to charities or nonprofit organizations. But charitable giving is definitely tied to how well the economy is doing. In 2011, during the severe recession, the number of people who said that they were going to stop all charitable giving increased from 6 percent to 12 percent. Do these statistics reflect only adults, or are kids cutting back too? We've read and heard about a growing number of preteens, teens, and young adults who have been inspired to help others in remarkable ways.

Making Change

In 2003, twelve-year-old Zach Hunter learned about the horrors of American slavery in his seventh-grade history class. He also learned that more than 27 million people were being held in a modern-day slave trade, all earnestly desiring freedom. The twelve-year-old decided to do something to help eradicate this plague, so he rallied friends in his school and youth group. Armed with yellow plastic cups, they fanned out across the city to collect spare change from others in the community. In the end, they raised more than $8,500 to help fund the work of abolitionist organizations such as Free the Slaves and International Justice Mission. Zach's efforts have since turned into a worldwide movement called "Loose Change to Loosen Chains," which continues to raise hundreds of thousands of dollars each year. He's also written a book entitled *Be the Change*. Learn more at www.ZachHunter.me. Who says you need to be old to make a difference?

Changing Proms

We were in Nashville, Tennessee, preparing for a TV interview when we heard about Archie's Promise, Claressa Johnson, and her dresses. In 2009, when she was a senior at Middle Tennessee State University, Claressa and several of her sorority sisters decided to collect their unwanted formal gowns and donate them to local high school girls who couldn't afford prom dresses. The initial drive was so successful that they were able to fully outfit about fifty girls. In 2011, when we heard about her story, the project had grown so large that a church donated space to store the gowns, and Claressa, along with fifty volunteers, was able to provide dresses for more than two hundred girls. Claressa told us that she was excited about the number of people she could help each year, but a little overwhelmed at how to manage the growing movement.

These are only two of thousands of examples of young people who are benefiting others while giving themselves a huge lesson in creating a vision, managing people, and running a charitable organization.

Teaching your kids to be generous doesn't need to start out with a huge fund-raising project, but it does need to start, and the earlier you begin, the better.

Generosity Is Important

Training our kids to be generous starts when they first utter that proverbial word *MINE!* If we can consistently help our children see the benefits that come with sharing the simplest things, they will be inoculated against greed and miserly thinking as they grow older.

And with more grade schools and high schools emphasizing volunteerism and more colleges weighing community service for admission and scholarships, teaching our kids to be generous with their time and possessions is more important now than ever before.

Giving Starts with Sharing

With five kids in our home, there were always toys or other things to be wrangled over. We would intercept any angry or distressed outbursts and help to mediate a workable solution. We also facilitated sharing by setting a kitchen timer. Our goal was to encourage our kids to think of their sibling's feelings and needs, not just their own.

Giving Reduces Clutter

Giving money and things away also helps with the curse of "stuff-itus"—that ever-increasing amount of clutter that occurs whenever several people inhabit a home year after year. To combat stuff-itus we hold an annual garage sale where the kids sell many of their unneeded things and afterward donate much of what is unsold to a local thrift store. This is an area that we constantly work on, because accumulating more stuff is as easy as waking up in the morning.

Giving Opens Their Eyes

From the outset of developing our MoneySmart Kids system, we required our kids to put some of their money in the Giving portion of their three-part "My Giving Bank" or their Giving envelope. Once your children have money set aside for charitable giving, they'll discover many opportunities for sharing.

When kids realize that some of their money is going to help others, they will gladly give and their sense of pride and compassion will soar.

How We Helped Our Kids to Give

We've heard of parents who give their children money on Sunday morning to put in the offering plate. While donating money is a commendable thing, when children give what isn't theirs, the joy of giving is usually missed. We've always encouraged our kids to give their own possessions, time, or money to those in need. Below are some things we've done to strengthen their giving power.

Setting a Percentage

Initially we set a specific guideline of 10 percent for charitable giving. Because they saw us or heard us talking about our own giving, there were never any arguments about how much or why they should give, but we did have many discussions about how to best help a family or an organization in need.

Raising Money

Sometimes the best solution has been to use our organizational skills to help raise money, rather than simply giving it. Working with our kids, we've taught them to organize, promote, and host fund-raising garage sales for our Boy Scout troop and drama group. We've also hosted several silent auctions, with the kids helping collect donations, label items, and administrate the auction. They'll never forget the time and effort they put forth. But more importantly, they'll always remember the fun and the success they had as hundreds of people came to the events and hundreds or thousands of dollars were raised.

Giving as a Family

Volunteering as a family is a fun and important way to give to others. Everyone, no matter how young, can play a small part.

WE'VE WORKED. When a single mom we were financially coaching needed help with some projects at her home, Steve took our older kids on the roof to repair her evaporative cooler and Annette and the other kids helped with projects in the house. We've also volunteered for community service projects; helped with church activities including vacation Bible schools, harvest festivals, and cooking for a family camp; and supported the Arizona State University men's gymnastics team (Steve's alma mater) by announcing at the meets and selling T-shirts.

WE'VE HOSTED. When any of our missionary friends are in town, we host a dinner where other supporters can gather. Our whole family helps to prepare, cook, host, and clean up afterward.

Helping Them Choose

There are so many needs all around us and so many good causes to support; how do you help your kids choose? When your kids are young, giving should start close to home: to a sibling, relative, or friend who has a need. Giving a toy, an article of clothing, a kind word, or help with a physical need is going to be the first step. Allowing them to physically interact and communicate with the recipient will help cement in their minds the value of giving much more than mailing off a few dollars to a large organization out of town. Here are three types of situations our kids have decided to give to.

Friends in Need

When our son Roy was sixteen and Joe was fourteen, their scoutmaster, Dave, shared that his nephew had a serious illness and that the family was doing a fund-raiser to help defray some of the medical costs. Roy and Joe decided to give some of their own money to help. At Roy's Eagle Court of Honor, Dave stood up and spoke about many of Roy's leadership qualities, then he shared about his nephew's fund-raiser. He choked back tears, saying that many adults had given, but our boys were the only kids who had. He knew that our sons had earned the money they donated, and that really touched their family. Also consider supporting friends who are raising money for missions, medical research, or relief organizations.

Groups That Touch Your Heart

When Abbey was eleven years old she had very long hair. Her best friend, Lauren, told her about Locks of Love—an organization that takes donated hair and makes wigs for kids suffering from a condition called alopecia areata that causes the total loss of their hair. Abbey fell in love with this group and read the rules on LocksOfLove.org. After several anxious months, her hair was long enough to donate and still leave plenty to be stylish, so we helped her set an appointment at Fantastic Sams (they do Locks of Love haircuts for free). We took pictures before, during, and after the donation, and cheered for her. Her generosity benefited an unknown child with a new head of hair, and encouraged many others too. Abbey still recalls her decision and smiles, and so do we!

Groups That Help Kids

A few great child-oriented organizations that we know of are Toys for Tots, Operation Christmas Child, Compassion International, World Vision, Samaritan's Purse, and the Salvation Army. Your kids will probably have an easier time connecting with the mission of these groups.

While many stellar national and international organizations provide great services, remember your local food banks, homeless shelters, churches, and soup kitchens. They often provide critical relief to people in your city. You might also consider orphanages, adoption and foster-care agencies, crisis pregnancy centers, 4-H clubs, and groups that your children participate in.

Helping your children select opportunities where they can successfully give will bless them and many others.

Rock the World by Giving

Both John and Becky went on short-term mission trips and their view of the world changed forever. John went to Spain with a high school singing group as a sound engineer and learned about planning and communicating in a hustling European metropolis. Becky went to Ecuador and used her drama skills to reach out to groups of people in Quito and children in orphanages.

Another family we know, decided with their daughters, to support a Compassion International child. They sent monthly checks and received updates about their "adopted" daughter. Years later they planned a vacation to meet the child they had grown to love. Lyn, Jim, and their daughters will never forget that experience.

Kids going and serving out of their comfort zone will return with a whole new perspective on what truly matters in life.

Watchdogs

Having a heart to give is good, but if your kids end up giving to a scam or an organization that doesn't have integrity, their money will be wasted. Help your kids research an organization before ever giving any money and check their standing with three watchdog groups:

Better Business Bureau (BBB)

The Wise Giving Alliance on the BBB website (www.bbb.org/charity -reviews/national/) posts evaluations of thousands of charitable organizations. The evaluations consider how the charity is managed and the percentage of donations used for relief efforts, fund-raising, and administration. If the group you're researching isn't listed, contact your local BBB; they'll have information on local charities.

The Evangelical Council for Financial Accountability (ECFA)

This group has stringent reporting requirements for their 1,150 members. Visit EFCA.org for more details.

The American Institute of Philanthropy

This group reviews hundreds of charities and ranks them on the percentage of money spent on administrative costs, tax-deductible standing, independent audits, and more. Visit http://CharityWatch.org/.

Acknowledging Our Kids

When a ministry that our kids love has a fund-raising need, many times we'll all pool our donations together. Whenever we decide to give a group gift, the kids give us their cash and we write a check. We always include a note to the organization letting them know that the gift was from our entire family and include the kids' names, ages, and amount donated. Sometimes we've received a personalized thank-you note that acknowledged our kids individually; that was really awesome.

We've fostered a culture of giving in our family and our kids have embraced it. No, we haven't always done it perfectly, but we are definitely a healthy body of water, taking in resources and sending them out. We don't want to be stagnant, overly salty water like the Dead Sea, and we're really excited to see our kids follow our lead by supporting a cause with their time and money. Teaching gratitude and generosity will always benefit the recipient *and* the giver. No matter how old your children are, start now to lay a foundation of giving.

Dealing with Giving at Different Stages

$5 Stage: Ages 0 to 5

Let them take some of their coins and put them in the offering plate at church or a Salvation Army kettle at Christmas. Talk with them about the groups you support and involve them whenever you can.

$50 Stage: Ages 6 to 11

Talk to your kids about who they could share some of their outgrown clothes or toys with. Encourage them to give their own money to people with a need.

For younger children we love using the three-part "My Giving Bank" because it has a separate compartment for Church/Giving. As your kids master simple math, move them to cash envelopes and encourage them to give at least 10 percent of what they earn.

Look for opportunities where your entire family can volunteer—Boy Scouts, 4-H, a food bank, Toys for Tots, or the Salvation Army.

$500 Stage: Ages 12 to 17

If your kids haven't yet started giving, help them put together a Giving envelope for their cash and put aside 10 percent of their earnings each week. Help them write a list of people and organizations they would like to assist. Aid them in evaluating unneeded toys, books, games, and clothes to be given to an organization or family who could use them.

Encourage them when they find new opportunities to give some of what they earn. If they have enough Giving money, or you want to pool your money together as a family, consider "adopting" a child through Compassion International or World Vision, or regularly supporting a foreign missionary.

Give your time by volunteering together in your community.

$5,000 Stage and $50,000 Stage: Ages 18 to 23 and 24 and Beyond

Be sure as you work with your young adults to set up or maintain a budgeting system that they include an allotment for charitable giving. Giving their money or time to causes that they believe in will help keep them from falling into a lifestyle of self-focused spending and living.

Whenever possible, introduce your young adult / adult children to people who are involved with nonprofit organizations. This can be done by inviting them to your home for dinner or through volunteering as a family.

CHAPTER 8

Saving: Banking on Their Future

Helping our kids think beyond their next meal or game is not an easy task. Neither is the thought of waiting more than a couple of days to be rewarded for hard work. Long-range planning and delayed gratification are not usually strengths of the younger generation (or some members of the older generation, for that matter).

If you want to retire and be able to live at 80 percent of your current spending, many financial experts recommend saving between 6 and 15 percent of your current earnings. But a 2011 report from the Employee Benefit Research Institute revealed that fewer than 50 percent of workers between the ages of twenty-five and sixty-five have more than $25,000 in retirement savings. It's obvious that many of us simply aren't very good at saving for the future. And if *we're* not sticking to a savings plan, how can we convince our kids that they should?

Other surveys show that the majority of kids (about 70 percent) do save some of their earnings. Unfortunately, most surveys don't detail what percentage or what they're saving for. If history is any indication, many youths may save some money, but the habit is quickly extinguished once they hit full-time employment.

Each of our kids is unique; some love to spend freely while others love to watch their savings grow. Because we've given them a tool—the MoneySmart Kids system—they've all learned that they can enjoy their spending money while putting money aside for the future. Even though, at times, they have resisted the idea of using the system, they still reached incredible savings goals. During their younger years they saved for small things like a special doll or baseball glove. As they grew, so did their goals, eventually saving for things like a nice leather jacket, a trip to Walt Disney World, Boy Scout camps, and cars. They've truly learned the rewards of long-range planning and delayed gratification.

If we expect to enjoy our retirement years, we've got to train our kids that saving a fixed portion of their earnings is smart and incredibly rewarding.

How We Taught Our Kids to Save

When kids grow up on a farm, the value of savings is much easier to comprehend than in an urban environment. If a farmer sells or consumes all of the corn that he harvests, the following year he will have nothing to plant and as a result, have no income. The smart farmer knows that some of what he harvests is to feed his family, some is to sell, and some is to be saved for seed. Teaching the concept of holding some of what is harvested (earned) as seed (savings) for the future is something every farmer's child understands.

Unfortunately, most of us aren't farm savvy. But at your dinner table you could use examples from any farm-grown vegetable that has seeds. Explaining that one kernel of corn produced a stalk with several ears and that each ear produced hundreds of kernels, can teach many principles: planning ahead, sowing and reaping, and compounded interest.

Years ago we read the book *The Millionaire Next Door* by Thomas Stanley and William Danko. The book gives great insight into the habits of hardworking, wealthy families. Of the many interesting statistics that the authors shared, one stood out to us: the average millionaire saves 15 to 20 percent of what he or she earns. If it's good enough for them, it's good enough for our kids and us.

Whenever we paid our kids, we had them divide up their money, first to Give (10 percent) and then to Save (20 percent), before depositing any money into Spend (70 percent). This communicated that giving and savings (paying themselves) were more important priorities than buying stuff.

As our kids grew older and wanted to save money for larger goals, we helped them in a number of ways.

A Savings Account

When our kids started earning money and putting it in their three-part bank, we encouraged them to accumulate $25 in savings. Once they reached that milestone, we went to the bank to open their first savings account—a monumental event for a six- or seven-year-old. Then as the quarterly statements arrived, we taught them to reconcile their account. Each one of our kids set a different threshold for when they would deposit cash from their Save category into the bank. For some it was $25; for others it was $50 or $100.

Tracking Their Progress

When John was young he wanted to buy a new bicycle, so Steve made a thermometer chart to track his saving progress (see figure 8.1). His goal was to save $60, and even though it took several months, the chart helped him to stay focused. We posted it in his bedroom, where he could see it every day. As your kids reach some smaller savings goals it will be easier for them to understand the value of longer-term savings for a car, college, a wedding, and eventually a house.

Abbey is a focused saver and always has one or two goals she's working toward. She'll usually create a separate envelope for each goal and track her savings on an envelope ledger or sheet of paper (see figure 8.2). She's purchased an iPod, a discontinued American Girl Doll, entrance to the Magic Kingdom, $100 dance shoes for clogging, and 4-H leadership camp fees. If she faced a specific deadline—like Magic Kingdom tickets—we'd chart out the number of weeks before the purchase and calculate what she needed to save each week.

I'm Saving for_____ By ___/___/___

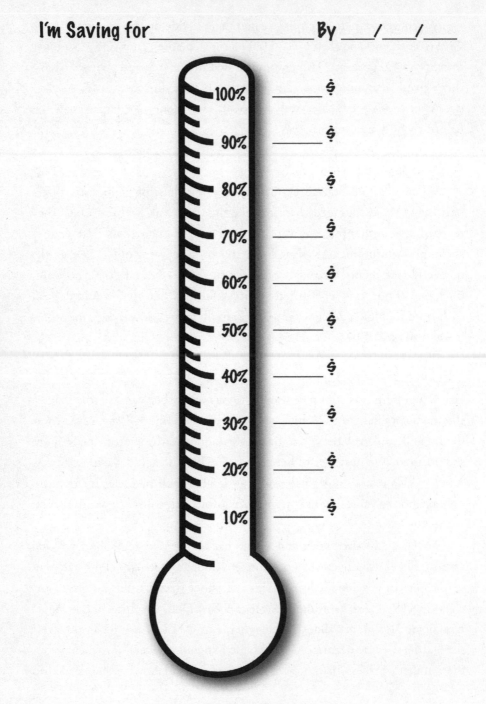

Figure 8.1 Thermometer chart used for John's bike goal.

Goal: *Magic Kingdom Admission*		
Today: *July 7*	Purchase Date: *May 7*	Trip Date: *May 22*
Amount Needed: *$300*	Weeks Until Purchase: *42*	Save Each Week: *$7.50*

Figure 8.2 Abbey's Disney saving envelope.

The Power of Savings

Albert Einstein described compound interest as "the most powerful force in the universe." When a bank compounds interest, it means that your money earns *more money* at a specified interest rate each month. The following month, your larger sum of money (the original amount plus interest earned) earns even more interest. Once our kids grasped the significance, they would eagerly tear open their bank statements to see how much their *money* had earned. Of course a few pennies of interest aren't going to encourage them to become prolific savers, but you could teach them with a hands-on, one-week experiment.

Follow the scenario below and you'll see the compound interest light-bulb go on.

Ten Percent Interest with Pennies

What you'll need:

- A clear plastic jar labeled "My Compound Interest Account"
- A second jar labeled "Bank of Mom and Dad"
- 200 pennies

Day 1

Put 100 pennies next to the "My Compound Interest Account" jar. Start off by asking your children how many pennies they think their 100 pennies could earn in one week if the Bank of Mom and Dad paid 10 percent interest each day; explain that they would earn 10 pennies the first day. Show them the bank jar and let them know that the bank has lots of pennies for them to earn. Most likely they won't have a clue, but write down what they say and stick it in the bank jar. Then have them count 100 pennies and drop them into the compound interest jar.

Day 2

Count the 100 pennies again and show them how to calculate 10 percent using paper or a calculator ($100 \times .10 = 10$). Take 10 pennies out of the bank jar and let your children count and deposit them into their jar. Ask your children how many pennies they now have. The total is 110, or $1.10.

Day 3

Do the same routine as on day 2: count the pennies, calculate 10 percent, transfer 11 cents from the bank to your children's jar, and count up the total, $1.21.

Day 4

Do the same routine. The bank pays 12 cents interest and the total is now $1.33.

Day 5

Do the same routine. The bank pays 13 cents interest and the total is now $1.46.

Day 6

Do the same routine. The bank pays 15 cents interest and the total is now $1.61.

Day 7

Do the same routine. The bank pays 16 cents interest and the total is now $1.77.

At the end of the week pull out the piece of paper with their interest guess on it and review what happened. Write down the numbers from figure 8.3 below as you review each day.

"The first day you only received 10 cents and on the last day the bank paid you 16 cents—that's 60 percent more money!" Count the accumulated total in the children's bank. Then share with them, "The total in your bank is now 177 pennies. That's almost twice as much as what you started with! Your money was working hard all week long earning more money, even while you were sleeping!"

Figure 8.3 Ten Percent Interest with Pennies		
Day	Interest Earned at 10%	Total
1	0	$1
2	10¢	$1.10
3	11¢	$1.21
4	12¢	$1.33
5	13¢	$1.46
6	15¢	$1.61
7	16¢	$1.77

With older kids (in their later teens) you could extend the experiment to thirty days—your total would increase to $15.86. You could also change the scenario by pretending each day is one year. At the start of each year they add one dollar to their total, just like an annual contribution to an IRA. After seven "years" they would have a total of $10.26 in their bank from an investment of $7. If you'd like to try a thirty-day version of this experiment, visit AmericasCheapestFamily.com/teaching-kids-save.

This would also be a great time to discuss the difference between *earning* interest on money invested and *paying interest on borrowed money.*

A website subscriber recommended a picture book entitled *Rock, Brock, and the Savings Shock,* by Sheila Bair, as a helpful tool for teaching kids the value of saving. Rock and Brock's grandfather gives the twins a ten-week summer challenge. Every Saturday he pays them each $1, plus a $1 bonus for each one that they saved from the previous week. It's like a 401(k) with matching! Rock spends like crazy while Brock saves his money. At the end of ten weeks, Brock has $512 and Rock has a bunch of cheap toys.

Our daughter Becky started working part-time at Barnes & Noble bookstore when she was eighteen years old. She was a mighty accumulator and within a few years had saved more than $10,000. When she turned twenty-one she was eligible to participate in their 401(k) program with employer matching. At first she wasn't thrilled with the idea, claiming, "It makes me feel old." She set aside 4 percent of her earnings and allowed her employer to match it dollar for dollar. Within a few months, her savings mushroomed and she started to enjoy feeling "old" as she watched her small deposits grow to well over $1,000—and they're still growing! She loves employer matching and compounded interest!

What to Save For?

As our kids started amassing cash, they asked the inevitable question, "Why am I saving this money?" We told them that they're saving for college, a car, and eventually a house. We reminded them that long journeys are completed one step at a time, and that saving money is the journey of a lifetime. Following our encouragement, their savings steadily grew, and both John and Becky bought cars with cash. Joe saved his money, and when combined with scholarships and grants, funded his college education with a very small amount from us.

Teaching our kids to save when they see no immediate reward is like encouraging them to eat spinach because it will make them strong. We know their forearms won't instantly swell like Popeye's, but good health, like savings, is built one day at a time. Another benefit to the savings process is the struggle they'll experience as they have to prioritize other spending and wait for savings to accumulate. They'll grow stronger and more convinced as they sacrifice today's desires for tomorrow's achievements.

A caterpillar released from its chrysalis through human intervention usually dies. The strain and struggle to free itself from a cocoon is the very activity necessary to vitalize wings and body for a life of flight. Making it too easy for our kids, won't provide them the strength they'll need to fly financially.

Share with your kids the things you've saved for, and help them establish a vision for their future goals. By teaching our kids to live on 70 percent of their earnings from a young age, they've learned that they can reach any savings goal they set. They're like a farmer planting seed, watching it grow, and waiting with great anticipation for the harvest of a greatly multiplied crop.

Dealing with Savings at Different Stages

$5 Stage: Ages 0 to 5

At three years old start using a three-part bank. They can put their money in the Save portion without knowing exactly why it's there; it's simply a discipline they should learn. Once they have $25, help them open a savings account.

Help them set smaller, age-appropriate goals like saving for a special toy such as a Lego model or baby doll that costs between $25 and $50.

$50 Stage: Ages 6 to 11

This is the stage to really help them develop their savings discipline. Once their math and writing skills are adequate, move them to cash envelopes with a ledger on the outside (see figure 2.4 on page 22). Encourage them to save 20 percent of all that they earn. As their savings accumulate at home, take them to the bank to make deposits. Be sure to help them record each deposit and balance their bank statements.

Help them set two or three long-range goals on a sheet of paper and store it in the Save envelope. Determine one goal to immediately pursue, regularly reviewing and tracking their progress with a chart or thermometer to keep them motivated, and plan a celebration when it is reached.

$500 Stage: Ages 12 to 17

This stage is the final preparation for independence. Setting and reaching savings goals should be routine by now. If it's time to go off to summer camp or some other costly activity and they haven't saved enough money, don't provide a bailout. Help them find other creative options, like working for you to earn the difference or doing odd jobs for neighbors and friends. Some extra effort now will go a long way toward helping them see the value of advanced planning and disciplined saving.

When they get their first job, aid them in developing their long-range savings plan for priorities like college or trade school and a car. This is also a great time to start researching career options and colleges. We'll discuss this more in Chapter 18.

$5,000 Stage: Ages 18 to 23

At this stage, young adults may be using their savings for college. Encourage them to continue to budget and manage expenses so they can either totally avoid loans or at least minimize them. If you've trained your children to manage their time well, most can work a part-time job during school and a full-time job during the summer. Once they graduate, help them work through the process of setting up a Roth IRA or, if an employer offers it, a 401(k), 403(b), or 457(b).

If they've accumulated debt, now would be a great time to encourage them to build an emergency fund and then obliterate their debt if they plan on getting married and having a family. (See Chapter 7 in our book *America's Cheapest Family Gets You Right on the Money* for strategies to eliminate debt forever.)

$50,000 Stage: Ages 24 and Beyond

By the age of twenty-four and older, the savings habit should be well established. If your kids are not saving, there will probably be emergencies in their life that cause them to come to you for help. For ideas on how to deal with these eventualities, read Chapter 19.

CHAPTER 9

Clothes Become a Money Tool

When your children are little, you can pick out their clothes and dress them up any way you want. It's a nice arrangement. You make the decision and they wear it—without an argument. You'll even be able to snap some excellent and sometimes embarrassing pictures for use at graduations or weddings. But when our kids get older, it's a completely different story. Clothes can become not only an expression of independence and identity, but also a source of terrible conflicts, consternation, and cost. Whether it's because of style choices (or the lack thereof) or the expense, dealing with your child's clothing decisions can be similar to walking into battle. In this chapter we'll share how we've disarmed the potential land mines and actually turned clothing into an alliance that teaches powerful lessons for financial autonomy.

What's Average?

The 2009 Consumer Expenditure Survey from the Bureau of Labor Statistics says that an average family earning $50,000 annually will spend $1,600 on clothes. For some families that may be a fortune and for others $1,600 may just cover shoe purchases. The same survey revealed that in

1950 the average family spent 10 percent of their earnings on apparel, while today we only spend about 3 percent. In truth, there is no formula for what is normal. With the retail price of gym shoes ranging from $15 to $200 and blue jeans selling for about the same, your expenses will be dictated by your taste and your bank account. But we've trained our kids from their tween years to buy clothes with money *they* have earned. And when they do make purchases, they're buying brand-name, quality clothes for a fraction of the retail price.

How We Started Clothing Our Kids

When our first child was born, our frugal skills were also in their infancy. We were blessed with lots of infant clothes from baby showers, but those were quickly outgrown. We shopped at discount retailers and found some good but not great deals. Later some friends with older kids began to share their hand-me-downs with us. We soon became a conduit for clothes, taking what we needed and passing the surplus to other families with young kids. No sooner would we finish evaluating a black plastic trash bag full of clothes and pass it along than another one would show up. It was unending—and fun. Honestly, we don't know how we would have survived without them. We also discovered that infant and toddler clothes were incredibly abundant and inexpensive at garage and rummage sales. There were many times that we picked up grocery bags full of clothes for a dollar or two.

Procuring clothes for our young kids wasn't as hard as keeping up with their constantly changing sizes. For that, Annette developed a storage system and determined to review all of the kids' clothes two times each year—spring and fall.

A Storage System and Swapping Network

The accumulation of discounted clothing is great, but if you can't find what you have, it's like not having it at all. Having an organized storage method is the key. We store kids' clothes by size in banker boxes in the tops of closets and the garage. Annette numbered the boxes and numbered a corresponding index card with the contents of each box. The index cards are kept in a green card file in a kitchen cabinet. If we needed to find the box with 3T boys' clothes, we'd simply thumb through the cards, find the box number and location, and pull the box. This system is especially helpful if you're planning on handing down clothes from one child to another or if you like to buy clothes well in advance of your child's need.

Before storing the clothes, we evaluate them carefully, eliminating things with stains or elastic (it becomes brittle after years of storage) and clothes that are extremely out of style. The balance of the clothes are cleaned, folded, and stored in a box.

The Fashion Show

Twice each year (spring and fall) Annette took a day or two to go through each of the kids' clothes with them. They would remove the clothes they had outgrown and store them, then they would model the "new" clothes pulled from the next-sized storage box. Annette made a shopping list of necessary clothing to complete their wardrobes. We won't tell you that this process was easy—there were times when one would fall to tears because they'd outgrown a favorite pair of pants, or another, weary of trying on clothes, would start whining—but taking inventory was critical to smart shopping. Another benefit to this biannual review was that drawers and closets were less crowded.

Setting a Clothing Standard

It's a lot of fun to dress up your little cherubs in fancy designer clothes and ooh and aah over how cute they look. If you can afford to spend the money on fancy duds, do it, but please consider the future ramifications. As your child ages, you'll establish expectations and habits. Expectations for the type and amount of clothes you'll provide, and habits of where and how to shop.

Years ago a popular TV talk show featured a couple, Matt and Melody, who were struggling with more than $200,000 of debt, accumulated through careless and indulgent spending. Their two daughters, Valerie (age seventeen) and Gail (age fifteen), had closets stuffed with expensive clothing, purchased by their parents. Valerie had twenty pairs of designer jeans averaging $60 each and twenty-five bras that cost $30 each—total spent: $1,950. Gail had her stash too, including 107 T-shirts at an estimated $20 each—total spent: $2,140. At one point one of the girls grinned slyly and said, "We've got our parents wrapped around our little fingers!" And they did too!

Parents who indulge their young children without considering the long-term consequences may well suffer the same fate as Matt and Melody—children with insatiable expectations, maxed-out credit cards, and the possibility of losing everything.

We aren't saying to dress your children like paupers in burlap sacks, but we are encouraging you to think carefully before you set a standard that will be difficult to sustain.

Clothes Become a Tool

Between the ages of nine and eleven, our kids started purchasing their own clothes from the money they earned each week. By this time they have learned to manage their Give, Save, and Spend envelopes. We increased their pay to 15 cents per point (a maximum of $7.50 per week), and they put 40 percent of their earnings into their Clothes envelope (reducing their Spending money to 30 percent) until they accumulated $100. Once they reached the $100 threshold, they could choose to distribute their clothing allocation elsewhere.

By linking their buying power to *their* income, rather than *ours*, we limited our exposure to the potential overspending experienced by the family we mentioned earlier. Having limits isn't bad; actually it's a good thing and teaches them to plan, save, and dig for great bargains. Unless you've inherited several billion dollars, we're all going to experience financial limits of some sort, so why not let our kids learn how to manage life with limited means in a very practical way, with clothing?

Having limited resources will most likely narrow the types of stores where your kids shop. Becky mentioned in one interview that some of her friends tried to "reform" her by taking her shopping at the mall. She walked with them, but bought nothing as she noted the prices: $40 for a pair of jeans and $20 for a basic blouse. Later her friends raved about a great-looking outfit Becky wore, and she gladly shared with them where she found it and how much she paid. They stood slack jawed at the thought of an entire designer outfit costing less than the price of one retail-priced blouse. They were impressed . . . but not quite reformed.

Initially we chose to train our kids on how to shop at thrift stores. It wasn't hard for the youngest ones, as they grew up seeing us shop there. We taught them to make a list of items they needed; to recognize good-quality clothes; to check the seams; to check for stains and worn spots; and most importantly, to ensure things fit well.

Lining Up Resources

Over time we've discovered a number of clothing stores—we call it our "Shopping Hit List"—within six miles of our home, where we can usually find any clothing item we need on a given day. We've taught our kids which stores are best for different types of clothes: consignment shops for dressier, higher-end clothes; thrift stores for jeans, casual clothes, and costume components—but sometimes you can hit the jackpot on dress clothes there too; discount retailers like Ross and Marshall's for dress clothes; and Walmart for socks and underwear. Having a list of ready resources makes clothes shopping with your kids a breeze. It also keeps you out of the mall, avoiding expensive impulse buys and food court temptations.

For the MoneySmart family, clothing becomes a great tool for teaching children real life lessons.

Getting through the Minefield of Clothing Choices

We shared in Chapter 3 how we trained our kids to choose what they'll wear on a daily basis. At the youngest ages, Mom made all of the choices, but as they grew older they made some of the selections. We called it "shared control," and it really worked. Mom picked three outfits and let the child choose one. Eventually the child pulled out a few choices and discussed them with

Mom. Finally the child made his or her own decisions and only on rare occasions did we intervene.

Making selections of clothes already in the closet is only the edge of the clothing minefield. The next challenge is to train our kids to purchase clothes that are appropriate so there are fewer "blow-ups" at home.

Even though the kids spend their own clothing money, they know that we have final veto power over what they buy. We don't abuse this authority, but wield it when necessary. When we're shopping it comes into play with clothes that might be too revealing for our daughters or T-shirts that might have inappropriate slogans for our sons. Over time they developed a good sense of what is allowable, so we'll laugh together at some unacceptable T-shirts or other items and put them back on the rack.

We shared an article with our kids that compared fishing lures to clothing choices. Experienced fishermen use different bait to catch specific types of fish. Some lures hang near the surface, good for catching fish swimming there, while others troll deeper behind a boat, jiggling and reflecting light to attract attention, and smellier bait is used to catch bottom-feeding fish. The article concluded that just as different bait attracts specific types of fish, girls who dress immodestly might unknowingly be using bait that attracts an undesirable type of guy. We want to help our kids send the right kind of message with their clothes.

If you don't set a standard for what makes an appropriate clothing purchase, you'll be doomed to the daily monitoring of what your kids wear. It's like being assigned to stand permanent guard duty at the front door.

The Color Zone

Shortly after we married, Annette discovered a book called *Color Me Beautiful*, by Carole Jackson. It describes the concept of color draping—knowing which colors enhance your appearance based on skin, hair, and eye color. For kids, buying clothes not in their color palette may mean that the clothes will sit in their closets unworn, which is a waste of money. When your kids know which colors look best on them and buy predominantly those colors, they'll spend their money more carefully, wear more of what they have, and feel better about their choices.

Helping our kids set reasonable dress standards is critical as they reach their later teen years. Of course, as a parent you must model good sense in your own clothing choices. We can't expect our kids to follow a specific standard we won't.

Off-the-Rack Clothing Tales

Because we've been training our kids to manage their own money since 1995, we've accumulated some family stories to illustrate the importance, fun, and value that come with allowing your kids to pay for their own clothes.

Dressing Up for Less

We have no lack of nice clothes for fancy events. All of the guys in our family have purchased used tuxedos and never paid more than $50 (including alterations) for them, and the girls all have drop-dead-gorgeous gowns. Joe was so jazzed about his black tux that he decided he wanted a second "killer suit" that you've got to hear about.

He had just started attending a small, private college where they had two formal banquets each year. He wanted to find a stylish white suit as an alternative to his black tux. Whenever we visited a thrift or consignment store, he always browsed the suit racks. Joe hit pay dirt while searching at a consignment shop for an upcoming TV appearance about inexpensive clothing. He found a classy, retro-styled, white frock coat suit with a vest, and it fit. A frock coat is long and is the predecessor to a cut-away suit with tails. It was marked down 50 percent to $25! Joe looked sharp in his "Mark Twain" suit and loved the price—no alterations needed.

When Becky was in high school she heard about a historic Victorian ball and we decided to go as a family. The attendees were encouraged to dress in period outfits if they had them. We all dressed up, and Becky wore a gown that she had made. After this dance Becky and Abbey started collecting thrift store gowns. Between the two of them they have purchased more than thirty fantastic gowns and are constantly looking for opportunities to wear them. Whenever they find a dressy event to attend, they usually invite a friend or two to borrow a gown and spend several hours prior to the dance primping and preparing. Most of the gowns cost around $20, many less than $10. They truly look like princesses heading to the castle.

Clothing Their Future

Decisions about clothing *can* become a battleground. But if you set an acceptable standard and are consistent in enforcing it, your skirmishes will be minimized. And if you let your kids pay for their own clothes, they'll be more influenced by their budget than by what their peers are wearing. Just as we've seen our kids swell with pride when they've saved and purchased a toy or an electronic gadget, we've also seen them enjoy finding the perfect outfit or addition to their wardrobe. We know that a book is not to be judged by its cover, nor are people by their attire, but our kids have learned that many in our society do classify you based on how you're "packaged." Dressing better will help them go farther, be more successful, and earn more.

Dealing with Clothing at Different Stages

$5 Stage: Ages 0 to 5

You buy the clothes, they wear them—it's that simple. If they want an outfit for a special occasion, you can search at thrift stores and let them pick the one they want to buy.

As your kids reach the older end of this stage, start applying the concept of shared control—Mom selects two outfits and the child chooses one to wear. Shared control is also a great way to help strong-willed children comply with your requests but feel like they still have a choice.

$50 Stage: Ages 6 to 11

Initially parents buy all of their clothes. As they earn more money, you can set a limit on what you'll buy. For example, if our kids need sneakers, we'll tell them that their budget is $25. Anything more than that will need to be paid for from their Spend envelope. When they demonstrate enough maturity, sometime between the ages of nine and eleven, create a Clothing envelope. They get a raise in pay and start buying their own clothes.

Let them know that there are limits to what they can buy or wear and that you have veto power. Setting a well-communicated clothing standard as early as possible will alleviate problems later on. Help your children keep their drawers and closets organized.

$500 Stage: Ages 12 to 17

As your children get older and their desires for more expensive items increase, you'll need to decide how you will be involved in their clothing decisions. Will you bail them out if they've spent all of their clothing money on expensive basketball shoes and need underwear? Continue to communicate your family's clothing standards and gently, but consistently apply your veto power on clothes that exceed your boundaries.

It's a good thing for them to keep a list of wardrobe needs in their Clothing envelope and review it with you every month. Schedule a shopping trip once they have the funds to cover the costs of what they need.

If you're just starting to have your teens purchase their own clothes and they have significant clothing needs, you may need to provide *some* funding to get them started.

Once your child reaches the age of sixteen, encourage them to get a part-time job so they can expand their wardrobe.

$5,000 Stage: Ages 18 to 23

If you've been paying for your child's clothes all through high school, you may need to change this gradually. Calculate a monthly average of what you've spent on your child's clothes. Select an amount to give that is less than what you have been spending. Once your children get a job, they should shoulder the entire cost of their clothes. They also need to be using a cash budgeting system to control their spending if they go away to college.

If they're working, not in college or trade school, they should cover all of their living expenses. If an expensive, unusual circumstance comes up where they need special clothing, such as a wedding, formal dance, or other event, you can help them find the clothes they need from thrift or consignment stores using money they have saved.

$50,000 Stage: Ages 24 and Beyond

There are no reasons why you should be footing the bill for an adult child's clothing unless they are severely physically or mentally challenged, or are going through rehab and have no ability to earn income.

CHAPTER 10

Spending: Living with Limits

Economists call us "consumers," "spenders," and "shoppers," and if we don't train them, our kids will emulate those titles—spending, or encouraging us to spend, *our money*! Marketers flood the media with ads enticing us to buy what they sell. Hopefully, as adults, we've learned to evaluate compelling advertising, only spending money on things that we truly need and can actually afford. But what about our kids? Are they able to withstand the persuasiveness of professional advertisers?

In the early 1980s, marketing to kids was a $100 million industry—that's small potatoes! Marketers quickly learned that targeting "Junior" was extremely profitable because children could not easily distinguish between regular programming and ads. In 1984, the Federal Trade Commission started to rein in extreme or deceptive advertising aimed at children. Even with greater restrictions now, marketers still spend more than $17 billion each year enticing our kids to buy. Kids see the ads; kids talk to their parents; kids convince their parents; kids go to the store with their parents; and the *parents* plunk down the money in ever-increasing amounts.

According to marketing industry experts, children influence their parents' spending to the tune of $400 billion annually. In 2010, there were 74 million kids under the age of eighteen living in 33 million households. If advertising generates $400 billion of child-influenced expenditures annually, then you're spending about $5,400 based on Junior's suggestions and desires ($450 per month). Add to that the estimated $200 billion that kids between the ages of five and twelve spend on their own and you're looking at more than $675 that marketers are hoping to siphon from your wallet each month.

While adults spend more money on cars or groceries each month, marketers see the money controlled by kids as low-hanging fruit, knowing that youths are easily influenced by ads and their friends.

In this chapter we're focused on the Spend envelope and how we teach our kids to evaluate the marketer's message, resist bad influences from their peers, and become wise hunters rather than merely consumers who "consume" whatever is set before them. We'll share the tools we've given our kids and some stories about how well those tools did or didn't work.

Wishing on a Star: How to Deal with the "Gimmes"

In Chapter 2, we briefly mentioned encouraging our kids to write down future purchases they'd like to make. We've always made lists: errand lists, to-do lists, baby-names lists, financial goals lists, Christmas lists—and the *lists* go on and on. But years ago, when we were "dirt poor," we started doing something that has stuck with us. This tool has helped us avoid impulse buys, kept us focused on what we really want, and has given our kids great satisfaction. We call it a "wish list." Nope, it's not rocket science, but it is very effective at keeping our expenses from going to the moon!

Danger in the Toy Store

Something terrible happened years ago, when the kids were much younger, yet we still remember the feeling of alarm as if it were yesterday. What were we thinking? The idea of taking three young kids into Toys "R" Us was utterly and totally ridiculous. Did we really expect that walking down those aisles of colorfully packaged toys—all at a kid's eye level—wouldn't stimulate an enormous, uncontrollable rush of desire in our children? Well, it did. And we had to think—and think fast. The prospects of either having to deal with whining kids for the rest of the week or managing expenses that would exceed the gross national product of Liechtenstein (a tiny country in the Alps near Austria) were equally disturbing. We looked at each other in panic and said, "Let's start a list!"

It was a stroke of brilliance, birthed in a moment of terror. Whenever one of the kids expressed an interest in a particular toy, we simply said, "That's a great idea, honey. Let's put it on your wish list." Amazingly, it seemed to calm their "wanters," and we escaped the toy store with our bank account intact.

Why Lists Work

This strategy worked for a few reasons. First, we didn't say absolutely no to their requests. Second, they had hope. Mom and Dad were taking time to write it down. They realized that we regularly made lists, and that items written on lists were very important. Plus, they remembered that each year we assembled Christmas lists for each of them so that when relatives asked what they should buy for the holiday (or their birthdays), we had an answer. As a result, most of the listed items found their way into their hands either at Christmas or at other times. Last, the strategy worked for *us* because we didn't have to cave in to impulsive choices. By putting the item on the list, we had time to talk with each child about the items and determine if their request was a deep-seated desire or merely a whim. It also gave us time to find the best price, if we decided to buy.

Many financial experts recommend putting expensive items on a list and waiting thirty days before making a purchase. We're always amazed at how many things kids *and adults* express a strong desire for, and then days later, they can't recall why it was so enticing.

Each of our kids maintained a wish list in their Spend envelope. It was especially fun to watch them pull out their lists at garage sales and ask the owners if they had any of the items for sale. Helping kids to write and maintain wish lists will keep them focused on what matters to them, and identify things that really don't. Here's an example of how well it works.

Four Steps to Spending Smart

When Abbey was about nine years old, she expressed a desire to buy an American Girl doll named Samantha. At the time they retailed for more than $120—a vast fortune for a child earning $7.50 each week. Initially we just let the comment go, but she persisted, so we wrote it on her wish list and agreed to help her take her first steps on a journey to smart spending.

1. Planning

Seeing her resolve, we discussed the process for making this kind of purchase. We talked about creating a special envelope where she could put a portion of her Spend money, separating it from the rest to more easily track her progress. On the outside of the envelope we would write the date of each deposit and the total saved. We told her that if she received any birthday, Christmas, or other unexpected money, she could put a larger portion into her Samantha envelope. As we talked, she realized that this goal could take a year to reach—more than 10 percent of her lifetime.

Even though the challenge was great, she had already seen her siblings tackle large purchases and she was ready to do it too!

2. Researching

Once an item is on the wish list, we help our kids research to find the best deal. We started by looking at an American Girl catalog, and Abbey was a little discouraged at the price with shipping. When Steve and Abbey looked on eBay and Craigslist, they discovered that the doll was selling for between $60 and $100, and wrote down several options. The higher prices included more outfits and accessories. Emotionally bolstered, Abbey determined to save $50 to $60 for her purchase.

3. Waiting

Patience is perhaps the hardest part of becoming a MoneySmart kid. Abbey stayed focused on her goal and steadily saved her money for many months. Some weeks it was merely pennies, while other weeks it was several dollars. Remember, she was still putting 20 percent in Saving and 10 percent in Giving. At some point in the waiting and saving process, Abbey realized that she was more than halfway to her goal. She had hope and went from mere resolve to total enthusiasm, deciding to accelerate her savings. We had to remind her that putting money into her regular Spend envelope was still important, but it was now less critical to her.

After about seven months she hit her $50 milestone. Earlier we'd offered to pay the cost of shipping, but now we wanted to reward her diligence, so we told her that we would contribute $10 to be used toward shipping and the purchase price. She now had $60 and was ready to buy her doll!

4. Buying

Once she had her full purchase amount in hand, we started searching in earnest. We put several dolls on our eBay watch list and confirmed that they were still selling for between $60 and $100. Of course many of the dolls sold for more than Abbey's budget. Initially, she was disappointed, but we encouraged her that we would eventually find the right deal. And after a couple of weeks we did.

On February 12, 2004, her bid was submitted in the last 15 seconds of an auction and Abbey won her Samantha doll. There was cheering and laughing and a little squeal too. The long wait was over—well, almost. The final price was $61.03, so she pulled the $1.03 out of her Spend envelope. We paid using our PayPal account and she reimbursed us.

The waiting continued until the UPS truck finally delivered her prize. We celebrated as Abbey finally held Samantha in her arms. The sacrifice and discipline were worth the effort!

Seven months to a nine-year-old is a virtual eternity. But to Abbey this successful expedition was one giant step toward financial maturity. In the ensuing years she's followed the same four steps—Plan, Research, Wait, and Buy—to make many other, more expensive purchases, but none of them rival that first purchase of Samantha, who is now gently and carefully stored in her box, waiting for the day when Abbey will allow *her* daughter to hear the story of how Samantha came into her life.

This same journey has been completed dozens of times by each of our kids. Every successive mission resulted in greater confidence, patience, and expectation. Our kids have saved for and purchased their own trading cards, bicycles, radio-controlled airplanes, stereo systems, special uniforms for Boy Scouts, Police and Air Force Explorers, and scores of other items.

Lessons in Spending

As the kids got older and their wish list items became more expensive, we taught them to write down the pros and cons of a particular purchase. Sometimes this would turn into an essay exploring the possible advantages and disadvantages of a particular purchase. Roy did this once when he was planning on purchasing a K'NEX Screaming Serpent Roller Coaster (retail price $80). He had seen ads for it on TV and in the newspaper. He was convinced that he would love it. We weren't so sure, but after several months of looking, talking, and writing his evaluation, he finally found it on sale for $60 and we acquiesced.

He was in his glory as he paid and hauled home his treasure. He immediately started assembling it in his bedroom. Two days later, the roller coaster, taking up about fifteen square feet of floor space, was complete. Roy inserted the batteries, mounted the car on the rails, and flipped the switch. Much to his delight, the car whizzed around the track flawlessly. It completed one, then two, then three and more trips around the brightly colored supports. It was fun to watch—for a few minutes. Slowly Roy's joy turned into boredom. The desire, research, and construction had been everything he'd dreamed. But now that the project was complete, he was disenchanted.

The roller coaster sat in the room for several weeks, with the car occasionally scooting around the track, but for the most part it gathered dust. Eventually it was dismantled, put back in the box, and taken to the garage to await its fate and Roy's next lesson.

Veto Power

As parents, we reserve the right to veto any purchase we deem detrimental or too distracting. But sometimes we need to let our kids work, save, and spend their money on something we *know* won't satisfy. Hopefully, Roy's disappointment with a $60 toy that didn't live up to his expectations will be recalled when he's facing a $600 or $6,000 decision. Allowing our kids to fail under our roof where we can help them pick up the pieces is an important part of raising MoneySmart kids.

Depreciating Power

We host a garage sale every year or so, and Roy was determined to recoup his costs, selling his roller coaster for $60. It received lots of interest, but didn't sell. Several months later at a homeschool family sale, he dropped his price to $50, then $40, and finally sold it for $30. He learned an important lesson in depreciation.

The Bouncing Deal

When Abbey turned sixteen she wrote the word *trampoline* on her wish list. She did her research and found that new ones with safety enclosures cost between $300 and $600. She checked Craigslist and told Steve that she could find them used for between $50 and $100. She started saving her money, shooting for the $50 mark, and within six months she had the money. Because we were in the midst of the final edits prior to the release of our second book, Steve didn't have time to go with her to check out the tramps that she found, so we put her search on hold for a few months. In September of 2010, just weeks before the book launch, we received an e-mail from our church. A family was moving and wanted to find a new home for several things, including their trampoline. The price: *free!* Steve read the e-mail in disbelief. When he shared it with Abbey, she screamed! We called Jonni and set up a time to pick up Abbey's new trampoline. Jonni was touched that Abbey had saved her own money, and was going to realize her goal and get a bonus too. Abbey learned that diligent savings and patience really do pay off!

Now, you may think that things like free trampolines are as rare as hen's teeth, but our kids have discovered that as they patiently save, wait, and pray, miracles happen on a regular basis. We've experienced these types of blessings too!

By this point in the book you realize that as a family, we aren't perfect. In our saner moments we have decided that failure isn't really a bad thing, especially if we can grab hold of a powerful lesson and learn from it. We view the Spend envelope and giving our kids more and more discretion over time as a wonderful teaching tool to help them learn from both their failures *and* their successes.

No matter what your child's age, start now and help them learn MoneySmart spending habits.

Dealing with Spending at Different Stages

$5 Stage: Ages 0 to 5

Once your kids have learned the names of the coins and started putting their money into a three-part bank, look for opportunities to teach them how to spend. We've found that the easiest lessons come when we take them to garage sales, where they can find many desirable items for pennies.

Before we leave home they get their bank and we help them take out some money from the Spend category. Mom or Dad holds the money in a zippered pouch or money envelope and supervises when it's time to pay. We talk them through the proper procedure for totaling the final price, haggling over the price, counting the money, and waiting for change. Usually the homeowner will talk directly to us, but we always redirect the conversation to our kids, saying something like, "Abbey is spending her own money for this. Could you discuss the price with her?"

Even at this young age, having a plan for what they will buy is important. If they have a wish list, review it or at least discuss what they want to buy *before* going to a garage sale.

$50 Stage: Ages 6 to 11

An exciting step toward financial independence occurs as your child develops the ability to write well and do simple math. When they're about eight years old, move your kids from the three-part bank to cash envelopes for Give, Save, and Spend. They'll love taking responsibility for "balancing their budget" each payday. But even more, they'll love being able to grab their Spend envelope and head out to the store.

A self-maintained wish list is also kept inside the Spend envelope along with a pencil for recording purchases and two smaller envelopes: one containing the cash and the other, receipts.

Every Sunday night when we do payday, we review each envelope, take out the smaller money envelope, and count the cash. We compare that total to the amount written on the envelope ledger. If they match, we mark the recorded total with a red check. If they don't match, we recount the money and recall the week's events to see if they forgot to record an expense. Some kids dislike the discipline necessary to record every expense and deposit. Having a time when they know that someone will be checking their work helps to keep them on track.

Remember this is the $50 stage. The "wanters" are going to be looking at more and more expensive items to buy. MoneySmart parents use their children's desires to help develop disciplined spending habits. If you "gift" them with expensive items too often, you'll derail their desire to plan, work, research, and save for those seemingly unattainable goals. Allowing our kids to struggle, save, and wait is one of the greatest gifts we can give them, and one of the hardest for parents to stand by and watch. If you do your job in this stage—becoming an advisor and encourager—you'll sidestep most of the financial pitfalls that come with the more expensive stages.

$500 Stage: Ages 12 to 17

Diligence and discipline are still the operative habits here. Grounding your kids in good financial skills during this stage is critical to their future independence.

Children who have been trained, from a young age, to manage cash, as we've described, should really be perfecting their cash-handling skills between the ages of twelve and fifteen. They'll be writing down all of their purchases, easily balancing their cash envelopes, targeting larger savings goals, and using their wish lists regularly.

Usually when kids get their first job, around age sixteen, and have regular outside income, you'll need to help them make a choice about how to manage their increased earnings. If your children are planning on going away to college, we recommend transitioning them to a system using a checking account, debit card, and individual account sheets instead of cash envelopes.

You should start this transition at least one year before they move out. It is entirely unfair (not to mention unwise) to send a kid off to college with a debit card in hand and without any formal training or experience in how to manage it.

We described this type of budgeting system in greater detail in our book *America's Cheapest Family Gets You Right on the Money.*

$5,000 Stage: Ages 18 to 23

While our kids were in college, they all worked part-time jobs to earn their spending money and some of their other expenses like auto insurance, textbooks, and gifts. Sure, it was a little more difficult for them to juggle their schedules and they had less free time, but they all earned scholarships and had great GPAs, besides earning a great sense of accomplishment and responsibility. It can be done.

Young Adults Not in School

College or trade school isn't for everyone. If you have children who want to work rather than continue their education, encourage them to work hard. If they are living at home and earning a paycheck, they should pay for rent and food, clothing, and all of their recreational activities. They should also be participating with the family in maintaining and cleaning the house. "Freeloading" is not a character trait that has any positive values. To determine a fair rent amount, research the price of a one-bedroom apartment in your area, then discount it a little. If an apartment rents for $500, we recommend charging about $300 to $400. The only exception to this rule would be an ill or physically handicapped child.

Young Adults at School

Communication and financial limits are the keys to minimizing spending casualties at this stage. If your children have learned from a young age to manage their own money, have earned their own income, and are paying for all or part of their college expenses, you'll have very few issues.

For a responsible young adult, a debit card budgeting system can be a great financial tool, but in the wrong hands, it can spell disaster . . . limited disaster. However, a limited disaster is much better than some of the problems we've seen with credit cards.

If your children haven't had the advantage of lifelong financial training, there are three things you can do to minimize your exposure and maximize their success at school. Give your child:

- *A joint checking account* to which you transfer a predetermined, limited amount of money each month.
- *A prepaid, rechargeable debit card* to which you add a predetermined amount of money each month. If the card is lost, it is usually covered by the provider's loss policy. Keep a record of the card number and contact the issuer immediately.
- *A secured credit card* with a low credit limit (this is our least favorite option).

We'll go into much greater detail on how MoneySmart parents should manage college spending and other expenses in Chapter 18.

Basically, our job as parents during this stage is to set up checks, balances, and limits to help our kids establish good spending habits as they venture on their own, without enabling bad habits that could sink both them *and us.*

$50,000 Stage: Ages 24 and Beyond

At this stage, adult children need to be paying their own way in life. A monthly stipend from Mom and Dad just increases their dependence on you and does not teach them to be self-reliant. Your position now is to be available to coach and encourage, not to fund their spending lifestyle. As we've said previously, if your child encounters a disability or injury that, for a time, limits his earning ability, you have a responsibility as a family to support and encourage him during a time of recovery and adapting to a new set of abilities or career options. If a financial crisis hits him either because of foolish spending or circumstances beyond his control, please read our suggestions in Chapter 19.

Establishing Credit

Many parents and young adults are overly concerned about establishing credit. The fear of a low credit score from FICO (Fair Isaac Corporation) compels countless people to make confused and unsound credit decisions.

The credit card industry inundates mailboxes with offers not only for you but for your high school student, college student, and young adult, whether they still live at home or not. Why would they offer credit to a person with no credit history, minimum work history, and little experience at managing money? For two reasons: First, research shows that most people remain loyal to their first credit card. Second, they know that many parents will cosign for their young adult's card, which virtually guarantees the credit card company will recover all of its money (and interest too!).

We don't recommend credit cards for high school or college students, but if your young adult is working full-time and shows self-control in the use of the debit card and Individual Account Sheet budgeting system, you could help her to add a credit card to the mix to help build her credit score.

When we'd been married three years, because we had no debt and put 15 percent down on our home, we had no problem getting a mortgage loan. We know that credit scores and loan applications are different today, so we did a test with one of our kids. Becky got her first credit card when she was nineteen years old. She really had no need for it—at the time she had more than $20,000 in the bank. She only used the credit card for her gas purchases. After six years of on-time, paid-in-full payments, her credit score from TransUnion was 816 (out of 990).

Another option for establishing credit is to get a secured credit card. Most banks offer to let you or your children deposit an amount—let's say $500—into a bank account. That deposit is held as collateral and the available credit will be equal to the amount on deposit. When they use the card and make timely payments, the bank will report their progress to the credit bureaus. If they don't make their payments, they'll be charged penalties and possibly have their credit card canceled, forfeiting their collateral.

If you are going to help your child get a credit card, there are a few important things you should do.

Don't be a cosigner. Let your child struggle though the hassles of applications, denials, secured credit cards, and low limits. A cosigner is responsible for paying back what was borrowed if the original borrower doesn't. Don't put yourself in this financially risky position. If your children can't qualify for a credit card on their own, they shouldn't have one.

Talk about the dark side. Take time to read the fine print of a credit card application, particularly where it says that they can change the interest rate anytime, especially if you're late for a payment. Discuss how some credit collection agencies use harassment, bullying tactics, and incessant phone calls to get back the money you borrowed (if you're unsure about this topic, just Google "Collection Agency Abuse"). Talk about how long it takes for someone to pay back $10,000 at 23 percent interest. Education about the dangers will hopefully keep your child from a credit card nightmare.

Explain protection limits. Your children need to know that if their card is stolen and used by someone else, they may still be liable for up to $50 in charges. Read the fine print on your credit card application because all VISA and MasterCard brand cards have a "zero liability" policy.

We're hoping that at this stage, you will be able to sit back and smile as your children exceed your training and example. They'll probably come to you asking your opinion on a particular purchase or plan. Take time to encourage and advise them—then revel in their success.

CHAPTER 11

Activities for Character, Strength, and Scholarships

Like the majestic oak concealed within an acorn, boundless potential is concealed within the spirit of a child. One of our most important jobs as parents or grandparents is to help children discover and develop their latent abilities or interests and turn them into a vocation, avocation, or simply a way to enrich the lives of others. Some kids naturally find their forte, while others, like young plants in the garden, need more tending and cultivation to achieve their potential. One way to determine the depth of a child's interest is through involvement in groups where like-minded kids can interact with expert adults. To find these experts and get your kids involved, look beyond activities that merely keep your child occupied; look for activities that develop character.

We want to raise successful kids with good habits. We teach them from a young age to listen to us and obey. We train them to say "please" and "thank you." We read to them, potty train them, encourage them, correct them, and send them off to school for academic instruction. But there's more to life than reading, writing, and 'rithmetic. There are songs to be sung and music to be played; debates to be won and speeches to be made; pictures to be drawn and painted; photographs to be taken; balls to be hit, kicked, dribbled, spiked, and carried; laps to be run and hurdles to be jumped; bars, mats, beams, and rings to be flipped from; arrows and guns to be aimed and shot; mountains to be climbed up and skied down—whew, there are so many possibilities.

Unfortunately, budgets are being cut at schools, and so are art, music, and sports programs. Activities that in the past were provided "free of charge" through the schools, now cost those who participate. Beginner lessons for music, sports, and the arts are relatively inexpensive, but if your child desires to achieve a state, regional, national, or international caliber, the costs really skyrocket and you'll need to do some serious financial planning.

Steve competed collegiately against a number of world-class and Olympic-caliber gymnasts. It took dedication, persistence, and lots of time, but today, it takes even more—lots of cash. Families of Olympic hopefuls have been known to use home equity loans or spend hundreds of thousands of retirement dollars paying for training and travel expenses. Even if international recognition isn't your goal, it's still possible to spend thousands of dollars annually pursuing your child's passion.

In this chapter we'll share how we select extracurricular activities for our kids and what we expect them to learn. We'll also talk about how to evaluate the leadership, what your involvement should be, and how to fund your child's pursuits.

MoneySmart kids don't necessarily have the biggest muscles or the most trophies, but they do have good character and work habits that they've practiced since their youngest days.

What Age to Start

Beethoven started playing music at the young age of four; Picasso painted *Picador* at eight years old; hockey legend Wayne Gretzky played against ten-year-olds when he was only six. Yes, there are child prodigies, kids who are self-motivated and destined for greatness. And cultivating that raw talent takes wise and discerning parents. Push too hard and you'll burn them out, push too little and their talent may remain undeveloped. However, what is most disconcerting is when parents push an unmotivated child into an activity because of the *parent's* interest.

Child development experts and homeschool pioneers Dorothy and

Raymond Moore believed that when it came to education and skill development, it was better to start late than early. Their groundbreaking analysis of more than eight thousand studies of children's senses, brains, cognition, and socialization determined that no concrete evidence existed for rushing children into formal study programs prior to eight or ten years old. This may fly in the face of the popular early childhood education movement or the Suzuki method for teaching music, but we see much validity in it. The Moores encouraged parents to read, sing, explore, and play with their kids, but to minimize formal, structured instruction until children are older.

Could this type of environment produce strong and capable athletes and artists? Steve didn't start training for gymnastics until age thirteen, somewhat old compared to today's standards, and was competing internationally by age eighteen, and Kurt Thomas, a world champion gymnast and Olympian, began training at age fourteen and competed in the Olympics only six years later. Starting younger may produce more burnout and injuries among young children instead of champions and well-rounded kids.

We met a man who was recruited in his college years by a large university and given a partial scholarship to play baseball, but unfortunately, all he ever did was sit on the bench and get an excellent education. When we met Mark he was about fifty years old, running a successful business, and his thirteen-year-old son was playing on the same baseball team as Joe. Mark regularly recounted his frustration with the college coach who never let him play and his determination that his son would do much better, no matter what it cost him. He put Riley in the best private school, signed him up for the best baseball leagues, set up a batting cage in his backyard, and trained his son relentlessly. He pushed so hard that his son actually ended up quitting baseball in high school and took up lacrosse. Pushing your children into an activity because of your passion, or starting them in an activity before they are mentally and physically prepared, creates frustration for the children, the instructor, and other kids in the group.

On the brighter side we've seen the result of an incredibly talented, patient, and careful parent who nurtured her daughter to a level that rivaled or exceeded her own. Annette took voice lessons from an exceptional college instructor named Rachel. In the past, Rachel has performed on concert and opera stages throughout the United States and Europe and has trained performers from Broadway, Las Vegas, Arizona Opera, and the Metropolitan Opera in New York. But we think her greatest claim to fame is the achievement of her daughter, Gina.

Rachel trained Gina to sing at a young age, and she sang very well—well enough to capture the attention of a very influential instructor in New York City, where they lived. Rachel was told that Gina's vocal training was so exceptional that he could immediately get the twelve-year-old cast to sing at Carnegie Hall throughout that holiday season, where she could earn great sums of money. Rachel was a veteran musician and with her contacts could have easily moved her daughter into the spotlight and great income potential, but instead, she took a longer view and decided to continue training Gina, delaying her professional debut until she had matured and completed her education.

Gina did eventually sing in New York, not at Carnegie Hall, but the Metropolitan Opera. It was the start of a long and worldwide performing career. Gina now is the director and owner of an opera company in a large city. Truly, starting young but moving slowly while focusing on skill and character can produce a well-rounded child with spectacular results.

If you've reached a level of expertise in a particular field—whether it's athletics, the arts, science, or business—please temper your enthusiasm for your children to follow in your footsteps. Nurture them along slowly, and if they're interested and have ability, then move forward. Our kids inherit our genetics, but their personalities, passions, and purpose may be different. Don't be disappointed if they choose a different direction. They can achieve great things if we are patient and gentle. The discipline and determination you learned can be taught in many different areas, and you can help them achieve prominence in all of their pursuits.

How Much Should You Spend?

The answer to this question is quite simple: spend only what your budget can afford. Extracurricular activities aren't a necessity, and they certainly aren't worth going into debt over. Because we're committed to living debt-free, when we've encountered costs greater than what we have available, we always pause and look for options. And we have always found several. Later in the chapter we'll share some.

We recently read the story of a single mom with a young daughter who could run like the wind. Lauryn participated in school-sponsored track and field events from grade school through high school. But when the costs for club teams, equipment, and travel exceeded her mom's financial ability, rather than borrowing money, family and friends in the community, seeing Lauryn's potential, helped sponsor her. As a result of their love and concern, fleet-footed Lauryn Williams earned a spot on the 2004 Olympic team, where she won a silver medal in the 100-meter sprint!

Limited finances aren't a curse; if your child's ability shines, opportunities and money will find you.

Sports aren't the only or best extracurricular activity for developing your child's character. We'll share several other groups that we've been involved with and some of the things we learned with each experience.

How Many Activities?

We limit our kids to one extracurricular activity at a time (on rare occasions we allow two). There are several reasons for this limit.

Schedule Coordination

It is a major task to coordinate the varied schedules of five active kids. Fortunately, by the time that Abbey, our youngest, started her dance training, the older two kids were pretty much on their own, leaving us with only three activity schedules to manage. But some days we had to "divide and conquer" with Steve taking one child and Annette taking another to their practices.

Cost

One activity at a time obviously keeps costs more manageable.

Focus

Waiting until our kids really want to be involved in an activity, and then making it the only one, helped them develop better skills in that area.

Burnout

We're talking about parental and child burnout if you have too many activities going at one time. We don't want to be a family who lives in a minivan going from one activity to another, day after day. We all need downtime at home to debrief and rest.

Life is full of limits. Teaching our kids to evaluate and choose one or two outside activities to be involved in will help them appreciate it and be more diligent in their efforts.

Character-Building Activities

If we're investing time and money into beneficial activities for our kids, we want to see a return on our investment. And we're not only talking about skills development. History is full of notable artists, athletes, and businessmen who were brought to ruin because of a serious character flaw. Developing qualities such as trustworthiness, loyalty, helpfulness, friendliness, courtesy, kindness, obedience, cheerfulness, thriftiness, bravery, cleanliness, and reverence are not just habits for Boy Scouts; they are vital to success in life. Your children should be learning these things at home, but participation in a club, program, or sporting activity can and should reinforce your family's values.

Evaluating Leadership

When John, our eldest, was young, we naively thought that any adult leader selected by a reputable group would have a positive influence on him. Boy, were we wrong. An organization's reputation for wholesome leadership doesn't necessarily guarantee that volunteers in your area will adhere to the same standards. One of the first groups he joined looked great initially, but we later learned that two of the leaders ridiculed kids for practicing personal hygiene and also used their position of authority to have kids serve them. We worked to influence change in the group, but after a time we realized that John's character development was more important than working to fix this group, so we left.

No matter the group, you need to keep your parental antennae poised to assess the integrity and character of the leaders. To better monitor the instruction our kids received, rather than dropping them off, one of us would stay at practices or meetings. And as our time allowed, we volunteered to help and therefore became better acquainted with the leaders. If we were really busy, we'd usually volunteer for projects of limited scope, such as a specific fund-raiser, rather than an ongoing role, such as treasurer.

Below are descriptions of some of the different clubs, programs, and sporting teams our kids have been involved with.

Clubs and Programs

We define these as groups that meet on a regular basis—usually every week—to focus on specific mental or physical skills. They usually have volunteer leaders, dues, and uniform costs.

Boy Scouts

Boy Scouts has had a profound influence on our boys and our family. Whether your child is an intellectual type or a more physical, outdoorsy type, scouting can fit his gifting. John loved the camping, hiking, and getting dirty part of scouting. Our second son, Roy, loved the academic or merit-badge side of scouting, investigating and completing any new merit badge that was offered. Joe loved the leadership aspect of scouting and was always mentoring the younger boys. Despite their differences, all of them achieved the rank of Eagle Scout.

Call your local Boy Scouts office and ask for a list of troops in your area, or you can visit their website at scouting.org. We interviewed five scoutmasters before deciding on a troop. Of course, Girls Scouts is an option for your daughters. Neither of our daughters has participated, but we know several families who have enjoyed their involvement. Visit girlscouts.org to learn more.

Explorers

The Learning for Life / Explorer program is an offshoot of Boy Scouts of America, focusing more on career development, citizenship training, leadership skills, life skills, and character education for young men *and* women. Some of the Explorer program career fields are arts and humanities, aviation, business, communications, engineering, fire service, health, law enforcement, law, science, skilled trades, and social services. To learn more, go to http://Exploring.LearningForLife.org.

4-H

Abbey, at the age of nine, joined a 4-H clogging club. She wore dance shoes with a double tap, producing a sweet sound as her feet clattered across the floor. The club held weekly practices and monthly meetings run by student leaders elected to serve the club. They performed exhibitions at nursing homes, state and county fairs, and at an annual holiday parade. Participants learned teamwork, the value of practicing, and how to teach younger students the various dance routines. There are dozens of different types of 4-H groups across the country, providing a broad range of experiences in science, citizenship, and healthy living. To learn more, visit www.4h-usa.org.

Congressional Award

From the time she was seventeen until she turned twenty, our eldest daughter, Becky, participated in the Congressional Award Program. We like this program because it had less impact on our weekly schedule. There weren't scheduled meetings, just a prescribed course of study or accomplishments that could be achieved at Becky's own pace.

Based in Washington, D.C., the Congressional Award provides great opportunities for young people, ages fourteen to twenty-four. There are six levels of accomplishment requiring varying levels of commitment. To earn the program's top honor, the Congressional Award Gold Medal, Becky needed to perform four hundred hours of volunteer community service, two hundred hours of physical fitness training, two hundred hours of personal development, and a seven-day exploration or expedition. The Gold Medal is presented annually, in June, by the U.S. Speaker of the House to qualifying students in Washington, D.C. Go to www.congressionalaward.org for more information.

Music

Surveys consistently show that involvement in music increases a child's ability to learn. School music programs are a great introduction for kids, but budget cuts have reduced some of their availability. As a homeschooled student, Roy was allowed to participate in a grade school jazz band and middle school district band. And in high school he played in a community college concert band with many excellent older musicians. Private lessons helped Roy's performances, but if money is tight, look for a college student to teach your young musician. It's the daily practice at home that truly improves a child's musical ability. Roy's music practice was part of earning his daily school point. The discipline music requires benefits all areas of life.

Sports

Competitive sports are excellent vehicles for learning physical discipline and character, provided the coaches are good examples. The "win at all costs" coaching philosophy truly taints amateur sports. Steve has helped coach many of Joe's lower-level baseball teams—coaching is a great way to influence good character values. One of Steve's assistant coaches, with three kids in Little League that particular season, said that between all of the practices and games, he basically "lived at the field." Sports activities can really strain a family's schedule.

Joe started with an inexpensive YMCA team, and as his interest and ability improved, we researched other opportunities. As he neared high school age, the more competitive teams became very expensive. One particular team looked great: excellent coaches, great organization, and good players. But about two months into the season the leaders decided to take the team to a higher level and started traveling out of town to tournaments. The costs skyrocketed, as did the requirement for parents' participation in fund-raising activities. Unfortunately, we needed to find a different team.

There are usually several options for any sports teams in your area. Research as thoroughly as possible by talking to other parents, interviewing various coaches, getting a list of the costs involved, and watching the teams practice. Keep in mind that many coaches are simply volunteers trying to create a great experience for their child and others, so be as supportive as you can. Remember that the team's win/loss record is less important than the physical discipline and the character traits that the coach instills.

Other Groups

We know that our experience is limited and that there are hundreds of other excellent clubs, programs, and sports for your kids to join. Look around and you'll find math, chemistry, and foreign language clubs at school, journalism clubs and school newspapers, Toastmasters (public speaking), YMCA youth and government, horse associations, National Junior Horticultural Association, Junior Achievement, rocketry clubs, handbell choirs, garden clubs, riflery clubs, astronomy clubs, turtle and tortoise societies, blacksmithing clubs, engineering clubs, and computer clubs. There are clubs and activities for everyone.

Religious Activities

We couldn't have a chapter on character-building activities for kids without including a section on faith-based groups. A strong moral compass will serve our kids well as they embark on a career and start a family.

Youth Groups

These can be a good place for character development, growing strong friendships, and receiving religious instruction. Get to know the leadership and their goals. There are a few potential pitfalls that we've seen:

CLIQUES Yes, these will exist in some church groups and can be difficult for a shyer child to navigate.

ILLICIT BEHAVIOR Just because it's a church or parachurch group doesn't mean that there won't be some kids who act out or attempt to suck others into their bad behavior: drugs, alcohol, sex, and rebelliousness. *Yes, these things happen, even here.*

TIMING The day of the week, frequency, and time of day for some youth activities can interfere with your family priorities.

ACTIVITIES While most activities will be wholesome and appropriate, there are times when the cost or timing won't fit with your family's priorities.

YOUNG LEADERS Youth leaders tend to be on the younger side (often having just graduated from seminary or college), and many don't have kids of their own yet. As a result, we've seen junior high and high school groups with activities that resemble reality-TV game shows rather than a character-building environment. We understand the need to have fun and attract kids to the group, but the problem comes when fun becomes the goal, rather than a tool to get kids to ponder the important issues in life.

Other Church Activities

Many churches offer other activities for youth education and growth, including Sunday school, choirs, discipleship groups, Awana, and confirmation-type classes. Be as involved as your schedule allows, watch what your children are doing, and evaluate if they are truly absorbing the message or merely socializing.

MISSION TRIPS Going on a youth group mission trip to a different city in the United States or internationally can be a life-changing experience. Being immersed in a different culture and learning how other people live can breed a deeper appreciation and greater satisfaction for life at home. Beyond that, it could open your child's heart to a possible career or avocation helping others in need.

Two of our kids have been involved in youth group international mission trips. We've helped them deal with fund-raising, planning, and buying health insurance. The teamwork and trials they experienced provided great opportunities to learn and grow.

Camps

According to the American Camp Association, more than 11 million kids and adults attend some sort of day or overnight camp each year. There are camps that cater to virtually any and every type of educational and physical interest you could imagine. Camp costs are almost as varied as the activities, with fees ranging from $100 to $800 for a one-week stay. We look at the camp experience as a time of developing new skills, honing old ones, having fun with friends, stretching the wings of independence, and especially living out the good character qualities that have already been developed.

All of our kids have attended a broad range of weeklong camps during their teen years. When they were younger, we'd attended as chaperones, but as our kids grew older and more mature in their decision making, we would send them off with trusted leaders on their own. Remember that the leadership of the camp will greatly influence your child's experience; plus they will have a profound effect on the attitudes and behaviors the child brings back home. We always planned on our kids coming home exhausted and allowed them a day to rest and several days to "de-brief" and tell us of their many camp adventures.

Age and Maturity

Our philosophy about camps is similar to that of sports and other club activities—start them later rather than earlier. Let camps be something that your child longs to attend rather than dreads. Your children will get more out of camp as their maturity increases, and they'll be able to cope with the common camp issues of bullying, homesickness, exhaustion, stealing, getting lost, and misplacing their possessions.

Ask yourself these questions:

- Can my child withstand negative peer pressure or will he cave in to it?
- Can my child reconcile differences with other children without fighting?
- Can my child submit to authority and a different schedule or way of doing things?
- Can my child follow rules when a parent is not around?

If your answer is no to any of these questions, your child probably isn't ready to attend an overnight camp.

Because camps are expensive and because the potential for negative influence is great, we don't recommend overnight camps for younger kids. We also don't encourage sending kids away for an entire summer; not only is it expensive, but families can only be built into strong teams if they spend time together. There are so many factors in our culture that want to segment or split up our families. Do whatever you can to preserve the cohesiveness of yours.

Allowing our kids to experience a week or more of independent living, focusing on activities of interest to them, is a perfect environment to foster the self-sufficiency and character we want them to develop. Sure, they'll make mistakes, lose things, possibly get bullied, but all of these issues can be used as priceless life lessons—teaching them things that simply talking or reading about never would.

Cost

Camps can be pricey. If you're convinced that your child should attend a specific camp, but you can't afford the fee, most organizations offer partial to full scholarships—just ask. Sometimes there are fund-raising activities you and/or your child can be involved in, and even opportunities for you to work at the camp in trade for your child attending. Do your research.

We truly believe that if a child is meant to be involved in a specific activity and the family can't afford the fees that somehow the money will be provided; if not, there is another, better activity that is a perfect fit for your child. Diligent searching and waiting are the best solutions; debt is *not* the answer.

Funding and Fund-Raising Activities

Initially, we pay all of the costs of the activities we've covered in this chapter. Over time, we encourage our kids to pick up some of the expenses, especially when they start working a part-time job. They create a separate envelope for their activity and make regular deposits. Since the age of sixteen, Joe has funded all of his baseball expenses, totaling upward of $1,500 per year. While that may be tame for some sports, for our family that's a significant amount of money. We know another family whose son plays hockey, spending between $4,000 and $6,000 annually. Fortunately for them, he has been recruited by a college and awarded a full scholarship.

Our philosophy is that the more your children have invested, the harder they'll work and the more they will accomplish.

Fund-Raising Ideas

Most of the activities listed in this chapter have costs associated with them. Some are minor and others can be excessive. There are numerous ways that we have helped our kids pay for their activities. Here's a quick list.

- Collecting discarded cell phones for cash. We've used PaceButler.com.
- Hosting or helping organize a group fund-raising garage sale. Every family donates, collects items, and helps, in some capacity, in all stages of the sale.
- Asking for scholarships from the hosting organization.
- Writing letters to friends and family, with the child offering to do yard or housework in exchange for a fair hourly wage, with the money going toward his or her activity fees.
- Helping with car washes.
- Helping coordinate fitness challenges where kids get sponsors to pay for various achievements: walk-a-thons, push-up-a-thons, dance-a-thons, etc.
- Selling T-shirts for the group.
- Selling treats at a bake sale fund-raiser.
- Organizing silent auctions. We also hosted fund-raiser silent auctions in conjunction with potluck dinners for a scout troop and drama club.

We don't look at character-building activities as "babysitting" for our kids, but as a down payment on their future. We will gladly invest our time and money in those things that help our child to mature; to grow strong in mind, body, and spirit; to examine possible career options; and to help others improve their lives. When kids excel in something they love, it stabilizes them much like roots do a tree. The stronger and deeper they grow, the more they will be able to withstand the gales of the culture that swirl about them. We need more noble and majestic trees in the forest of our nation's youth. *Character counts!*

Dealing with Activities at Different Stages

$5 Stage: Ages 0 to 5

In this stage, most of the character development happens at home. Don't worry about putting your young child into organized sports, day camps, and music or art lessons yet.

$50 Stage: Ages 6 to 11

If you've observed an interest in a particular activity, begin researching groups in your area. Start a notebook where you can store the information. Visit the group on a meeting night and observe how kids respond to the leaders. As your child nears the older end of this range, the cost of activities will start to escalate; adjust your budget to accommodate the costs or start fundraising and discuss the future with your child.

$500 Stage: Ages 12 to 17

If your child becomes proficient in a particular skill and is seen as a potential regional or national contender, start looking for additional ways to fund his or her pursuits. Monitor the effects that peers involved in various activities are having on your child. If you start to see bad habits developing, quickly discuss the issues or remove your child from the activity or to another group. As your child nears college age, you may find scholarships or grants being offered through the activity's sponsoring organizations. Fill out any and all applications.

$5,000 Stage: Ages 18 to 23

During the college years, allow your children to self-fund their activities if they are pursued for purely recreational reasons. At this stage, school and employment should be their top priority; however, if an activity will enhance their future employment opportunities, and they don't have enough funding, consider contributing, but only if they are showing diligence, persistence, and academic excellence.

$50,000 Stage: Ages 24 and Beyond

The only reason you as a parent might consider helping to fund a young adult's character-building activity would be the pursuit of national or international experiences. There may also be instances where you're called upon to assist financially with some sort of physical or emotional rehab as the result of addictive behaviors. Approach this with great care. If your adult child is truly willing to change, then by all means help as much as your budget allows. We'll cover this in more detail in Chapter 19.

CHAPTER 12

Playing and Paying: Toys, Recreation, and Technology

Raising MoneySmart kids requires that we help our kids juggle learning, working, earning, *and* playing. In our recreation- and technology-obsessed society, this is no easy task. Kids may spend between six and eight hours each day doing school and homework and then spend even more in recreational pursuits. Playing can easily become an addiction, sidetracking good kids and derailing promising futures. As parents we must diligently create an environment that helps children balance fun with a focus on the things that matter most. If we don't take this issue seriously, we could well raise a generation of kids who know how to work at their play, but only play at their work—if they work at all!

The $20,000 Game

Several years ago we met a young man named Jim. He was an energetic twenty-something who had moved to Arizona to be close to his brother. He started playing video games when he was young, but in his late teens became addicted. He was incredibly smart, and lazy—a bad combination.

Without putting forth much effort, he managed to graduate high school and was accepted into a small private college where he easily procured a student loan. He went to his college classes regularly for a few weeks, but then started hanging out with a group of gamers. Studying became his second priority while friends and gaming became his first. He was put on probation after his first semester, but during his second semester he became obsessed with an online game that he played continuously. He failed all of his classes and eventually dropped out. When we met Jim, his car had recently been repossessed; he had no college degree, was earning a little more than minimum wage, and had a school debt totaling $20,000.

We know this is an extreme example, but the truth is that many young men today are falling victim to their own lack of self-control, jeopardizing their employment future and their future marriage. Jim did eventually get married, and now he *and* his wife are working to dig their way out of debt.

We want to arm you and your kids with information and attitudes that put play in the proper perspective so that, as a family, you can develop limits that lead to a balanced and productive adulthood.

Playing to Develop MoneySmart Kids

We view toys and games as more than simple diversionary activities. From the youngest ages, kids are sponges for learning, and we want them to absorb good things, so we're careful about what activities we provide them. The problem with some toys is that they can be trendy or expensive, or can teach values that we would rather not have our kids learn. Toys can help kids develop problem-solving skills, creativity, and increased attention spans. They can also provide hours of constructive, wholesome activity. But if you aren't selective, you could end up spending money on toys that are never played with and provide no real learning value for your children.

When John was born, we discovered a great resource book, *The First Three Years of Life* by Dr. Burton White. Dr. White breaks down child development during the first three years into eight different phases and, among other things, challenges conventional thinking regarding appropriate toys for each stage. We remember well the "hinge phase," when one-year-old kids are fascinated by swinging doors, and the "water phase," about eighteen months to two years, when our toddlers happily splashed away in the bathtub.

Based on Dr. White's book and our own observations, we've implemented eight strategies to maximize the beneficial aspects of toys and play for our kids while minimizing our costs.

1. Be Involved.

Stevanne Auerbach, PhD ("Dr. Toy"), says, "When you become your child's 'Play Tutor' you are creating the quality time he or she craves and needs." We never realized the importance of Steve building tall block towers with our kids, who would scream with pleasure as they "just happened" to knock them over. It was fun, but they were also learning logical consequences and cause and effect. Later on, we played Wiffle ball in our cul-de-sac, basketball on the driveway, word games at the dining room table, board games in the family room, and even invented games in the swimming pool. Playing with our kids taught them to think more maturely and to play better with others.

2. Provide Problem-Solving Toys.

Toys can help MoneySmart kids learn to solve problems. A favorite toy of our toddler-aged kids was a bright yellow bucket with a blue lid that had three cutout shapes: circle, square, and rectangle. They spent hours putting the correspondingly shaped blocks into the bucket.

As our kids grew, we introduced them to puzzles, starting with wooden ones with shapes that had to fit into similarly shaped openings. They progressed to 35- to 70-piece floor puzzles. A favorite of four-year-old Abbey was a Winnie the Pooh puzzle that was as tall as she was when she lay next to it. Now, a couple of times each year, our family pulls out a 1,000-piece puzzle, whooping when we find an elusive piece and cheering when we finally complete it.

Duplos, Legos, K'NEX, Lincoln Logs, Tinker Toys, and Waffle Blocks provide practice in following instructions, sequencing, and working step-by-step through projects.

Playing with Barbie dolls challenged young Abbey to solve many problems. She had about twenty dolls and developed an organized storage system for the multitudinous outfits and shoes she'd collected. She even fashioned a throne room for "Queen Rapunzel" and her princes and princesses.

All of these things helped our kids develop organized thinking and perseverance.

3. Focus on Creativity.

Solving the challenges of life requires creativity. Selecting the right toys can help develop creative thinking skills.

Make-believe and dressing-up develop kids' imaginations. We kept an extensive costume collection in a large trunk, which the kids would regularly use for skits and plays performed for the video camera. The inexpensive costumes were either given to us or purchased at garage sales.

When it rained, the kids built forts in our living room using cushions from chairs and couches, giant waffle blocks, and every available blanket and pillow in the house. A child's creativity can transform a large cardboard box into a tank, lawn chairs into a maze, and blankets into mountains for army men. Common household objects became uncommon instruments for inexpensive creative thinking.

We hired a college-age babysitter who introduced our kids to colored modeling clay, which they fashioned into small clay animals. They built farm scenes on metal trays and crafted amazing stories about their menageries. At twenty years old Becky was still sculpting phenomenal horse models, because years earlier, a college student taught her to make a simple dog.

When kids are small, they love when a parent colors with them. When Becky was about eight years old, we took a 36-inch-wide sheet of brown craft paper, laid it on the floor, and did a complete body tracing of her. We colored it for a whole day. Now every time we see a picture of it, we giggle—she was so tiny!

Roy, Joe, and John all loved playing with Hot Wheels cars. Annette found a rug that had city streets printed on it, and the boys added Lincoln Log and Lego buildings. They also made jumps out of books or pieces of wood and played daredevil driver with their cars.

Inspiring creativity doesn't require expensive toys.

4. Plan for Play on the Go.

Annette took some large pieces of scrap fabric and sewed drawstring toy bags for our young kids. The bags were filled with several of each child's favorite toys, coloring books, and crayons to be used whenever we went to a friend's home or an event where they might need to sit and wait. Rather than being bored or getting into mischief, they always had things to do and share with other kids.

Whenever we traveled by plane or car, each child had a backpack full of things to keep them occupied. In their teen years they would always bring things like books, lanyard material, and playing cards whenever we went out, and usually found other kids to join them in not being bored.

Planning ahead and having constructive activities available makes outings much more productive and enjoyable.

5. Build Attention Spans.

Our young kids had longer attention spans than most of their peers because we didn't allow them to run from one uncompleted activity to another. It took time and discipline—on *our* part—to help them complete puzzles they thought were "too hard," to finish a game, or put away one toy before going on to the next. But these habits served them well as they became involved in more complex activities, like a competitive team, club, part-time job, or college classes.

Other activities that encourage a longer attention span are playing with Fisher-Price or Playmobil town kits or Perler beads, knitting, model building, setting up battles with army men, building a doll house, and listening to audiobooks.

6. Turn Constructive Activities into Play.

Making things can be fun and educational too! Consider crafting, sewing, gardening, making beaded jewelry, decorating Christmas ornaments, woodworking, or repairing furniture. Our kids loved entering craft projects in the Arizona State Fair. Their creativity often garnered blue ribbons (and prize money)! Consider buying kits—moccasins, wood burning, car models—from a craft store. We buy many of these items from local craft stores with 40-percent-off coupons from the newspaper. Our kids have also learned to make lanyards into key chains, bracelets, belts, and Boy Scout neckerchief slides. The boys enjoyed building model rockets. We've had a few wild flights, but for the most part we've been awed by their power and speed.

Hobbies allow a child to develop excellence in a skill and sometimes profit from it.

7. Play Family Games.

We've always been a game-playing family. For younger kids, we played games that focused on counting, colors, memory, or matching. As they grew older the games became more strategy oriented. Some of our family favorites are:

- Younger kids: Candy Land, Pizza Party, Hi Ho! Cherry-O, Yahtzee Jr., Checkers, Mousetrap, and Ker Plunk
- Teens: Scotland Yard, Clue, Settlers of Catan, Puerto Rico, Rummikub, Stocks and Bonds, Monopoly, Risk, American Dream (out of print), Farkel, Scattergories, Taboo, Catch Phrase, Pit, and Mille Bornes

We've reviewed more favorite games on AmericasCheapestFamily.com, under book reviews. Now that our kids are all college-aged and above, we still get together to play board games. The games they choose are more about planning and strategy than they are about just relaxing fun. Playing games with our kids and helping them learn to follow rules, play fairly, be creative, and plan strategies provided them with great life skills.

8. Buy Used.

We have found inexpensive toys and games at consignment stores, thrift stores, garage sales, homeschool curriculum sales, Craigslist, and eBay (particularly helpful for out-of-print games). Slightly used items prove just as enjoyable as new ones! We check the parts carefully and wash anything we can prior to playing. Purchasing toys that kids love doesn't have to be costly.

The Value of Inexpensive Play

Can we calculate the benefit of being able to solve problems, think creatively, and develop solutions? Many people can find a flaw in an idea, but of greater value are the few who see a problem and can develop a solution. Allowing kids to experiment and create is worth both the mess and the time. The creativity within a developing mind is incalculable—our job is to nurture, train, and encourage it. Fostering creative thinking doesn't require expensive toys or pricey technology. If you simply provide a nurturing home, lots of time, and plenty of encouragement, creativity will blossom.

Recreational Activities

Some people may think we're a bit on the radical side, but we evaluate what recreational activities our family will participate in with four purposes in mind: the cost, the time involved, the educational benefit, and the physical benefit. There are times when we do things just for fun, but for the most part, the activity needs to meet at least two of our four criteria.

We'll present a number of recreational activities that we've enjoyed as a family—these are above and beyond any formal character-building activities mentioned in the previous chapter. We hope these ideas will get you thinking beyond taking your kids to the mall or a movie when you're looking for some fun. Building great memories and family enjoyment is worth a little extra effort.

Many of these activities are free, but when it comes to paying for recreation, we'll cover most of the costs until our kids turn sixteen and get their first part-time job. There are some exceptions, and we've noted those on the specific activities.

At Home

Movie Nights

We have built a collection of quality classic movies that promote heroism, patriotism, and positive values (okay, we do have some that are just hilarious too). If we want to watch a movie that we don't own, we borrow it from a friend or check it out from the library. Sometimes we watch a movie that falls short of our ideals and take that as an opportunity to have a discussion about the issues it raises. If there's a movie we think our family would like but we haven't screened it yet, we read the review from PluggedIn.com.

Movies regularly appear on our kids' wish lists and as a result are included in many birthday and Christmas presents at our house.

Reading

Our kids are voracious readers. When we checked out library books with five young kids, it was a massive operation. Each child brought a canvas book bag to the library, which could hold ten to twenty books. When the kids were too small to carry that many books, we brought our red Radio Flyer wagon and loaded the book bags and a kid or two into it and pulled it through the library. At the checkout, each child stood in line with Mom or an older sibling to scan their books, and then put them into their book bag with the library receipt.

Each summer we signed up the kids for the Summer Reading program. The program gave them an incentive to read, plus prizes for reaching different levels. They all received things like Major League baseball tickets, movie and restaurant coupons, pencils, rulers, stickers, and other little trinkets.

LIBRARY FINES Checking out large quantities of books can be a budget buster if you miss the due date. Our libraries allow phone or Internet renewal, which makes it much easier to avoid fines.

If missing a due date was our fault, we paid the fine, but as our kids got older, they helped with online renewals and many times would pay their own fines. Interestingly, each year our library allows fines to be paid with donations of canned food to support a local food bank—we usually chose this option.

Sports

We've collected an assortment of inexpensive sporting equipment: basketball, soccer ball, baseball, Wiffle ball, croquet, volleyball, and more. With a large family, there always seemed to be two or more people who would be willing to go outside and play a game. We've purchased sporting equipment at garage sales and thrift or consignment stores.

Friend Sleepover

This is something that our daughters have truly enjoyed doing. They invite a friend or two over for a girls' night, complete with manicures, pedicures, makeup makeovers, chick flicks, a special dinner, and of course, very little sleep—although we always instituted a lights-out time.

To keep the cost down, we do a pasta dinner cooked from scratch or grilled cheese with tomato soup and get movies from the library. We expect that the following day they won't be very coherent, so these events can't be scheduled when there are important activities or chores to be done the next day.

Away from Home

Inexpensive Local Outings

We often have out-of-town visitors stay with us, so we contacted our local convention and visitors' bureaus and consulted a AAA tour book to assemble a list of sites of interest in our area. We were amazed at the list and have had a great time visiting or doing many of the items on it. To encourage you to look for great opportunities in your area, we've made a generic version of our list. Almost every one of the outings is free or very inexpensive. We'll usually pack a lunch and some snacks and head out for a day of fun.

Seasonal Activities
- ❏ Winter: ice skating, sledding, building snow forts and snowmen
- ❏ Spring: biking, hiking, bird-watching, parks, arboretums, botanical gardens, geocaching
- ❏ Summer: swimming, berry picking (free in parks and forests), picnics, biking, sand volleyball, art walks, camping, lakes, and beaches
- ❏ Fall: jumping in leaf piles, hiking, pumpkin picking (buy one for the entire family), cornfield mazes, harvest festivals, and making baked apples, apple pies, or apple crisp

Annual Events

❍ State and county fairs (look for discounted tickets)
❍ Horse/livestock shows
❍ Parades and rodeos
❍ Hot air balloon races

High School / College Activities

❍ College music recitals and art exhibitions (usually free)
❍ Drama productions
❍ Sporting events
❍ University bowling alleys
❍ Concerts—band and orchestra (usually free or inexpensive)

Other Concerts

❍ Many churches produce musicals or other concerts around the holidays (usually free or inexpensive).
❍ If your older kids want to hear a favorite artist in concert, let them purchase their own ticket. If you see value in the message that the artist presents, pay for a portion of the ticket price and let them pay for the rest.

Nature

❍ City, state, and national parks
❍ Fish hatcheries
❍ Lakes
❍ Mountain preserves
❍ Wildlife preserves

Field Trips

❍ Factories—candy, bread, milk, pretzel, tortilla
❍ Farms and orchards—dairy, egg, horses, vineyard, citrus, avocado, cotton gin, organic farm
❍ Tours—newspaper, post office, private airport, radio and TV stations, recycling and waste processing facilities, community college,

university, city bus ride to the central library. These are especially valuable to create potential career or educational vision.

Museums

Many museums have free admission days periodically. Check websites for details and plan your outings on those days.

- Science
- Children's
- History (local, state, national)
- Musical instrument
- Air and space
- Military

Political/Patriotic/Historical

- State capitol tour
- Meet your legislators
- Courthouses
- Presidential museums
- Historical reenactments

Holiday Celebrations

- Easter—church musicals
- Fourth of July—fireworks and picnics
- Looking at Christmas lights
- Christmas caroling to friends and neighbors
- Parades

Tools

Here are several tools we've used to find great recreational opportunities.

- Entertainment book (discount coupons)
- AAA tour books
- Convention and visitors' bureaus
- Parks and recreation offices

◯ College and university calendars
◯ Local newspapers
◯ National Parks pass

FAT Nights

Our kids have watched us plan and host events for years, and now that they're older, they've created their own popular recreational event. They originally called it a "fun awesome time," but it soon became FAT night. They invite dozens of friends in person or through Facebook (around twenty will come) to play flag football, volleyball, or some other sporting activity and ask each person to bring a snack. They plan the evening and we provide transportation and the main dish (usually pasta) for dinner. During a break we give each team thirty minutes to create a "halftime" commercial that we videotape. Abbey or Joe would pick an item, like Speed Stick or Raisin Bran Crunch, for the teams to "sell." While the teams are finishing up, Steve adds music and sound effects to the commercials. The laughter rings through the house. These nights are hugely successful, cost very little, and are especially fun because our kids do most of the work.

Things We Don't Encourage Our Kids to Do as Recreation

Hang Out at the Mall

Some parents we know send their kids to the mall and provide them with $20 to have a good time. We've never allowed our kids to simply "hang out with friends at the mall." Without adult supervision kids often end up getting into mischief, become the victim of a predator, or squander their money. By teaching them to buy things with their own money and make lists of expected purchases, their desire to hang out and waste money is non-existent. Besides, our kids much prefer "treasure hunting" with family or friends at thrift stores.

Movie Premieres

As our kids entered their teen years and the influence of friends became more prevalent, there were often requests to go to the premiere of the newest blockbuster movie at midnight. We rarely, if ever, agreed to this type of event. Not only is it an ungodly hour for our kids to be out (especially if they needed a ride there and back), but it's also a time when many more accidents and other dangerous behavior occur. Plus, arriving home at 2:00 a.m. basically renders them unproductive the following day. We want our kids to evaluate the total effect these types of decisions have on them not only fiscally but physically.

If the movie is important to them, they usually go a week later, when the lines are shorter and the times more reasonable. Of course, at this age, our kids paid for these excursions with their own money.

We don't rent (or download) movies very often at all, but if your kids do, let them pay for the movies they want to watch. Our kids have discovered that they can get virtually any movie they want to watch from the library or very inexpensively from Amazon, eBay, or Half.com. They only buy movies they would want to watch several times.

As you can see, recreational activities for your kids don't need to be costly or boring. Because we were totally involved in our kids' recreational activities when they were younger, as they grew older they knew our expectations and also knew how to plan a fun and awesome event to enjoy with friends. We've been so impressed with the creativity our kids are exhibiting—it's awesome to see!

Taming Technology

The use of technology can be a blessing or a curse to a MoneySmart family. There are always newer, faster, and more expensive electronic "must-haves" being advertised. Our kids are besieged with messages from their friends that if they don't have the latest and greatest techno-gadget, they are social outcasts. Technology has, in many ways, become a status symbol for this generation. We need to have a balanced and intentional approach to the use of technology in our homes, or we'll find that the technological appetite of our culture will take us to places we don't want to go. In this section we'll share how we've tamed the techno-monster in the areas of TV, gaming, music, computers, and cell phones.

Media Consumption in Our Homes

Sixty years ago, a television was a rarity in the American home; today it is rare to have a room without one. We have only one television and rarely watch network programming on it, because we know that much of the information presented teaches rampant consumerism, discontentment, and a host of values that aren't commensurate with becoming a self-sufficient, MoneySmart adult.

Recently we discovered an insightful study from the Kaiser Family Foundation entitled "Zero to Six—Electronic Media in the Lives of Infants, Toddlers and Preschoolers." It shares the results of a telephone survey of more than one thousand parents of children ages six months through six years. We can't review the entire study—you can on our website www.AmericasCheapestFamily.com/KaiserStudy—but we've highlighted some of the most pertinent findings. The study was not very supportive of young children using most types of media. Because we have seen the potential dangers, we created technology limits for our family too. Here's what we learned from the survey:

1. Children today (six months to six years old) are immersed in media:

- 50 percent have three or more TVs in the home
- 36 percent have a TV in their bedroom
- 73 percent have a computer in the home
- 49 percent have a video game system

2. Children (six months to six years old) spend an average of

- 2 hours per day with screen media (TV, video game, or computer)
- 2 hours per day playing outside
- 39 minutes reading or being read to

3. Homes where the television is

- on at least half of the time: 65 percent
- used to occupy the children when the parents are busy: 45 percent

The survey revealed that even very young children are highly exposed to TV and other screen media.

4. Children under two who have ever

- watched TV: 74 percent
- watched videos/DVDs: 70 percent
- used a computer: 11 percent
- played video games: 3 percent

The American Academy of Pediatrics recommends that children under the age of two not watch any television at all and that children between the ages of two and six years old be limited to two hours of educational screen media per day.

A 2010 Kaiser Family Foundation study entitled "Generation M^2" researched the media use of children between the ages of eight and eighteen and revealed more startling information. As more media was consumed, grades declined, as did good relationships with parents and overall satisfaction with life. A link to this study is also available at www.AmericasCheapestFamily .com/KaiserStudy.

Hopefully information like this will help you evaluate the media you allow to infiltrate your home and influence your children. For our family, this survey completely validated our decisions that we should limit screen time, spend more time reading to and with our kids, play more board games, and definitely not have a TV or computer in any of our bedrooms (including parents').

Following are the things we do with our kids to manage technology and media in our home.

Managing Television

When we were first married, we had a television given to us as a wedding present. We decided that the TV lifestyle—watching other people live an exciting life—was not what we wanted as a family. So we put the TV away and eventually sold it.

As we started having kids, our views changed a little and we ended up buying a VCR and borrowing a small TV from Annette's parents. We started to see some redeeming value in allowing select, screened media to influence our kids. We eventually bought a larger TV and DVD player, but are by no means a savvy, cable channel, hi-def, TV-watching family.

We share this history with you because we believe that *too many kids* are influenced by *too much time* spent watching *too many unmonitored* television programs. It's more than simple entertainment choices. They're being fed a constant stream of moral, materialistic, consumerist, and scientific messages that usually don't fit with our family values. Do they fit with yours?

Television viewing will affect your finances. As we mentioned in Chapter 10, child-targeted advertising has long been an area of concern for child development experts. Kids between the ages of two and five don't easily distinguish between the actual TV show and a commercial. Even if they realize that some programming is a commercial message, they don't have the cognitive ability to determine if the advertised product is something that would truly be beneficial to them.

Given this information, we made some choices:

1. Our kids would mostly watch known content on recorded media (VHS or DVD).
2. If network television was viewed, one or both of us would be there to screen and comment on what was being watched.

Because we enforced a limited viewing policy, our kids spent more time reading, playing outside, playing board games, and doing other creative projects that they wouldn't have done if they had been planted in front of the TV or computer for hours at a time.

Many of the most successful people we know have put time limits on their recreation and entertainment choices to ensure that they accomplish the things that matter most to them and their families.

To help our kids track their TV and computer time, we created a chart that allowed them three hours of screen time each week (see figure 12.1). If one of the kids was watching a movie or playing on the computer and another child walked by and started watching, the second child was required to deduct the time also. Initially we gave grace and reminded the kids to record their time on the Weekly TV and Computer Time Chart, but after several warnings we needed to implement stricter controls. If they didn't write down their time, they forfeited their entire week of viewing and playing. That solved the problem.

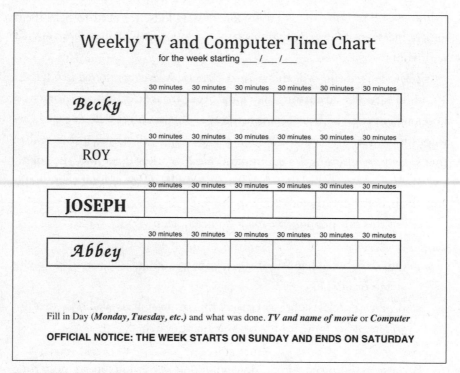

Weekly TV and Computer Time Chart

for the week starting ___ / ___ / ___

	30 minutes	30 minutes	30 minutes	30 minutes	30 minutes	30 minutes
Becky						

	30 minutes	30 minutes	30 minutes	30 minutes	30 minutes	30 minutes
ROY						

	30 minutes	30 minutes	30 minutes	30 minutes	30 minutes	30 minutes
JOSEPH						

	30 minutes	30 minutes	30 minutes	30 minutes	30 minutes	30 minutes
Abbey						

Fill in Day (*Monday, Tuesday, etc.*) and what was done. *TV and name of movie* or *Computer*

OFFICIAL NOTICE: THE WEEK STARTS ON SUNDAY AND ENDS ON SATURDAY

Figure 12.1 TV and computer time chart.

Another family we know issued each of their kids personalized poker chips. Each chip was good for a half hour of TV or computer time. They had a limited number of chips for the week and were responsible for turning them in to Mom when they watched or played. Tagalong viewing needed to be paid for also. Each one of the kids in this family did well in school, earned college scholarships, and two of the four have already graduated.

Managing Video Games

According to the 2009 Pew Internet & American Life Project, more than 80 percent of kids between the ages of twelve and seventeen own either a Wii or PlayStation gaming system. The Kaiser Family Foundation "Generation M^2" study, which we referenced earlier, found that more than 60 percent of kids between the ages of eight and eighteen played video games on a system, cell phone, or handheld device each day.

Playing video games has become a predominant way for kids to occupy themselves. If we're going to raise MoneySmart kids, we need to help them manage their time and the all-consuming urge to play. We've seen far too many boys become young men addicted to video gaming, and as a result, were unmotivated to find productive work or to pursue marriage and raising a family. The pursuit of the video adrenaline rush is emasculating our young men. Real life simply can't hold a candle to the drive to conquer in the fantasy realm. On the positive side, we have seen several of them shake off the shackles of virtual living and join the real world, but it didn't happen until late in their twenties.

Because of these reasons and several others, we have decided not to have a gaming system in our home. We do have some select computer games that we researched and discussed before purchasing, but these are more educational or vocational directed. Even these "good" games were subject to our Weekly TV and Computer Time Chart, and as a result we never had to deal with addiction issues.

We really do try to keep an open mind, but it seems that many of the more popular games have themes that present evil and illicit activities as desirable and good. Spending hours at a time, week after week, reinforcing the thoughts that murder, stealing, or pillaging are the way to winning does not align with our family values.

Most of these video games contribute nothing to our child's future career or mental well-being. We understand that these are *merely fantasy* games, and not reality, but surely some of the thought patterns of our youth are influenced by these games—and that's not a good thing.

Whether or not you have the same convictions about gaming as we do, we hope you recognize the value in moderating children's video gaming to allow them to pursue other productive interests. Here's what we recommend.

Creating Limits

If gaming is part of your family's life we strongly encourage you to develop some family limits. Don't simply give up and allow your kids to set their own schedule.

- Require that all homework and chores be completed before any gaming starts.
- Put strict time limits on gaming each week. Consider only allowing it on weekends for a specified amount of time.
- Totally prohibit games that allow interaction with unknown participants. The pressure from these gamers can truly suck a child in.
- Keep all gaming equipment in the main part of your home so you can supervise.
- Have your kids turn in gaming equipment (phones included) before going to bed.
- Encourage computer games that are more educational and don't focus on adrenaline-pumping activities.
- Review game choices at PluggedIn.com or Parents-Choice.org before you or your kids buy them.

Paying for Games

We have purchased a few computer games for our kids, but the vast majority have been discussed as a family and then purchased by the child who wants it. We know one family who purchased a new gaming system for their son each time he reached a significant educational goal. Buying a computer gaming system for a child as a reward for good grades or some other accomplishment is something we wouldn't consider. If your kids want to play, allow them to pay or earn it.

Managing Computers

We provide our kids with shared family computers and Internet access. We don't have superfast, gaming-speed Internet, and we don't buy the latest, most expensive computers. If our kids want a laptop or tablet of their own, they'll have to save their money to purchase it. If your household budget can fund the purchase of computers and Internet access, they will definitely help your kids, but high-tech gear is not worth going into debt over. Talk with your child's high school administration about making use of school-provided computers and labs, or use those available at public libraries.

Safety

Some families pay for website filtering services like Bsecure.com, NetNanny.com, or the free k9webprotection.com. We've chosen to permanently block certain websites using our router and to regularly monitor the history of our kids' surfing. Regardless of how it is done, parents must monitor and protect their children from harmful choices during their teen years.

Social Media

We've seen social media become as addictive as video gaming for some kids, easily devouring dozens of hours each week that could be better spent studying, working, or interacting with family members. Facebook's rules require children to be thirteen or older to create an account; we hold our kids off even longer. We've established a few other Facebook rules:

- No Facebook until schoolwork is completed.
- All friends must be people you have physically met.
- No friends of the opposite sex until you're sixteen years old, except relatives.
- Parents are given passwords and access to all social media accounts.
- Parents are "friends" with their kids so they can monitor behavior.
- Friend lists will be purged every six months of people you no longer interact with.

Parental involvement is critical, and so is honesty. We know one family who allowed their eleven-year-old daughter to lie about her age so she could have a Facebook page. She learned an "important" lesson from her parents—she doesn't need to follow the rules.

And then there's the dark side of social media. We've personally been a part of a single mom's tragedy when her sixteen-year-old daughter was lured away by a predatory older guy, leaving home with him for two years. Fortunately this story had a happy ending. She finally returned home and received some much-needed counseling. Not all families are as fortunate— there are predators and members of the sex-slave industry actively looking for innocent children. The potential for deception and harmful behavior are epic; parents must be diligent.

Surfing Limits

Laptop computers are kept in one room of the house and may not be taken into a bedroom without a specific purpose, and then only for a limited amount of time and with parental approval. Steve regularly checks the kids' e-mail accounts and reviews file downloads and history. If you have a computer, you need to take a class or have a friend teach you how to monitor your kids' activities; we want to be aware of what they're doing.

Managing Cell Phones

We simply don't pay for our kids to have cell phones. But with more than 85 percent of kids between the ages of fifteen and eighteen "owning" a cell phone, we are definitely going against the flow. We know that it is easier for some families to keep track of their kids with phones, but we don't think that way. Spending $100 to $175 each month for a family plan with multiple phones, texting, and data is not within our budget. Once again, if you do this and can afford it, are you setting your kids up with an expectation that you will continue providing well into their twenties? Or are you setting them up for an expense that they may not be able to afford when they're finally on their own?

If you think your child must have a cell phone for safety reasons, consider a limited, prepaid phone. It's cheaper and can't be easily abused—too much talking or texting simply turns the plan off earlier and they'll have to do without. It's kind of like teaching them to budget their money, except they're managing texts and talk time. We have a very limited prepaid cell phone plan on what we call the "family cell phone."

It costs us less than $60 per year and is only used to communicate with other family members.

Phones at Night

It's important to limit your kids' use of cell phones at night. One family we know "docks" all phones, including the parents', at 9:00 p.m. in a specific spot in the kitchen. No phones in the bedrooms at night. Kids need their sleep and to be able to set boundaries on communicating with friends.

Managing Music and Music Downloads

We let our teens purchase their own music with our approval and our iTunes account. If your kids have their own music collection on an MP3 player, be sure you're screening their purchases and listening habits. We've heard some pretty raunchy lyrics and don't think that listening to songs that promote violence, disrespecting authority, or illicit sexual behavior should be part of the listening diet for our children. Helping kids evaluate their private listening habits is important.

Who Pays for MP3 Players?

We've seen parents give their young children expensive cell phones / MP3 / smart devices that were soon dropped, broken, or lost. Kids should pay for their own devices and repairs or replacements. When Abbey wanted an iPod, she researched, planned, and saved for it. We helped her decide what and when to buy, but she paid for it. Letting your kids pay for their electronic toys virtually guarantees that they will care for them better.

The End Game for Recreation, Toys, and Technology

As a family, we all love to relax in different ways and really love to play. But we also get a thrill from setting and reaching tough goals. Limiting our kids' time for play has helped them reach many goals that their peers simply haven't even tried to accomplish. MoneySmart families limit exposure and time spent using technology and monitor it carefully.

Dealing with Recreation, Toys, and Technology at Different Stages

$5 Stage: Ages 0 to 5

Pick a few carefully selected, age-appropriate toys that help your child develop. Communicate with relatives about toys and games that you think would be beneficial so you can minimize those that aren't. Get on the floor and play with your child as often as you can. Please don't use the television or computer as a babysitter for your child. Technology at this stage in life does more harm than good. You're setting recreation expectations and standards at this stage; think carefully about the future.

$50 Stage: Ages 6 to 11

Develop a system to control your child's TV and technology time. We limited our kids to three hours per week. Monitor online activities by using blocking and filters, and keep all computers in a common room. We didn't allow our kids to use any social media websites until they were well into their teens.

If you choose to use cell phones for all members of your family, control your child's usage with a prepaid phone.

Monitor your child's recreational activities with their friends, and be sure you know the family and home rules where they visit. Ask questions and be involved.

Consider building onto existing toy sets or collections rather than buying a multitude of different toys. Encourage toy choices that are constructive or educational.

$500 Stage: Ages 12 to 17

As your children near the start of their college years, limited TV and technology time is going to help them succeed in their studies. They may complain, but stand firm—for their own good. Have a cut-off time for technology each night and a cushion period to decompress from all media. Kids at this stage need lots of sleep to function well in school.

Host a board game or FAT night with your kids. Teach kids to plan events and activities that are constructive rather than just "hanging out."

When it comes to cell phones, your child should be paying for some or all of their usage. It's part of adult life; every techno-gadget comes with a price.

$5,000 Stage: Ages 18 to 23

If you've spent time training your children and helped them set limits on their recreational activities, they'll probably stray for a little while when they first live on their own, but most will soon find their equilibrium. They should pay for their own cell phone and other technology needs.

$50,000 Stage: Ages 24 and Beyond

There are no reasons why you should be footing the bill for recreation, toys, or technology unless you're giving them a birthday or Christmas present.

CHAPTER 13

Gifts and Gratefulness

When it comes to gifts, most kids would say that it's better to receive than to give. But at our house, the kids have learned to sing a slightly different tune. Sure, they love to receive presents, but they also have discovered the joy of planning, saving, and giving gifts to each other and to those outside of our family. In this chapter we'll share some strategies we've used with our kids when we give them gifts, how we train them in gratefulness, and how we help them to give gifts from their hearts.

Giving Them Gifts

You're probably going to give gifts to your kids—homemade or from the store—but regardless of where the gift *physically* comes from, one thing is usually true: *emotionally* it comes from your heart. We want to give our kids good gifts that will bring them joy and help them grow.

Here are some dos and don'ts we follow when giving gifts to our kids:

Do

Focus on their interests. If one of our kids loves horses (Becky), then we'll constantly be watching for horse items (books, movies, décor, riding gear, special ornaments, games, etc.) and buy them when the price is right.

Yearlong shopping reduces stress at holiday time and helps us find more appropriate, reasonably priced gifts rather than last-minute, costly items.

Add on to collections. If your child loves Legos or some other expandable building item, buy new models or parts each year instead of buying a completely unrelated toy.

Give disappearing gifts. If clutter is an issue or space is limited, give a consumable or disappearing gift like favorite special foods, music lessons, sports lessons, a zoo or museum membership, or a special date to a restaurant or favorite location, or give them your time—your undivided attention to help them complete a long-desired project or goal. If you're creative, make up a personalized gift certificate so they have something to unwrap.

Use wish lists. We shared in Chapter 10 how we help our kids create and update their wish lists. It provides a record of things they want or need to shop for, or gift ideas to communicate with inquiring relatives or friends.

Be creative with birthday invitations. As our kids grew older and invited a broader range of friends to their parties, inevitably we'd receive phone calls from well-meaning parents wondering what type of gifts the birthday child would enjoy. We simply went to their wish list and rattled off a few items. Then in their teen years, we took it a step further. Because our kids had their own money and no real "needs," they truly wanted to have a party, not for the sake of presents, but to spend time with friends. This idea may seem a little tacky, but at the bottom of Joe's printed invitation for his sixteenth birthday party, he wrote:

Suggested gift list: All I want is to have a good time with everyone, so gifts aren't necessary, but since I know some of you will ask, here are some things I like:

Beef jerky
Corn Nuts
White Cheddar Cheez-Its
Sour Skittles
Big 5 gift cards
.20-gram airsofting ammo

The friends who did choose to give Joe gifts made them consumable, inexpensive, and delicious.

Keep it even. With five kids in our household, we don't want to be perceived as playing favorites (especially at Christmas), so we carefully watch how many presents we give each child and strive to keep it similar. We also watch the total amount of money we spend on each child. While it's not always possible to make it exactly the same, we do the best we can. We buy lots of smaller presents, things like books, music, or movies (often preowned) from their wish lists and then try to find one "larger" present that costs around $30 or $40. We'll spend about $70 per child, but since we shop all year long and pick up bargains, we usually end up with a much higher "retail" value.

For birthdays we usually spend around $30 per child. This is what we've been comfortable spending as it fit into our annual gift budget, and our kids have been happy with it. If they are saving for something more expensive, then we give them the $30 in cash to be used toward their goal.

Don't

Give them their hearts' desires. While this may sound unloving, don't give them everything their little hearts desire. Often our kids (of all ages) will want things that simply aren't going to be beneficial for them. You're the parent. You can say no or wait, and your children will learn that you still love them.

Keep it all. There have been times when well-meaning birthday party guests or relatives at Christmastime have given our kids presents that are not age-appropriate, are items we already owned, or are toys that would have necessitated starting a new collection. Abbey loved Barbies and had an extensive collection of dolls and accessories. One year at a birthday party she received a Polly Pocket doll. It was cute and there was nothing wrong with it, but after some consideration, she decided to exchange that doll for other Barbie accessories, so we helped her make the trade. Our kids have learned that they don't have to keep everything that is given to them. As a result, when they unwrap presents, they don't immediately unbox them. After the presents are opened and the guests are gone, we discuss each gift and decide if it will be kept or exchanged.

If you start this habit when your kids are young, you'll receive very little resistance. We'd put the gifts to be returned in a box and pick a day to go gift exchanging. Before we went out with the kids, we'd review what they would like to buy and if the gift was exchangeable. We tried to guess where the gift came from and went to those stores first. You've got to know each store's return and exchange policy. Some require receipts, others give the lowest recent advertised price, and some only give store credit. There were a couple of times when we simply couldn't trade a gift and ended up putting it in our gift closet (to be re-gifted) or out at a garage sale (our kids got the money for it).

Teaching Them to Be Grateful

We've helped our kids from the youngest ages to show their gratitude. Before they could write, we would write down the presents they received and who gave it. Then Annette would write thank-you notes and the kids would sign their name and draw a little picture or put fun stickers on the card. When they got a little older, she'd have the kids dictate what they wanted to say. Once they were able to write, they would record in their journal notebooks what they received and from whom; then Annette would address and stamp an envelope and the kids would write the card. At Christmastime when relatives or out-of-town friends gave us gifts, Annette would address a larger sheet of paper with the relative's name—"Dear Aunt Dianne"—and then each of us would write a sentence or two thanking her for her gift and the note would be mailed.

Several people have commented that the notes they received from our kids truly touched their hearts, and that our family was the only one that took time to say thank you. As our kids have grown older, they continue the practice and have expanded it to writing notes to businesses or foundations that have awarded them scholarships. We also help them thank their college teachers and club leaders by baking and giving them homemade loaves of pumpkin bread during the holidays.

Teaching Them to Give Gifts

Annette manages our household calendar and has always been a long-range planner. The kids have watched her start Christmas shopping in January and know she is always watching for discounted deals on things that others would enjoy.

We don't know when it started, but John and Becky at some point in their young lives decided that they were going to start giving gifts, but they didn't have much money. We had just returned from taking them around the neighborhood trick-or-treating for Halloween. They were sorting and trading their candy when John said, "Hey, Aunt Jenny really likes Tootsie Rolls and Uncle Billy loves Smarties. Let's give them all that we have!" They both got excited as they rummaged through their piles of candy. When they were done sorting it, Annette boxed it up and helped them wrap the presents. When the gifts were distributed on Christmas Eve, Uncle Billy and Aunt Jenny were really surprised that John and Becky had given them each a present, and more surprised when they each found dozens of pieces of their favorite candies inside the child-wrapped box. Since that time, their enthusiasm for finding inexpensive yet perfect gifts for their siblings, relatives, and even close friends has continued and spread to all of our kids. They each maintain a gift box in their closets where they gather perfect presents to be given away to those they love.

There are seven lessons that our kids have learned about gift giving:

1. **Cost.** It doesn't need to be expensive to say, "I was thinking of you" and "I love you." The candy they gave away was free, but the fact that they knew what their aunt's and uncle's favorite candy was, was priceless.
2. **Relationships.** They learned that it's really easy to find the perfect gift when you know the person well. They had spent so much time with Uncle Billy and Aunt Jenny that they knew what they loved.
3. **Watchfulness.** They learned that perfect gifts appear if you're looking, so they started watching more carefully and gathered gifts throughout the year.
4. **Storage.** Having a place to keep their gifts allows them to start early and not lose track of what they have gathered.
5. **Wrapping.** The kids loved to wrap their presents to immediate

family members in the Sunday comics. Childlike wrapping doesn't diminish the love that is communicated with the perfect gift.

6. **Homemade.** Abbey learned to sew when she was about eight years old. That year she made an apron for both Becky and Annette and pillowcases with fabric that reflected each of the boys' favorite pastimes: for John, army camo; Roy, airplanes; and Joe, baseball. The gifts were prepared with thoughtfulness and received with surprise and gratitude. John noticed that Grandpa (Annette's dad) had lots of keys on his dresser for his cars, house, workshop, and other things. He asked Steve to help him make a key rack out of some nice scrap wood and screw-in hooks. Together they sanded and finished the wood, then measured and screwed in the hooks. Twenty-five years later, the key rack is still in use. John smiles each time he sees it—so does Grandpa.

7. **Certificates.** On occasion, each of our kids has been a little short on gift money for Christmas. Instead of buying or making a present, they gave a gift of their time. Things like "Good for one long back rub" and "Good for making your bed five times." But our all-time favorite was when Abbey at ten years old had saved six dollars and wanted to "treat" Mom and Grandpa to lunch. She wrote, "Good for one lunch at McDonald's from the dollar menu, but you have to drive, you'd be scared if I did."

Being an example of generosity and helping our kids express their love through giving gifts is one of the greatest skills we can impart. As our kids have been generous to others, they have discovered there *is* more joy in giving than in receiving!

Dealing with Gifts at Different Stages

$5 Stage: Ages 0 to 5

Help your children "write" thank-you notes for birthday and holiday gifts that they receive. Encourage them when they choose to give away a toy or candy to a friend or relative.

$50 Stage: Ages 6 to 11

Writing thank-you notes is a habit that should be encouraged. If your kids don't have a journal, buy them one to record gifts that they've received and gifts that they've given. Help them write a list of things they would like to give as gifts to siblings, relatives, and friends. Then establish a place to store the gifts they accumulate.

$500 Stage: Ages 12 to 17

At some point in this stage, your kids will probably want to create a Gift envelope where they can put away a little money each week for gift buying. Having money set aside serves as a constant reminder to be on the lookout for gifts to buy. It also encourages a generous lifestyle. Keep encouraging the writing of thank-you notes. In this age of Facebook, texting, and e-mails, a handwritten note is so much more meaningful.

$5,000 Stage: Ages 18 to 23

If your young adult children live with you and are working while going to school, encourage them to set aside a little money for giving gifts. Be available to help them come up with ideas if they are stumped about the perfect gift to give. If they are short on cash, work together to find things they can make from resources around your home.

$50,000 Stage: Ages 24 and Beyond

If your adult children are living at home, follow the previous recommendations. If they live on their own and they need help coming up with inexpensive gift ideas for family members, provide them with ideas from everyone's wish lists. Making the holidays more about family and less about spending gobs of money, is what matters most.

CHAPTER 14

Miscellaneous Expenses: Essentials, Electives, and Extravagances

A s much as we dislike miscellaneous categories in a household budget, we've come across a few issues that needed to be included but didn't fit within the confines of other chapters. Some of these expenses should be considered essential to survival in our society, several are elective, while others we consider extravagant or even decadent and the total responsibility of the child who desires them.

Before your kids reach the ages where their "wants" start to exceed their earnings, it would be wise to develop a game plan for who will be responsible for various expenses. Communicating this in advance will definitely curtail many discussions and arguments.

This chapter will cover several expenses in the miscellaneous category, including school items, personal care items, medical expenses, and pets. Many thanks to our Facebook Fans who helped us with ideas for this chapter.

School

We highly value education and encourage our kids to embrace learning as a lifelong habit. However, you should not be expected to pay for all expenses that are encountered during the education sojourn from preschool through college. We've divided this list into three categories: parents should pay, parents could pay (if they can afford it; otherwise kids should pay), and parents shouldn't pay.

Parents Should Pay

School Supplies

Your annual trek to pick up school supplies doesn't need to break the bank. Before you head out to the stores, gather the supply lists from the school and do a household inventory of what you already have in stock. Make a list of things that are missing and then check the ads. Most office supply chains and discount retailers have huge sales during the month before school starts. Be sure to stock up on those items that are "staples" each year.

If your child wants to have an upgraded superhero notebook, a flashier backpack, or some other more expensive item, set a limit on the amount you will fund and let him pay for the difference. As your children are old enough, involve them in the planning and budgeting process for school supplies. It's a great exercise in planning, comparison shopping, and finding deals.

School Lunch

Parents are responsible for feeding their kids, but that doesn't mean that you should buy them lunch every day at school. We make lunches at home; it's usually more nutritious and definitely less expensive. If you feel like bringing a lunch to school is depriving your children of an important life opportunity, determine if you have the money available to let them buy it once a week. Remember that each time we completely fund an optional expense, we create an entitlement attitude—an expectation that this is what they deserve. Be wary of raising your household overhead for lunch money.

Field Trip Fees

In the younger years, parents are going to have to foot the entire bill for these. As your kids get older and start working part-time jobs, the expenses could be shared.

Teacher Gifts

Teacher appreciation gifts are incredibly important, but not important enough to warrant spending money that you can ill afford. We've always given homemade gifts of cookies or small loaves of pumpkin or banana bread to our kids' teachers. They are always appreciated, and many times eagerly anticipated.

School and Team Portraits

Selling portraits through school and sports groups is a big money operation. Here's a quote from the PhotoPreneur Blog: "An average size elementary school generates over $20,000 in sales over the course of a year for the photographer that takes advantage of all the opportunities there: portraits in fall and spring, events and yearbooks. . . . Some of the wealthiest photographers in America are school photographers!"

Know that the photo day is coming once or twice each year and research your costs. Many parents we know buy only the basic package, once each year, so they can receive a group class photo. If your child wants to have a more expensive photo package, or have a photo twice each year, let him pay the additional costs.

Senior portraits are a milestone event for most kids, but they don't have to cost hundreds of dollars. If you can only afford a minimal package, don't feel bad, but you might want to research other sources outside of your child's school.

One website visitor (Debbie from Phoenix) shared that she found a great deal at JC Penney's for her son's portraits. Several years ago the school photographer offered a package deal for $275. Debbie did her research and spent $42 at JC Penney's and received three 8 x 10s, three 5 x 7s, four 3½ x 5s, eighteen wallets, and nine billfolds. One 8 x 10, one 5 x 7, three wallets, and three billfolds were imprinted with his name and year of graduation. Prices have changed since then, but the idea is still the same. Research outside options like Sears and JC Penney's and look for coupons; you'll find great savings. Another option is to find a friend who does photography as a hobby and pay him or her to shoot some photos—that's what our daughter Abbey did.

Once again, set your budget, and if your children want a more expensive package or photographer, allow them the privilege of investing in their photos.

When it comes to sports team photos, if a league hires a professional photographer, we usually opt for buying only a team photo. Other years, Steve offered to take the team photo, retouched it, and e-mailed it to everyone on the team.

Graduation Fees

While the fees for high school and college graduation can be pricey, we've paid for all the costs (fees, cap and gown) and hosted a party (we did the cooking and provided the food) at our house to celebrate.

Parents Could Pay

Prom: The Big Dance

A senior prom or some other "once in a lifetime" formal event is truly a special memory for our kids, but still there is no reason to spend exorbitant amounts of money. Talk with your teen well before the event and set a budget that you both can live with. It may mean that your teen works a part-time job or does odd jobs to start saving money months in advance. The teen's efforts will make the night that much more important and memorable. Here's how we would handle other prom-related expenses.

OUTFITS As we mentioned in the clothing chapter, we've found tuxes for all of the young men in our family at thrift or consignment stores for less than $50 each (including alterations) and gorgeous gowns for our daughters for between $10 and $30. If you have children who refuse to buy used clothing, give them a small amount of money to spend on an outfit and let them earn the rest.

HAIR If your daughter wants a fancy "do" for prom, help her save her money to pay for a professional stylist. Another option is a do-it-yourself "do"— YouTube and Google searches provide plenty of how-to and technical info.

TRANSPORTATION Offer the use of the family car or to chauffeur the couple to the dance, but don't spring for a limo. If your young adults want that experience, they should research it, save for it, and decide afterward if it was worth paying for. It's a great opportunity for them to experience the true cost of the lifestyles of the rich and famous.

Yearbooks

For most high schoolers, a yearbook becomes a time capsule for a special period in life. Pay for one senior year, but if your budget can't truly afford it, tell your child early in the year so she can save for it. If your kids want a yearbook each year, once again, let them have the satisfaction of buying it.

Study-Abroad Costs

A child who wants to participate in a foreign-exchange or study-abroad program should also be involved in the planning and funding of an undertaking of this magnitude. While these types of programs can be incredibly beneficial, we don't see them as necessities or something that parents should go into debt for. See the fund-raising section in Chapter 11 for ideas on how your child can earn the money necessary to fund the trip.

Parents Shouldn't Pay

Class Rings

We simply don't see the purpose of spending this money; most people don't wear them in the years following graduation and/or eventually sell them to gold scrap dealers. But if your children want class rings, at the very least allow them the added pleasure of paying for these. If you want to give them a graduation present, make it something that will help them further their education—money toward college or a laptop or tablet.

Personal Care

Parents Should Pay

Haircuts

Parents should pay for inexpensive cuts at Great Clips, Fantastic Sams, or a beauty college. We learned to cut our kids' hair at home. Once the girls got their first job, they started paying for their own haircuts. If your children want to go to a fancier salon, give them the amount you would normally pay at a lower-priced shop and let them pay the difference. Hold firm on this, folks. You've got a long way to go before they are completely financially independent.

Parents Shouldn't Pay

Cosmetics

When our daughters were younger, we purchased makeup for them as presents for birthdays and Christmas. If they needed something at other times, they used money from their Spend envelope. Cosmetics go on sale regularly at grocery stores, and there are usually coupons to help make the price reasonable. We also shop at Ulta because they often offer a coupon for $3.50 off of a $10 purchase, plus they sell many other items at reduced prices and honor manufacturer coupons. If your daughter wants higher-end cosmetics, lotions, conditioners, and more, let her find the money to buy them.

Sunglasses

These items are so often bought and lost or broken that unless they are a medical necessity, parents should allow their children the "joy" of seeing their money depreciate, break, or get lost.

Tints/Colors

If your kids want to change their natural hair color, it's completely natural for you to let them pay for it too. A decision to continually color, tint, or frost is truly a lifestyle choice, an ongoing expense, and something your son or daughter can learn to do themselves. Abbey wanted to have her hair highlighted. A friend came over and showed her how to do it. They had a great time and the results were fantastic. If you don't have a friend who can teach you, there are DIY videos all over the Internet.

Other Professional Services

Let your kids spend their own money on these salon items: pedicures, manicures, and waxing. We've never heard of any of these things being a medical necessity.

Perfume or Body Spray

We've noticed many teen boys (and a few girls) using body sprays (and perfume) to replace good hygiene. The person who "needs" these items should be allowed to pay for them. If your child is conscientious about cleanliness and truly enjoys specific scents, buy it as a birthday or holiday present or let the child pay for it.

The amazing thing about all of these optional expenses is that kids who truly value these items will find a way to either do it themselves or pay the full price. Dealing with a finite amount of money encourages the establishment of priorities and lots and lots of creativity.

Medical

Parents are responsible for the health and well-being of their children. There is no question that we should fund their health insurance payments, doctors' visits, medication, and any necessary medical equipment. But there are some nonessential medical-related costs where your kids should be involved in the expenses.

Parents Should Pay

Doctor, Dentist, and Emergency Room Visits

This includes sick visits, annual physical, annual teeth cleaning, X-rays, sealants (one of the best health care investments you can make), fillings, and wisdom tooth extractions. Parents should pay for all of this until your child is out of college or has a full-time job.

Sports Physicals

Pay for these, but be smart about it. If your insurance covers an annual physical for your child, most doctors' offices will fill out sports physical forms for no charge as long as they are submitted within a year of the last exam. We've done this multiple times for baseball, volleyball, and various summer camps.

Glasses

Corrected vision is critical for children to grow and learn properly. Parents should pay for eye exams and glasses. But this doesn't mean that you have to pay for the trendiest frames and most expensive types of lenses. We always purchased basic single-vision lenses and frames. We only purchase additional items like UV and anti-scratch coatings for our kids who wear glasses every day. If your child regularly loses or breaks his glasses, have him participate in the replacement costs.

Contact Lenses

Hard or rigid contact lenses shape the eye better, but are more difficult to get used to. We'll pay for these when the kids are younger, but once they start working, they pay some of the costs. Becky started wearing disposable lenses when she got her first part-time job and paid the entire cost.

Parents Could Pay

Braces

If your child's teeth need aligning and you can afford it without borrowing money, great, but if you can't afford to spend the money, look for other options: negotiate a discount, save the money over several years' time, sell assets, or allow your child to help. If braces are not a medically prescribed necessity, you could simply do nothing, and let your child fund a smile makeover when he or she is older and can afford it. We know many loving, wealthy, and highly successful people who don't have Hollywood smiles but do have hearts of gold.

Parents Shouldn't Pay

LASIK

The FDA doesn't recommend LASIK for anyone younger than eighteen years old, but most doctors won't perform the procedure on anyone younger than twenty-one. The reason most often cited is that a person's eyesight needs to be stabilized, and many children between the ages of eighteen and twenty-one are still experiencing significant vision changes. In any event, LASIK is not totally covered by insurance companies and it is costly. Let your young adult pay for it.

Cosmetic Surgery

We live in Scottsdale, a wealthy community where many people spend money to improve their looks. We've seen and actually know a few families who have paid for cosmetic surgery like breast implants or nose jobs for their children. Unless there are huge appearance concerns that result in self-esteem issues, as in the possible need for a nose job, don't do it. As parents we need to convince our kids that appearance is not nearly as valuable as good character, which will last forever.

Pets Are a Child's Responsibility. *Not!*

Many times families we coached who were getting their finances in balance after months of working to pay off debt would one day announce, "Oh, by the way, we just got a new _____ (fill in the blank with your favorite animal) for our kids." There were two problems with that decision:

1. Usually it was impulsive and they hadn't fully counted the cost of pet ownership. We informed them of the expenses related to a pet's grooming, boarding, and medical care and discussed how much of their budget to allocate for it. It's more than simply food and water.
2. They got the pet for the kids! This is not only our opinion, but pet experts everywhere agree. Please don't allow a living creature to be an "experiment" to teach your child responsibility.

Pets Don't Teach Responsibility

If you have children who want a pet, please don't buy one for them expecting that they will be fully responsible for it. Some children may well be nurturing and gentle enough to truly love and play with a pet. But it is unrealistic to expect most children to be fully responsible for feeding, exercising, and cleaning, and to have enough experience to know when something is wrong. Parents should get a pet for their family because they have enough time, patience, and money to care for it. Pets will not train children to care for them; that's a parent's job. Over time, your kids can take on some of the tasks related to pet care, but ultimately the responsibility falls squarely on your shoulders. So before you make any decision about adding a living creature to your household, please consider the cost.

Success and Failure with Our Kids

When Abbey was about five years old, she assisted in cleaning hamster cages, scooped doggie doo, and helped feed and brush the dogs. Annette assigned the chores and at that young age Abbey did them. One of our sons wanted a pet, so we started him off with a hamster. He loved the idea of having a pet of his own and loved the pet. What he didn't love was the regular schedule that had to be maintained: feeding, checking water, and cleaning the cage. It quickly became evident that he didn't have an adequate level of responsibility to care for a pet. His younger sister adopted his hamster.

Can kids be taught responsibility? Some can and some can't—at their current age. They can be told to do things, but the drive to be totally responsible for nurturing an animal seems to be a character trait that is not easily taught. It simply isn't worth the nagging, reminding, and stress that are created when an unmotivated child is given a responsibility she isn't equipped to handle.

The Pet Progression

If you think your child is ready to help care for a pet, we've proposed a progression of sorts from those that are less expensive and easier to care for to those that take more time and money.

When buying pet equipment, check thrift stores, Craigslist.org, garage sales, feed stores, and discount retailers. When buying pets, we stay away from expensive pet stores and search for rescue groups, visit the pound, and check home breeders, the classified ads, or Craigslist.

These are various pets that we've had. Use this list as a guide to determine what type of pet is right for your family:

FISH We did have goldfish for a while, but our kids eventually became bored with them. Kids can feed fish with supervision, but cleaning the bowl or tank takes adult involvement until the kids reach the teen years.

TURTLES We've raised three-toed box turtles in an enclosed atrium in the middle of our house for the past fifteen years. They're low maintenance.

The kids help make up a special food mixture every two weeks and put it out a couple of times each week when the turtles aren't hibernating. The kids love hunting for newly hatched babies once a year.

BIRDS We had parakeets for a while and they would chatter anytime we were near. They required daily checks for food and water and cleaning their cage every few weeks. The kids couldn't interact much with them, so we sold them at a garage sale.

MICE We had these for a while too. It's a long story, but we'd never do it again. It might work for some families, but not for ours. They don't require much more than food, water, and a clean cage (escape proof is always a good idea).

HAMSTERS These critters require regular food and water monitoring and cleaning the cage every few weeks. Our kids loved holding and playing with them. They'd build Lego or Lincoln Log forts for the hamsters to play in or let them run around the house in a plastic rolling exercise ball. The hamsters broke out of their cages regularly until we used metal twisty-ties to lock the cage doors.

RATS A family friend of ours had a rat and loved it. We were told it was incredibly intelligent and very docile. Maybe for some families, but not for ours.

CATS There is allergy in care, so we haven't had one, but they are definitely low maintenance and kids love interacting with them. Count on vet costs, food, water, and litter. Don't expect your kids to be thrilled about cleaning the litter box.

DOGS Annette grew up with German shepherds and we've had three sets of them since 1986. They are great pets (we're a little biased), but do require a large amount of family involvement. Our kids have worked on exercising and training them, and we all scoop doggie doo. For our family, kids and dogs work well together.

Pets can enrich your life and teach your children many things, but please be sure you have the time, space, budget, and temperament to care for them well.

Beware of the Varied Varieties of Miscellany

Parents need to constantly monitor the expenses that their children ask them to pay for. We know that some of what we wrote in this chapter may fly in the face of the expectations your kids bring home from being with their friends. But the truth is that you are helping your children establish their baseline lifestyle by what you will and won't fund.

There is nothing harsh or unloving about setting a limit on what you will fund and allowing your child to pay for those things that you won't. We are actually empowering our kids to find themselves—their lifestyle, their spending level, and their dreams—by giving them the opportunity to carry the price of their miscellaneous desires. Cut the cords of entitlement and lower your overhead.

CHAPTER 15

To Work or Not to Work?

Do you remember your first paying job? Was it babysitting, yard work, flipping burgers, bagging groceries, or something else? Receiving that first paycheck was a milestone that most of us fondly recall. But regardless of where you first worked, you embarked on a journey of learning and accomplishing that has defined a part of who you are to this day.

Unfortunately, many in our society view the teen years as a holding pattern between childhood and adulthood. A time when expectations are low and expenses are high. A time where irresponsibility is accepted and play is expected; video gaming and texting are virtually unconscious behaviors; and consuming immeasurable amounts of junk foods and energy drinks are the standard fare. But the teen years haven't always been this way. A century ago teens were vital to the productivity of the family farm—their labor helped to clothe and feed the family. Children were an asset to the family.

Have our teens lost the physical ability or technical knowledge to be an asset in today's world? Or are we simply expecting less of them? Many parents believe that school is their teen's full-time job. While an education is vitally important and mastering the discipline of learning is critical to a child's future success, we believe that most kids have the time and ability to work around the house and work a part-time job, once again becoming a contributing part of our families and society.

Learning to work a real job, with real pay, in the real world, is a positive and important component of raising successful and savvy MoneySmart kids. And we're not alone in our beliefs; there are scores of incredibly successful people throughout history who embarked on their life's mission in their teen years. Here are just a few: Billionaire Warren Buffett at the age of ten started selling icy-cold Coca-Cola to thirsty beachgoers and chewing gum to neighbors and delivered newspapers. Thomas Edison went to work on a railroad when he was only twelve years old. Wolfgang Puck, a chef and owner of sixteen restaurants and eighty bistros, quit school at the age of fourteen and went to work. Richard Branson, the founder of Virgin Records, Virgin Atlantic Airways, Virgin Mobile, and several other companies, quit high school at the age of sixteen and started his first successful business—*Student* magazine.

The teen years are a launchpad for adulthood. In this chapter we'll talk about how to prepare your teens for getting that first job and what to do once they do start working.

Working Student

According to the Bureau of Labor Statistics, teen workers comprise about 3 percent of the total U.S. workforce. That means that almost 5 million kids between the ages of sixteen and nineteen are working part- or full-time jobs. Of your child's friends, you'll find that 37 percent of them have jobs (1 in 3). It used to be more (46 percent), but economic conditions have caused many adults to take the jobs that teens once held.

A large number of studies have been conducted to determine if high schoolers who work part-time jobs have lower grades. The results are mixed. Basically the statistics show that teens who have a strong, supportive family, work between ten and fifteen hours each week, and get enough sleep, will earn grades that are higher than the average student or only slightly lower. But working more hours definitely has a detrimental effect on grades.

What Good Is It?

All of our kids have held part-time jobs in high school, and we like the idea for a number of reasons.

It's a real-life experience.

It would be great if we only had one job to do and one role to perform in life. But life is more complex than that. We need to juggle a number of different priorities and roles each day, and in slowly increasing proportion, our kids need to learn this too. Taking on more responsibilities as one grows older is a natural part of becoming an adult. Some kids are ready for it at age fourteen or sixteen, while others never feel ready and need to be "pushed out of the nest."

It teaches responsibility.

Working for a well-managed business is a great way to develop a strong work ethic. Your child will need to learn and adhere to company policies, arrive on time, follow instructions, serve others, and deal with the responsibilities of managing a larger paycheck. These are all good lessons for a maturing teen to learn!

It may lead to a career.

A grocery bag boy (or bag girl) could become a grocery store manager, but a bagger could also say, "That was fun for a while, but now I know that I really don't want a career in the grocery business." Eliminating several types of jobs from a list of possibilities helps our kids narrow their thinking until they discover their life's passion.

It takes them off the family payroll.

Once our kids get their first job, we stop paying them from our payday system. They still budget their money, but it is money they've earned from outside our home.

What Age?

If your children are self-motivated and reliable, follow instructions well, and receive correction without becoming defensive, then they're probably ready for a job. If they're fourteen or younger, see if they can get a job in your neighborhood babysitting, dog walking, scooping doggie doo, house-sitting for a neighbor (watering plants, bringing in mail, taking care of a pet), washing cars, mowing lawns, or shoveling snow.

Child Labor Laws

According to the U.S. Department of Labor (DOL), the minimum age for nonfarm employment is fourteen years. The following rules apply to teen workers:

1. Youths fourteen and fifteen years old may work outside school hours in various nonmanufacturing, nonmining, nonhazardous jobs. Their hours are limited to:
   - three hours or less per day on school days, including Fridays
   - eighteen hours or less per week during a school week
   - eight hours or less per day on nonschool days
   - forty hours or less per week when school is not in session
2. Youths sixteen or seventeen years old may perform any nonhazardous job for unlimited hours.
3. Youths eighteen years or older may perform any job, hazardous or not, for unlimited hours. We limited our kids to working no more than ten to fifteen hours per week during the school year and twenty to thirty hours during the summer.

For more information visit the DOL website: www.YouthRules.dol.gov/. Also check with your state labor department for any specific restrictions in your area. Go to www.YouthRules.dol.gov/states.htm.

If your children are ready for a job, there are several things you can do to help them prepare to find one.

The Job Hunt

By the time our kids looked for their first jobs, they were seasoned researchers. They knew that it was a matter of being prepared, evaluating several options, and learning as much as possible about the companies where they wanted to work. We helped them put together their first résumés prior to filling out applications.

There were a few things we discussed to prepare them as they searched:

The Right Attitude

We reminded each of them that starting at the bottom was okay. Some kids think that they deserve more than minimum wage and that mopping a floor is "beneath them." As we've trained our kids to work at home by doing chores, they've understood that cleaning toilets, sweeping floors, and scooping doggie doo *are* menial jobs, but can be endured. And as they become more and more capable, they'll be given more challenging and rewarding jobs. Og Mandino, author of several awesome books, including the best seller *The Greatest Salesman in the World*, wrote, "Do more than you're paid for and soon you'll be paid for more than you do." We've taught all of our kids that having a willing and helpful attitude will bring huge blessings.

Where to Look

When our kids start looking for a job, we always start searching close to home. While this isn't always possible, it is extremely practical. Our kids get their first job because they want a driver's license—which means they need enough income to pay for their auto insurance. Since they aren't yet driving, Mom, Dad, or an older sibling will need to drop them off at work, or they'll need to bike or rollerblade. It's helpful to make a list of businesses within a two-mile radius of your home. Unless you live in a rural area, you'll be surprised at what you'll find. Within one mile of our home there are three grocery stores, several fast-food and pizza franchises, three ice-cream parlors, a bookstore, several doctors' offices, a dozen restaurants, and many more options.

Sometimes It's Who You Know

If the prospects near your home aren't as plentiful as ours, then make a list of people you and your child know well enough to serve as references or employers. This list should include teachers, guidance counselors, coaches, family friends, club leaders, scoutmasters, organizations you've volunteered for, and business owners. Have your child contact every one of them in the hopes of getting a lead for a job. A kid who shows initiative and diligence will catch the eye of many employers.

Keep a Lifelong List

Business owner, author, and syndicated columnist Harvey McKay wrote that from the youngest age, he kept a list of every person he met (with phone, date, and address). When he was looking for his first sales job, he contacted almost everyone on his list. Then when he started his own printing business, he did the same thing and many of them became customers. Encourage your kids to keep a list of contacts and to continue building it over the years. They may say that they've got it on their phone or in their head, but phones can be lost and memories can fail and if either happens, the list is lost too.

Help expand your children's network by introducing them to your friends and business associates over lunch. Prepare your children to ask questions about your friends' line of work and family. We've done this with several friends and our kids have learned much from them. Being disciplined in building a lifelong networking list can pay huge dividends when applying for scholarships, internships, employment, or even starting your own business.

Family Businesses

If you own a family business, it's important that at some point your child works for another business or at least under the leadership of a trusted nonfamily employee who has full authority to treat your child as a regular employee. While the family dynamic is a central theme to raising MoneySmart kids, all of our kids have benefited greatly from working outside of our business. We understand that there may be exceptions, but we've seen too many cases where children, given unearned positions in a family company, become a hindrance to the productivity and morale of other employees.

If your kids do work for you, please pay them a normal and customary wage. Pay them too little and they'll lose incentive. Pay them too much and they'll have an inflated view of their worth and find it hard to work anywhere else.

Safety

While we encourage our kids to work near our home so they can bike or rollerblade, we always keep safety in mind. We live in a large city, in a relatively safe neighborhood, but we like to minimize our kids' exposure to harassment or accidents by not allowing them to bike or rollerblade after dark. We've taught our daughters to calmly request the help of another employee if a male customer approaches them with a pickup line or unwelcomed attention.

Checking Out the Business

Before your children apply for employment at any business, visit the workplace together. While there, help them observe the culture, the dress code, how the work is done, and how the managers treat employees. If it is a grocery store or restaurant with several assistant managers, you'll probably want to visit a few times at different hours. If the business passes your first inspection, it would be appropriate to help your child introduce himself or herself to the manager.

It's a good idea to practice with your children before the introduction. Teach them to have a firm handshake, look in the manager's eyes when speaking, and have two or three prepared questions to ask.

If the business is hiring, filling out the application is the next step.

The Application

Many larger businesses and franchises require applications to be completed online. Be sure you sit with your teens when filling out their first few applications. Mistakes in answering questions can automatically kick them out of automated screening systems.

If the application is to be handwritten, we always ask for (or print out) two copies: one for practice and one as the final. Printing neatly is a must for these types of applications.

Practice Interview

Role-playing can help your children fly through an interview and relieve some stress too. Have them sit on the other side of a desk or table and ask questions like: What do you know about our business? Why do you want to work here? What other jobs have you had? What have you learned from the work you've done? (If this is a first job, the answers should be about volunteer work and chores.) Tell me three of your strengths and one weakness.

Also discuss what your child will wear to the interview, selecting clothes that are slightly nicer than the dress code of employees in the store.

Schedules and Availability

Most job applications ask for your child's availability. Since you probably won't know what normal shift times are, this will be a little difficult to gauge. What we typically do is offer times based on our child's normal school and activity schedule combined with our family dinnertime schedule.

If one of your kids is regularly assigned a shift that overlaps your dinner hour, talk with your teen and his or her manager about doing it less frequently—perhaps once each week. It might be helpful to find a job where your teen can work afternoon shifts or after an early dinner. We've helped two of our kids negotiate this issue, and both times they have received the schedules they wanted. One employer actually changed a scheduled shift time permanently after we explained our family mealtime priority.

Many first-time jobs are at businesses with several shifts, numerous employees, and one person trying to keep every employee's availability in mind when creating a weekly schedule. Because Joe's and Roy's availability sheets were lost or not followed several times by their managers, we taught them to submit it handwritten on a large sheet of colored paper (8 ½ x 11 inches) with their name written conspicuously on top—and they kept a copy too. Training our kids to communicate well so they get what they need is an important part of working in the real world.

Managing the Job and the Income

There's always a lot of cheering at our house when our kids land their first job. It's truly a major milestone! But employment does bring with it several new issues to be managed.

Family Staff Meetings

Our kids need to make sure they have their schedule for the upcoming week before our Sunday staff meeting because we need that information to coordinate car usage and rides to work.

Money Issues

With greater earning comes greater responsibility. Our kids love the increased income, but they need to learn to deal with Uncle Sam too.

The Great Awakening

When Joe received his first paycheck from working for one week as a courtesy clerk at a grocery store, he looked at the $54 check, and then looked at Steve and said, "Dad, you've been ripping me off!" He had worked for eight hours and received more than five times what he earned in one week from our payday system. We explained that as parents no one was paying us to run the house or cook meals, and that we allowed him to earn points so that he could learn to manage money. We congratulated him on getting paid, took him to the bank to cash his check, and helped him distribute his "fortune" into his envelopes.

Taxes: A New Reality

When we told each of our kids that they wouldn't be able to keep all of the money that they earned, they were crestfallen. We explained that some money is taken out for state taxes, federal taxes, and Medicare.

W-4 New employees are required to fill out a W-4 form. On the form, they'll be asked to select a number of withholding allowances. Employers use the number of allowances to determine how much money is withheld from the paycheck. Guidelines for choosing the number of allowances are provided with the form's instructions, but since most teens are claimed as dependents on their parents' taxes, they claim either 0 or 1.

FILING TAXES If your teens earn enough money, they will be required to file taxes, and will need your help doing it. Since your children's income will be below $31,000, they'll qualify to use TurboTax for free through Free File, a philanthropic partnership between the IRS and the tax software industry. It's what we've used with our kids for years. TurboTax walks you step-by-step through the complete filing process, including state taxes (if applicable). We submit the form online and enjoy watching the kids get their small refund.

Dealing with Tips

Several of our kids have worked jobs where they've received tips. Many employees view tips as free money, but they are actually considered self-employment income and must be reported to the IRS. Steve taught our kids to record their tips each day on a handwritten sheet of paper (see figure 15.1). They also start a new envelope in our payday system that they title Tips. We instruct them to put 15 percent of all earned tips in this envelope. At the

Date	Tip Amount	Running Ttl	Grand Ttl	TAX
6/10/09	$13	$13	$13	
6/14/09	$10	$23	$23	
6/16/09	$9.10	$32.10	$32.10	
6/20/09	$9	$41.10	$41.10	$6 15
6/23/09	$8.80	$8.80	$49.90	Tax =
6/25/09	$5.78	$14.58	$55.68	4.24
6/26/09	$3.25	$17.83	$58.93	
6/28/09	$10.47	28.30	69.40	
6/30/09	$14.00	14.00	83.40	
7/2/09	$8.81	22.81	92.21	
7/4/09	$1.21	24.02	$93.42	$3.60
7/9/09	.65	.65	94.07	
7/11/09	11.31	11.96	105.03	
	3.10	15.06	109.13	3.60
7/18/09	9.58	24.64	118.71	
7/21/09	$11.50	$11.50	130.20	
7/23/	$3.45	14.95	133.66	20,25
7/8/09	11.43	11.43	145.09	1.75
8/4/09	14.73	14.73	159.82	
8/8/09	9.00	23.73	168.82	3.60
8/11/09	9.00	9.00	177.82	
8/14/09	4.36	13.36	191.18	2.00
8/20/09	$5.84	5.84	197.02	
8/29/09	$3.47	9.31	$200.49))	

Figure 15.1 Joe's record of his tips.

end of the year, we input all of their daily tips onto an Excel spreadsheet. We summarize the tips in monthly totals and then input the self-employment earnings into TurboTax (see figure 15.2). Usually they have enough money withheld from their regular pay to cover the amount of tax owed on tips,

Joe Tips Calculation 2010

Date	Total Earned	15% amount		Monthly Totals	
01/11/10	$18.24	$2.75			
01/17/10	$17.94	$2.75		$57.18	JAN
01/24/10	$5.00	$1.00			
01/31/10	$16.00	$2.40			
02/22/10	$11.00	$1.70		$11.00	FEB
03/07/10	$17.32	$2.65			
03/13/10	$5.40	$1.00			
03/21/10	$10.50	$1.50			
03/23/10	$7.60	$1.26		$40.82	MAR
04/17/10	$8.27	$1.25			
04/26/10	$8.00	$1.20		$16.27	APRIL
05/02/10	$20.67	$3.10			
05/09/10	$6.80	$1.05			
05/24/10	$33.33	$5.00			
05/31/10	$16.00	$2.40		$76.80	MAY
06/20/10	$16.33	$2.45		16.33	JUNE
07/11/10	$8.33	$1.25			
07/18/10	$5.00	$0.75			
07/25/10	$10.00	$1.50			
07/25/10	$0.33	$0.05		$23.67	JULY
08/06/10	$20.00	$3.00			
08/14/10	$15.00	$2.25			
08/28/10	$11.67	$1.75		$46.67	AUG
09/06/10	$20.00	$3.00			
09/14/10	$14.00	$2.10			
09/19/10	$12.00	$1.80			
09/26/10	$20.00	$3.00		$66.00	SEPT
10/13/10	$14.67	$2.20			
10/24/10	$8.67	$1.30		$23.33	OCT
11/07/10	$6.67	$1.00			
11/19/10	$11.67	$1.75			
11/26/10	$7.33	$1.10		$25.67	NOV
12/19/10	$16.67	$2.50		16.67	DEC
TOTALS	$420.40	$63.76		$420.40	

Total months earning $20 or more	$360.13
Total months earning $20 or less	$60.27
TOTAL	**$420.40**

Figure 15.2 Tax calculation for Joe's tips.

and as a result the 15 percent that they've stashed away in their Tax envelope becomes a windfall for them. But there have been a few years when some of that money was needed to pay the government.

Monitoring the Money

When your kids start earning more money, you'll need to be more diligent in monitoring what they do with it. Using our MoneySmart Kids payday system has allowed us to check our kids' spending and saving on a weekly basis. They will be relating to many different people at work, some of whom could influence them to do things with money that could be detrimental. Other teen workers have enticed our kids to gamble or spend money on video games that they knew we wouldn't approve of. We know this is pretty mild stuff, but the potential is there for being lured into drugs and other illicit behavior. When kids know that there is accountability, it actually helps them walk the straight and narrow. And like we said earlier, there are very few times in anyone's life when they are completely unaccountable for their actions.

Saving for the Future

We still require our working kids to save 20 percent of their increased income. Refer back to Chapter 8 if you want more details.

Helping the Family: Sending the Paycheck Home?

In these tough times there may be situations where some or most of your teen's earnings will be needed to help the family survive economically. It may be a hard decision to make, but the upside of the family working and struggling together will be the unbreakable bond and great memories it produces. If at all possible, teens should be able to utilize some of their earnings, but as a family you'll have to decide how to structure it. Just be sure that you are being thrifty and working as hard as your kids are.

Internships

Work isn't always about earning money. Sometimes it's about not wasting time or money on unworkable career choices. Changing careers at the age of thirty-five or fifty, when you've got an established lifestyle and a family to support, is difficult, but trying several different types of career paths during the teen and young adult years can help your child avoid costly changes of majors in college and career changes later in life.

We like the idea of helping our kids find paying or volunteer situations in career fields of interest to them. As we mentioned in Chapter 11, we use club activities to investigate their interests as well. Before Becky started taking college classes, she thought she wanted to be a veterinarian. Annette called several vets' offices near our home and found one nearby that allowed Becky to volunteer there three hours each week. Becky learned that vet work wasn't her calling and moved on to earn an equine science degree.

Abbey thinks she wants to become either an athletic trainer or physical therapist. This past summer she spent two days each week volunteering/interning at a physical therapy (PT) practice. Most of her time was spent observing how the head therapist dealt with various patients' needs, but she also interacted with a college PT student who was doing her "clinicals" (spending several weeks working in various clinics around the country) and several other staff members. Abbey peppered them all with questions about colleges, various certifications they had to earn, and the rigors of training to be a physical therapist. She came away from this summer experience energized and more certain of her direction for college.

If your children are considering several fields of study or career choices, help them get an internship to flesh out their desire and see if it is a fit. Two added bonuses that come from volunteer work or internships are wonderful reference letters from the business owner and putting the work experience onto a teen's résumé. Most employers would rather hire someone who has practical, real-world work experience *and* an education over someone with only academic knowledge.

Cheer the Big Step

Getting a job is one of those happy *and* sad moments in life. On one hand your "baby" is growing up and moving closer to leaving home. On the other hand your child is becoming a contributing member of society, earning real income, and providing a necessary service. Cheer your kids on as they take a big step toward complete financial independence from the family.

Dealing with Work at Different Stages

$5 Stage: Ages 0 to 5

Teaching your children to do chores is the only thing you need to do at this stage to prepare them for the world of work. Assign age-appropriate chores, then instruct, correct, and praise their efforts (see Chapter 5).

$50 Stage: Ages 6 to 11

Introduce your children to different friends or relatives and talk about the kind of work they do. If you can visit them at work during the summer or other times when your child is not in school, do it. During the summer take field trips or tours of different businesses that provide services in fields that interest your child. If your employer will allow it, taking your children to work with you is always a good way to introduce them to the employment world. Be watching for talents or interests that you want to encourage as possible career choices.

$500 Stage: Ages 12 to 17

Help your children start a networking contact list of different people they meet. When it's time to look for that first job, help them identify the various businesses near your home that might provide a job for them. Help in preparing their first résumé and filling out various job applications. Role-play meeting the manager and the interview process. Review how things will change once they start earning their own money—what they will be expected to pay for and what you will continue to fund. Be sure to talk about taxes, tips, and W-4 forms. Be diligent to monitor the distribution, saving, and spending of their earnings.

$5,000 Stage: Ages 18 to 23

By this stage, managing a job, their income, and school should be a normal part of life. Encourage your children to continue building a list of networking contacts and to keep in touch with those people who might be able to influence their school or career paths. If you have business associates who are willing to mentor your young adult, facilitate that relationship. If the employment picture in your area is dismal and your young adult is finding it hard to land a job, encourage pursuing internships or volunteering—it could lead to a full-time job.

$50,000 Stage: Ages 24 and Beyond

Work for the young adult is a must, with the exception of someone who is mentally challenged or recovering from some sort of life-changing trauma. Your job at this stage is to serve as a coach and encourager.

Be a cheerleader and a safety net, but don't enable your young adult child to come back to roost in the nest unless there is a written contract with mutually agreed-upon terms, and a predetermined time frame (more in Chapter 19).

CHAPTER 16

Transportation: Getting Around

From the youngest ages we encourage our kids to transport themselves: crawling, then walking, and finally running. They graduate to little ride-on cars, tricycles, bicycles, skateboards, rollerblades, and scooters and experience more and more freedom as they deliver themselves under their own power. For many of our kids, getting their driver's license is the ultimate rite of passage, not being dependent on Mom or Dad to get around anymore.

We love the idea of our kids being independent, but when it comes to transportation, independence has greater actual and potential costs associated with it than many other activities that our kids are involved in. Actual costs include gas, insurance, and maintenance. The potential costs include higher insurance premiums due to crashes or violations; emotional distress and physical harm to themselves and others caused by accidents; and repairs from hitting other objects.

In this chapter we'll share what ages our kids start driving, what costs they are responsible for, and how they get their first car. Because the financial and personal stakes are extremely high when it comes to transportation, we're very slow to relinquish the car keys until our kids demonstrate a proper amount of maturity and responsibility.

When Should They Drive—Later or Sooner?

We made a mistake with our first child. We were excited about him turning sixteen, so we immediately helped him get his driving permit and taught him to drive. Mechanically, he learned to drive just fine, but what we didn't anticipate was his lack of maturity. Don't get us wrong, John was a good kid, an Eagle Scout, and a great student, but we simply didn't count on his desire to use a car to express himself. Within two years he racked up two speeding tickets, one hit curb ($900 damage), and a second accident that wasn't his fault. His insurance rates went up and so did our apprehension.

Maturity

So what is the best age for a child to start driving? The law may say age sixteen, but insurance industry statistics say older is better. We agree, especially if you live in a larger metropolitan area where accidents are more common. We uncovered these statistics on the websites of Allstate and the Centers for Disease Control regarding two significant issues to consider before allowing your child to drive.

Younger versus Older

- The fatal crash rates among sixteen- to nineteen-year-olds is four times higher than that of older drivers.
- Sixteen-year-olds are 40 percent more likely to be involved in a fatal crash than an eighteen-year-old.
- The risk of a crash is particularly high during the first year that a teen gets behind the wheel.

Boys versus Girls

- The death rate for male drivers and passengers between the ages of fifteen to nineteen was almost 200 percent greater than that of female drivers.
- Among male drivers between fifteen and twenty years of age who were involved in fatal crashes, 37 percent were speeding at the time of the crash and 26 percent had been drinking.

Knowing the tragic statistics, many states are now requiring sixteen-year-old drivers to take either a school-sponsored or commercial driver's education class. If they wait until they're seventeen or eighteen, the requirement is dropped. Since our first foray into teens driving, we've revised our standards. We allow our kids to get their driver's permit when they are sixteen or seventeen years old. They spend at least one year, sometimes longer, learning to drive with Steve in the car. As they exhibit better skills, we slowly extend the time and distance they drive. When their skill level and bank account (see the insurance section) are adequate, they can get their license.

Getting Around

Before they can drive on their own, they get around on foot or bike, or we give them a ride where they need to go. Sure, they're a little embarrassed to be seventeen years old and being dropped off at a friend's house or a sporting event. But because we've fully discussed the costs and responsibilities of driving, and they know that they will get to drive eventually, they're okay with it. Plus, we get to spend extra time with them while they're driving, keeping our relationship stronger through their teen years. We don't encourage our kids to ride with friends their age unless we know the family, the character of the driver, and how many kids will be riding along. And there's always public transportation, which our kids have used.

Driver's Education

Unfortunately, due to funding cuts, many schools no longer offer driver's education classes. If your school does, give it a try; if not, you'll have to research other options. Commercially provided driver's education classes with classroom and on-the-road training cost between $300 and $600. The only upside of paying for the class is that many insurance companies give a discount for successful completion. The discount probably won't pay for the course, but it will reduce some of the sting from insurance costs.

Rules for the Road

A 2009 Temple University study of teens' behavior proved that young drivers took greater risks when their friends were watching. Distractions, encouragement to take risks, and showing off are several of the reasons that we and many other parents, along with some states, have created some specific driving rules for teens:

- Turn off the radio and iPod for the first six months.
- No friends in the car for the first year. One family member is okay (they're usually pretty good at policing an older sibling).
- Minimize driving at night.
- Call when you arrive at your destination and when you leave to come home.
- Discuss the route you're taking with parents. This helps in case of car trouble.
- No phone calls or texting while driving—pull off the road if you must answer.

If you think these rules are unreasonable, consider these Centers for Disease Control statistics:

- 11 percent of teens said they drive more safely without friends in the car.
- 67 percent of teens said they have felt unsafe when another teen was driving.
- Almost 60 percent of teens' nighttime auto deaths occur before midnight.
- 56 percent of teens make and answer phone calls while driving. Talking on a cell phone doubles the likelihood of an accident and slows a driver's reaction time to that of a seventy-year-old.

We love our kids and want them to experience freedom, but for their safety and the safety of others, we must put carefully monitored rules in place. You're not being unreasonable—you're being a parent. It's your car and their life that are at risk. Your teens will simply have to get over it or walk.

Paying for Insurance

Our kids pay for their own auto insurance. Yes, it's expensive, and yes, it takes them quite a while to save for it, but it's all part of teaching them the cost and the privilege of driving. If we insulate them from the real-world costs by paying their insurance, they'll quickly learn that they don't have to be responsible and that they can depend on Mom and Dad to pay for their living expenses. If you're uncomfortable with your children paying for the entire premium, at least let them pay for half. Having some "skin in the game" will help them act more responsibly.

It's a good thing to explain how insurance works, what a deductible is, and what kind of coverage you have on your cars. If you don't know all of the answers, take your child to meet with someone from your insurance company.

Earning Income

Paying their auto insurance obviously requires a source of income. In Chapter 15 we described how we help our kids find a part-time job and how we limit their work hours so school doesn't suffer. Once our kids get their learner's permit, they start looking for a job and socking away money for insurance.

Six Months at a Time

As a family, we pay our auto insurance premium once every six months, saving the monthly processing fee. Because of this, we require our kids to save enough money to do the same. When they're learning to drive, we call our insurance agent and get a firm estimate on the new premium with an added driver. We calculate the increase and pass that expense on to our teen. It's interesting to watch them start calculating how many hours of work it will take to fund an amount around $100 each month, just for the privilege of driving.

The Wrong Question

When John was learning to drive, Steve took him to meet with our insurance agent, Paul. During the meeting, John learned how insurance coverage worked, what it cost, and what he should do in case of an accident. He listened respectfully and asked a few good questions.

As we finished up, John decided to ask one more question. He said, "What if I drove a Dodge Viper?" Paul whistled as he opened his eyes wide and then rolled them. He typed quickly on his keyboard as he spoke in choppy sentences, "Primary driver. Sixteen-year-old. Dodge Viper. Drives to school and work. Full coverage." He smiled slyly and looked up at John, saying, "Well, after you paid about $70,000 for the car, your insurance premium for six months would be . . ." He paused for a more dramatic effect, then slowly continued, emphasizing each "nine" as he spoke, "Nine thousand, nine hundred and ninety-six dollars or about $1,700 each month. Will that be cash, check, or Dad?" Steve laughed at the absurdity of it as he picked up John *and his jaw* from the floor. We still laugh about that question today!

Get a Discount

Paul did inform us that if John's grades were good enough, he could qualify for a Good Student discount. Insurance statistics prove that kids who get better grades have fewer accidents and tickets. Being homeschooled and attending community college for some classes did present a unique situation, but we wrote a letter and the insurance company granted the discount, saving John about 20 percent.

What to Do in Case of an Accident

You hope that it never happens, but it's always good to review this list with your teen and keep a copy in each of your vehicles along with your insurance information.

1. **Stay calm.** You'll probably be very shaken up. Take some deep breaths and remain at the scene.
2. **Be safe.** Check yourself and others for injury.
3. **Dial 911.** Contact police and medical services; ask a passing motorist to call if you're unable.
4. **Get info.** Gather the following information:
   a. Date, time, and location of the accident

     b. Other driver's name, address, phone number, and insurance information

     c. Year, make, model, and license number of the other vehicle

     d. Name, address, and phone number of any passengers or witnesses

5. **Call home.**

6. **Call your insurance agent or claims department.**

7. **Keep quiet.** Do not make any admissions of fault or sign any written statements until you have talked to your parents or insurance company.

8. **Arrange for towing.** If your car is disabled, ask your insurance company to contact a towing company.

Helping Them Save for a Car

Of course, you've probably guessed by now that the only time our kids will wake up in the morning to find a shiny new car on the driveway with a big red bow and their name on a gift card will be in their dreams. We simply won't be that unkind to any of our kids and deprive them of the pride of earning their own car.

But that's not the case for every family we know. It was a Tuesday—99-cent scoop night at Baskin Robbins—right after our weekly scout meeting. Several Boy Scout adult leaders were sitting and talking at a table while the kids were getting ice cream. One dad looked at Steve and said, "My sixteen-year-old daughter has put a full-court press on me to give her a car. All of her friends at school are getting them—and we're not talking used Chevys. It's more like BMWs or Mercedes [after all, this is Scottsdale, Arizona!]. What do you do for your kids when it comes to cars?" Steve replied with one word, "Nothing." Then he explained that from a young age we teach our kids to pay their own way for clothes, recreation, and auto insurance. If they want a car, they save their own money to buy one. We'll help them research and shop, but it's their responsibility to buy and maintain their own cars. By the time they leave our house, they can handle the full weight of real-life responsibilities. The dad just shook his head.

Eventually each kid will want his own set of wheels. Here's how we help.

Research and Planning

We start the process by discussing what type of car they're interested in and why they want it. John wanted a Honda Civic or Accord, while Becky, because she rides horses, wanted a Toyota Tacoma pickup truck.

Then we review *Consumer Reports'* annual car reliability guide. We check out the specific model and look back over a three- to six-year period to get a gauge on other owners' experiences with a specific model. We also call our family mechanic and get his perspective on the strengths and weaknesses of the vehicle we're considering.

Websites

To establish a specific savings goal, we look at Cars.com and AutoTrader .com to see the asking price for cars in our area. We also look at Edmunds .com and KBB.com (Kelley Blue Book) to see what they estimate sellers should expect to receive for their used cars. We've never bought a car from a dealer, preferring to deal with private sellers, avoiding the 9 percent sales tax in our state (sales tax rules differ from state to state). Remember that for kids working lower-paying jobs, the number of hours they'd have to work to save $150 to $900 of sales tax is enormous!

The Budget

Once we have a dollar value, we talk about how much money they expect to put aside each month and how soon they want to have the car. Then Steve helps them understand that when you buy a used car, you need to have some money set aside for repairs and unexpected maintenance. Becky and John both added $1,000 to their goal amount.

John's car budget was about $6,000, while Becky decided she wanted to buy a newer truck and set her goal at $13,000. It took John about one year to save his money and we bought his Honda in 2003. Becky started her savings plan in 2006. It took her two years and nine months to hit her target.

John was disappointed when his "new" used Honda wouldn't start one morning. The battery was dead, and fortunately the $1,000 in his maintenance account more than covered the $60 cost.

Inspecting and Buying

Once the money is saved, we search Cars.com and AutoTrader.com in earnest. With cash in hand, we've got negotiating power, but we also remind our kids that they may have to walk away from a deal because of price, condition, or a shady seller.

Before you go too far in the buying process, be sure you know your state's rules for purchasing and transferring the title for a car with a lien (outstanding loan balance) and a car owned by a private individual.

When we do locate a good prospect and set an appointment to look at the car, here's what we teach our kids to check.

- Always inspect the car in the daylight. Scan down the side of the car to look for paint irregularities or surface unevenness.
- Bring your research file folder and some blank paper to write notes on.
- Cover a magnet with a piece of cloth and check out various areas on the car to see if the magnet sticks to the metal. If the body has been repaired with Bondo or some other filler material, the magnet won't stick.
- Bring a mirror to check the underside.
- Bring a dollar bill with you. Close each door on the dollar bill and try to pull it out. It should hold the bill snugly. If it easily slips out of some areas but not others, the car has probably been wrecked.
- Check all fluids. The transmission fluid should be reddish in color but transparent. If it smells burnt, that's not a good sign. Oil should be golden in color; if it's black, it hasn't been changed in a long time.
- Ask to see the title to the car. If it is a salvage title (meaning the car has been considered a total loss by an insurance company), we may consider buying it, but only for a reduced price. We prefer a clean title and a car that hasn't been wrecked and repaired.
- Ask to see all maintenance records. We discovered in the records of one car we bought that it had been hail damaged, but repaired.

For a more in-depth checklist for how to inspect a used car, visit Samarins .com/Check/Index.html.

If the car passes our first inspection, we take it for a test drive. If it drives well, we ask to take it to our mechanic for an unbiased inspection. Usually the owner will drive over with us; other times we've been allowed to take the car for a few hours to have it inspected. Based on our mechanic's recommendation, we make an offer. One time, a truck that Becky liked checked out well, except for the shock absorbers—several were leaking, and replacing them was going to cost about $500. We came back to the owner with a lower offer, but he was unyielding, and we walked from that deal. It was okay, because Becky ended up buying a newer truck with fewer miles and more accessories for only $1,000 more.

Once the agreement is made, we get a cashier's check and bring it to the seller. In Becky's case, we negotiated the price down to $11,500 for a five-year-old Toyota Tacoma with 70,000 miles on it. We accompanied the owner to her bank to pay off the loan and start the title transfer process. She was so desperate to sell her truck that she accepted $700 less than she owed. The strange part of the story was that she was a mathematician for a company that made slot machines and her husband was a bank manager— they gambled on borrowing for a car, and lost. Becky won and really loves her truck.

If you're buying a car from an individual versus a dealership, create a bill of sale with the date, VIN number, and description of the car, including any known defects and the amount paid. Have both the buyer and seller sign it. Be sure to inspect the title for authenticity and take it with you to start the transfer process.

Gas and Maintenance

Kids should know what it costs to maintain a car, but when they're first driving, we pay those costs. They pay for insurance, and as long as they respect our rules, we'll pay for the gas and maintenance. If they start doing a lot of driving for school or sports, we make some adjustments. Joe's college baseball team has practices at various fields, sometimes a thirty-mile round trip from home. He ride-shares with other players to save gas and build team unity.

When they're earning more money and saving for their own car, they pay for gas. We usually ask them to fill up every other tank and keep track on a gas mileage card in the car. For a copy of our mileage tracker, visit AmericasCheapestFamily.com and search for "Mileage Tracker."

Another frugal family we know keeps a mileage-tracking notebook in their cars and requires their kids to log the miles they drive. The kids are charged a per-mile fee, which is put into a car maintenance budget account.

Teaching about Maintenance

As your kids start driving, be sure that they know how to:

- Check the oil and other fluids
- Check tire pressure
- Wash, wax, and vacuum the car
- Change a flat tire

If you don't know how to do these things, ask a friend or a mechanic to teach you. If it is physically impossible for you or your child to change a tire, purchase a AAA membership for both of you.

A Car Loan?

You've probably picked up that we dislike—no, hate—the concept of debt. We know that's strong language, but nothing in our culture has created so much distress, discord, and destruction as debt has. We know that credit is a modern convenience, allowing us to buy now and pay later, but we've seen so many people end up upside down in cars that we simply won't encourage any parent to put an unprepared and un-creditworthy teen under a pile of debt.

We feel just as strongly about cosigning. Don't do it—period. Once you enable your children to head down the path of debt it will take almost superhuman strength and determination to reverse that direction. Allow them to struggle and save and work and figure and pray. They'll develop character qualities that our debt-laden society has long forgotten—determination, self-responsibility, diligence, focus, and frugality.

One thing we've seen repeatedly is that those who wait and save are always rewarded. When you have cash in hand, a deal will come your way and the perfect car will end up in your garage.

You've done a great job so far raising MoneySmart kids. Stay the course, help them climb this mountain—on the other side is a car and the confidence that if they can conquer this goal and pay cash for a vehicle, they can triumph over any financial goal.

Driving Off into the Future

Helping our kids be MoneySmart about cars did cost us as parents. We bought cars for cash and our kids put thousands of miles on them for us. They burned our gas and dented our fenders and bumpers. Sure, they paid for their insurance, but we bore many of the other costs. It's our way of giving them a running start into adulthood. If they can get through college and buy a car, both without the ball and chain of debt, they'll be miles ahead of their peers.

Dealing with Transportation at Different Stages

$5 Stage: Ages 0 to 5

Keep your kids safe when you drive by always using a sturdy car seat. Be sure you buckle your seat belt too, as an example to them.

$50 Stage: Ages 6 to 11

As your child gets older and starts self-propelling themselves, be on the lookout for opportunities to allow them to pay for part or all of their transportation purchases (i.e. bikes, scooters, rollerblades, skateboards, etc.), reminding them that one day they will want to drive a car and eventually buy their own.

$500 Stage: Ages 12 to 17

Start talking about the real costs of driving—insurance, gas, and maintenance—and the responsibilities of protecting yourself and others by driving safely. Carefully consider the right age for your children to start driving and spend lots of time teaching them. Help them get a part-time job to cover expenses. Let your children know what their portion of the auto insurance will cost so they can save for it. Have your insurance agent explain what auto insurance covers and what affects the cost. Teach basic maintenance: changing a flat, checking fluids, filling with gas. Review how to safely use public transportation.

$5,000 Stage: Ages 18 to 23

If you can, allow young adults to use your vehicle while they save to buy a car; be sure that they are paying for their auto insurance and gas. Help your child research, set a savings goal, quote new insurance coverage, and buy that first car.

$50,000 Stage: Ages 24 and Beyond

At this stage, you're a resource for help and advice, not a bank or car leasing service. If your young adult needs to borrow a car while hers is in the shop, you'll have to make a decision about her driving ability and the use of your car. We've loaned our car to our older kids when they've had a car crisis, but it's only been for a short-term need. Be a safety net, not a crutch.

CHAPTER 17

Friends, Love, and Marriage

We realize that this chapter might seem out of place in a book dealing with money, but trust us, who your children hang out with could well affect not only their financial direction but the direction of their life compass. Who we associate with has a huge impact on who we become. If you pause for just a few seconds, you'll easily recall several people who had positive and negative influences on your life. We've all heard about the danger of negative peer pressure. What we're proposing in this chapter is that we encourage our children of all ages to build strong, positive peer relationships that will influence them to pursue great and virtuous goals. We'll share how we've done it with our kids.

Building Lasting Friendships

Temple University psychologists conducted an experiment to determine why teens took more risks when surrounded by their peers than adults would. They used magnetic resonance imaging scans of several parts of the brain while various aged teens and adults engaged in a car-driving, decision-making video simulation. When teens (ages fourteen to eighteen) knew that their friends were watching how they performed, they ran 40 percent more yellow lights and had 60 percent more crashes. The MRI revealed that areas of the brain associated with *rewards* showed much greater activity when their peers were watching. Researchers saw no meaningful difference in behavior when college students or adults knew their friends were watching.

The changes in our youngsters' thinking and actions are greatly affected by who they spend time with. Is it okay for a parent to train a child in all areas of finance, work, and school, but leave the area of relationships— friends, dating, and eventually marriage—to the child's sole discretion?

Be My Friend?

Facebook may have redefined the word *friend*, but not the significance of having true friendships. The total number of friends your child has is less important than the character of those friends and how deep the roots of relationship have grown.

We have helped our kids establish relationships with children from other families with similar values and similar economic backgrounds. Relating to families with different values would mean that we'd have to constantly retrain our kids on what was and wasn't appropriate. And if there was a great difference in household income, there likely was a large disparity in the things kids were and weren't allowed to do and buy. Friends can greatly influence us.

Strangely enough, even though the term *friend* is much more prevalent now due to Facebook, as a culture we actually have fewer close friends than previously. The American Sociological Review published a study recently revealing that the average American had only two close friends or confidants, whereas in 1985 that number was three or four. The saddest statistic was that 25 percent of the respondents said that they had no one they could confide in at all.

Having friends whom you've related to for many years through many changes in life is truly precious. We both have a few of those "call anytime, tell anything, cry on my shoulder" type of friendships, and it's been heartening for us to watch our kids develop some special relationships too.

There are several ways we've invested our time and some money to help foster those types of relationships for our kids:

Family Events

When our kids were younger, we'd host a few families (children and parents) for a picnic, barbecue, or game or movie night and spend time together. We selected families who had children similar in age to ours. We'd play games together, supervising the kids' interactions. Sometimes the boys and dads would go on the driveway to play basketball. The girls would play with dolls, do makeup makeovers, or dress up in costumes from our costume trunk.

As our kids grew older, they'd plan and lead some activities for other families attending. As we got to know the families better, we'd let the kids go off unsupervised, but with frequent "checkups" from the adults. Even the best kids, left alone, can do some goofy things.

As a result of supervised, selected family interaction, our kids have developed some deep and trusted relationships.

Playtime

There are some friendships our kids have developed apart from family associations, through school groups, clubs, or kids in the neighborhood. When we're unfamiliar with new friends, we encourage them to pick an activity that they can do at our house. We help our children think through what they want to do when their friends come over. We try to keep a low profile, but stay within earshot during the initial times together until we're sure that this new friend has positive character traits.

After an initial time together, we debrief our kids, asking questions about how the other person played, what they talked about, and other things to help them understand how to evaluate the character of a new friend. This is especially important if you have a child who has a more timid, following personality. That child needs to learn to assess behavior in terms of right and wrong rather than simply going with the flow.

If a friend passed the "play at our house test," we'd allow our child to go to the friend's house for a short playtime, provided the parents were home and would supervise. We'd discuss the things they intended to do and debriefed when they got home. Some of the families our kids played with differed from our standards regarding video gaming and acceptable TV viewing habits. If we knew there were differences, we'd encourage our kids to be mentally prepared to talk about limiting video game time (to something like forty-five minutes) and then offer other options for activities they could do. Helping our kids think ahead helped steer the relationship in a more productive direction.

Going in Groups

In the teen years there can be a lot of pressure on kids to "couple up" and start dating. We encourage our kids to minimize pressure from the opposite sex by doing things in groups. We know this isn't a foolproof method of protection from relationship pressure, but it certainly helps. Having a group of like-minded friends to spend time with, combined with strong personal convictions, will help protect your kids from any unwelcome relationships.

Your Friends

Another important way to provide a positive influence and instill a desire to seek out quality friends is to introduce your kids to your friends. Our kids view our closest friends as "aunts" and "uncles" and can approach them to talk about work, dating, money, fears, and hopes—basically anything or anyone that they are struggling with.

Remember that who your children select as their closest friends can and will have an impact on their future, and also on your life and finances. Help them choose wisely.

Just a Date?

What is the right age to start dating? With the media attention on the stars and who they're dating this week, TV shows glamorizing guy/girl relationships, and society telling you that you're not complete unless you have a boyfriend or girlfriend, the pressure to couple up is relentless. We've read news stories of a six-year-old being suspended from school for kissing a classmate, as well as parents allowing eleven-year-olds to date. Is this a good and healthy habit to encourage? And does encouraging young children to date lead to strong, long-lasting marriages and financial security?

After much reading on the subject, years of thinking, and numerous discussions with our kids, we've all decided to challenge the norm (are you surprised?) and establish a different view of dating. We don't think that having a significant other makes you more *or less* significant. We don't think that becoming an experienced "dater" better prepares you for a better marriage. And we don't think a person needs to "test-drive" lots of guys or gals to find the right one.

Looks Aren't Everything

Developing a deep, loving, and secure relationship takes lots of effort, care, and most importantly, time.

Today there is so much emphasis placed on external appearances. While we agree that there must be a physical attraction between marriage partners, this cannot be the major motivation for a relationship. Character is a critical component that is often overlooked by kids, but we've discovered that no matter how people dress, talk, or look, if they aren't honest in small things, it usually indicates other problems.

Our daughter Becky, age twenty-seven, has been patiently watching and looking for a hardworking, ethical, and financially responsible young man and has yet to find one, as of this writing. She's discovered that a lot of guys under the age of thirty have checked out of reality and checked into the adrenaline-filled, ultracompetitive world of computer gaming. She has had several men in their late thirties and forties approach her—it appears that by this age many of them have awoken from their gaming stupor.

Developing a Family Dating Philosophy

If the relationship landscape is so rife with craters and canyons, how do we help our young adults navigate? Many faith-based families we know have adopted a courtship mentality, basically eliminating dating during the high school years and waiting until a young man has a career and can support a family before pursuing a relationship with any girl. Some parents have gone so far as selecting a spouse, like the arranged marriages of old, while others encourage their kids to marry children of their friends or only someone who attends their specific church. We are not criticizing any of these choices. We encourage you to do your research, read, pray, and take time to develop your family's philosophy—don't just go with the latest trend.

For our family, we've asked our kids if we, as parents, could be involved as a coach in their dating choices. We've talked for years, from their early teens until now, about the importance of not finding the right person but of *being* the right person—encouraging our own kids to develop their character and work skills and to become "other minded." Having in-depth discussions with our kids about the bonding process that occurs when you spend hours upon hours with another person has been a real eye-opener for them. They've learned the importance of carefully and slowly building a strong and lasting friendship first with the person you love. We discovered this powerful material in a book called *Bonding* by Dr. Donald Joy. We've also encouraged our kids (and lots of their friends) to read several books on dating and marriage so they can be fully informed about the consequences (both good and bad) of pursuing a deeper relationship with someone of the opposite sex.

As Becky was moving toward deeper involvement with a guy named Jim (not his real name) a few years ago, we noticed some red flags. We liked Jim, he was a good kid, but his past was full of careless spending, lots of debt, video game addiction, too much alcohol, and a few other things. After spending much time with Jim, we carefully shared some concerns with Becky without condemning him or her. We told her that she could be happily married to Jim, but that it would take lots of work and several years to overcome the issues in his past. We didn't "forbid" her relationship. We knew that if we did, it might simply drive her away from us and into his arms, regardless of the facts. Over time, as she related to Jim, she started to see the differences in attitude and character as deal breakers and decided to end the relationship. They still remain friends, but Jim has moved on and married someone else.

Have you established a dating philosophy and communicated it with your child?

The Cost of Sex

Our society advocates sex education in schools as the ultimate protection against unplanned pregnancies and sexually transmitted diseases. The reason we bring up this topic is because of the potential financial costs to you as parents and the emotional and financial costs to your kids. According to 2010 research data provided by the National Campaign to Prevent Teen and Unplanned Pregnancy, 60 percent of teenage moms never graduate high school. Most are supported by their families or by the state in which they reside. The earning potential for the following fifteen to eighteen years for teen parents is reduced by more than $20,000 per year when compared to couples who wait until their twenties to have children.

And the problem doesn't stop with the teen pregnancy. The children of teen parents pay a high price too. The National Campaign study showed that the majority of them are raised below the poverty level and usually struggle with school. Sons are more likely to be arrested and jailed, and daughters are three times more likely to become teen mothers. Plus, many of these children end up being raised by their grandparents (us!).

The cost of a sexually transmitted disease is virtually incalculable, but it can mean a lifetime of heartache and ongoing medical issues and expenses.

So is the solution more school-based education, condom distribution, bodyguards, or locking our daughters in "Rapunzel-esque" towers? We think the solution to this issue is the same as teaching kids to handle money: it's up to the parents to be involved and teach their kids by example and through a lifetime of discussions.

A study published in the *Journal of Marriage and the Family*, conducted by Stephen Small and Tom Luster, revealed that teens whose parents carefully supervised their activities, knew who they were dating and where they were going, and set moderate and reasonable rules experienced the lowest occurrence of sexual activity. Teens whose parents set strict rules had more occurrences of sexual activity, but not as much as those with parents who set no boundaries on their behavior.

We don't want to treat our children like criminals or potential deviants, but clearly the presence of parents who are involved in their kids' lives is a huge deterrent against inappropriate, detrimental, and costly behavior.

If you want to raise MoneySmart kids, talk with your children about how to build appropriate relationships and how to withstand the pressure to have sex outside of marriage.

Relationship Resources

We've read some excellent books that have helped us navigate this stage in life with our kids:

- *Bonding* by Dr. Donald Joy
- *Life on the Edge* by Dr. James Dobson
- *Lady in Waiting, A Man Worth Waiting For*, and *The Right Guy for the Right Gal* by Jackie Kendall
- *Boy Meets Girl* by Joshua Harris
- *Marriable* by Hayley DiMarco
- *How to Know If Someone Is Worth Pursuing in Two Dates or Less* by Neil Clark Warren
- *Too Close, Too Soon* by Jim Talley and Bobbie Reed

If you and your teen or young adult child read these resources, you'll both be prepared to make decisions that will have positive influences on your lives.

Wedding Bells

If you've spent time talking with your kids from the youngest ages about relationships, communication, and money, a wedding can be one of the most exciting times of life. If you haven't prepared your child, it may still be a joyous time, but it could turn into an expensive experience for both you and your child—after all, weddings usually occur in the $50,000 stage from age twenty-four and beyond. Here are a few things to consider.

Premarital Counseling

Many churches or denominations require engaged couples to attend a marriage prep class or series of counseling appointments with a church leader. During the several weeks we attended our marriage prep class, we covered topics including communication, conflict resolution, sex, and money. It was the foundation of our marital and financial success.

If you don't belong to a church or if your church doesn't offer this service, help your soon-to-be-married children find a source for premarital counseling. Just make sure that you choose an experienced counselor who shares your values.

Becoming an In-Law, Not an Out-Law

If your adult child chooses to marry someone who doesn't quite meet your standards, what will you do? Constant criticism and warnings will only cause a broken relationship. We've found that love and acceptance keep relational doors open and can do much to heal wounds and misunderstandings.

It's so hard to stand by and watch your children make decisions that you know aren't in their best interest. Remember, if you've invested in your kids when they were young, good seed was planted, and it's just waiting to sprout. Give them space and time—they usually come around. If you can, be an encouraging in-law. It will keep lines of communication open and will usually give you the opportunity to help if there is ever an emergency.

Wedding Budgets

We've been in extravagant weddings where the parents spent a boodle, and smaller, less expensive ceremonies where the decorations were home-made and the food was "potlucked." Both ceremonies and receptions were wonderful and memorable. If your child wants a wedding that is beyond your means, let the engaged couple earn the money or help the bride find creative ways to get the look she likes for less. The book *Bridal Bargains* by Denise and Alan Fields is full of creative, frugal ideas. Also be sure to read etiquette books so you know your responsibilities as the bride's or groom's parents, and discuss these with your child. Yes, weddings *are* once-in-a-lifetime experiences, but in reality, the reception is really just a big, memorable party and not worth going into debt for.

Rich Kid Syndrome

Years ago, when marriages were arranged, couples seldom married outside of their economic station in life. The wealthy married the wealthy and got richer; the poor married the poor and stayed poor. While financial barriers are easier to cross today, the financial lifestyle we experienced in childhood is hard to forget.

Perhaps you've seen or experienced what we call the rich kid syndrome—a marriage in which one partner was raised in a wealthy or indulgent home and the other wasn't.

Golden Handcuffs

The scenario we've witnessed most often occurs when a young lady, raised in a wealthy or indulgent home, marries a fun-loving guy from a lower income family. The husband will never, in many cases, have the earning potential of her father. But they love each other and she is willing to make sacrifices—for a while.

Soon the babies come along. She remembers the luxuries her parents provided, things *she* can't afford for her own children. Inevitably, the little sacrifices start to add up. So she begins pushing her husband to get a different job, a second job, a completely different career, or a higher education. It is a recipe for disaster.

Beating the Syndrome

Some "rich girls" realize that their "golden handcuffs" can be removed. The chafing can be healed with large doses of contentment and creativity. One wife we know didn't give up her Pottery Barn tastes, but she stopped dreaming about shopping there and decided to go to garage sales instead. Rather than throwing away her marriage, she made her home a designer showcase fashioned from other people's castoffs. Her marriage is strong, her kids are happy, and she refers to herself as a reformed "spoiled brat." The cure for the rich kid syndrome is never easy, but it is always rewarding.

Helping your children select great friends and encouraging them to build strong relationships may take a lot of your time and buy you some grief too. But you'll never regret introducing your kids to a compass that will head them in the right direction for the rest of their life.

Dealing with Relationships at Different Stages

$5 Stage: Ages 0 to 5

Focus on building relationships with families who have your same values, with kids the same ages as yours. Don't send your kids off to play unsupervised. Parental involvement and supervision may not get you the break you want, but it will help your kids develop stronger relational skills and deeper friendships.

$50 Stage: Ages 6 to 11

As kids in this stage become more independent, they'll start making neighborhood and school friends that you don't know. Inviting those kids to spend time at your house when you're home will allow you to monitor the relationship and the character of the new friend. You'll need to assess the outward spending habits of the kids your child plays with. If they come from wealthy or indulgent families, you may need to minimize contact or discuss the differences with your child. Help your kids plan fun activities when they spend time with friends.

$500 Stage: Ages 12 to 17

This is a great stage for interacting with your child's friends. Being a visible and involved parent will keep the relationship from heading the wrong direction. Minimize the emphasis on dating by encouraging your child to spend time in larger groups at church and school or by planning game nights or sporting events at your home. When hosting an event in your home, be aware that kids in this age group can really eat, so if you can't provide dinner, just have lots of snack foods. During this stage our kids developed some long-lasting relationships with great friends. We've enfolded these kids into our family, taken them on vacations, and truly enjoyed seeing their positive influence on our kids.

Set aside time to read some of the recommended books on bonding, dating, and other relational topics. This is an important time to have deep and honest discussions with your teens about their goals for life, school, and relationships.

$5,000 Stage: Ages 18 to 23

Heading off to college, trade school, or work will expose your young adult to relationships well beyond your influence. If you've invested time in educating your teen on building strong relationships, few problems will arise. If you haven't, you may be in for a tumultuous ride. Be sure you've discussed your expectations for dating, pregnancy, and marriage. But if your young adult children choose different values than yours, love them with healthy financial and relational boundaries. Love can always win over the strong-willed, hard-hearted, or wayward child.

$50,000 Stage: Ages 24 and Beyond

Remember that relationship issues—weddings and divorces—can be very costly. It is possible that young adults may want your input or involvement in some of their relationship issues. Just be sure that you can provide objective help without becoming an enabler for unhealthy behaviors and choices. If you can't, refer them to a relationship professional and keep loving them. We'll discuss this more in Chapter 19.

CHAPTER 18

College and Trade Schools

College attendance has become the norm for the majority of high school graduates, but it wasn't always this way. In 1960, only 40 percent of graduates attended college, and the majority were young men. Today nearly 70 percent of high school students will attend a trade school, community college, or university, and 55 percent of them will be our daughters.

Most kids start their post–high school education sometime between the ages of seventeen and twenty-two. They may be physically mature, but for most, their fiscal acumen is undeveloped and they are unprepared for the monumental monetary decisions they will make. Unfortunately, many parents lay the full responsibility of selecting and paying for this academic adventure squarely on the shoulders of their young adult. Would you give a five-year-old $100 to spend without your supervision, or allow your fourteen-year-old to drive your car unsupervised, or give your eighteen-year-old $50,000 to manage without your input? The answer to all of these questions should be "No!" Placing the entire weight of a serious undertaking on someone who is unprepared for that responsibility is unfair and a recipe for disaster. Yet allowing and sometimes encouraging our barely informed children to enroll and commit to spend *or borrow* $40,000 is occurring regularly in the lives of America's young adults.

Most college graduates have greater earning potential and lower unemployment than young adults with only a high school diploma. But a diploma is no guarantee of success, and the lack of one is no curse either. History books are full of highly successful "dropouts," including Christopher Columbus, Abraham Lincoln, Thomas Edison, Frank Lloyd Wright, George Eastman (Kodak), Ray Kroc (McDonald's), Walt Disney, Colonel Sanders (KFC), Dave Thomas (Wendy's), Debbi Fields (Mrs. Fields Cookies), Rush Limbaugh, Mary Kay Ash (Mary Kay Cosmetics), Michael Dell (Dell Computers), and Bill Gates (Microsoft), just to name a few (for a list of more than one hundred dropouts, go to AmericasCheapestFamily.com and search for "dropouts"). These people were uneducated by academic standards, but were diligent workers and became savvy business leaders.

With college costs skyrocketing and enormous student loans becoming the norm, it's more important than ever to make sure your child has the motivation to go to college and a fervent desire to search out the highest-quality education at the best available price. Without this mind-set, your child may well graduate in four years but be paying off that expensive sheepskin for the next decade or two. In this chapter we'll share many of the things we've done to help our kids get a debt-free college education.

What about Perpetual Students?

Recently we met a young man who, at the age of twenty-six, was still attending college and still spending his parents' money. He was chasing his dream of becoming a major-league baseball player and had transferred from school to school, following different coaches, taking time off to play in semipro leagues, and looking for his "big break." At twenty-six years old, he has no undergraduate degree, no baseball contract, and no idea what his future holds, now that he has played his final year of college eligibility.

Helping our kids to target an education goal, while setting a limit on our financial involvement, will motivate them to work more efficiently and conscientiously. Plus, setting financial limits will safeguard our retirement savings from being siphoned off by a perpetual student.

Investing for College: A Parent's Part

Most financial planners say that the best way to pay for college is to start saving before your child is born. If you save $208 per month per child, by the time they're eighteen years old, you'll have $45,000 saved, hopefully more with a well-performing investment.

When we were first married, earning about $14,000 per year, a financial planner told us that we should save $200 each month for our son's education (16 percent of our income). We had money for only the most basic necessities, and saving for an event eighteen years in the future was impossible. Instead, we invested our time and efforts into our kids with the hope that they'd find a way to get through college without debt.

Here are three other ways we've seen parents provide for a child's college education.

The Costly Mistake

A wealthy friend of ours saved diligently for his two sons to go to college. By the time they graduated high school, he had enough money in separate investment accounts to fund each child's entire education. The mistake he made was structuring the investment to become their sole property when each child turned eighteen years old. One son did well, attended school, and graduated with some money left over. The other son took the hard-earned, carefully saved money and squandered it on fun and frivolity—and a really nice car.

Just because you're frugal and disciplined with your money doesn't mean your children will be. Be careful about how you structure any tax-deductible, college savings account. Your best intentions may well handicap your child—and break *your* heart.

50-50

Steve's parents encouraged their four sons to attend college, offering to fund half of their college expenses if they would fund the other half. Mom and Dad contributed their portion; Steve garnered an athletic scholarship to pay for his part. This arrangement provided incentive to keep his scholarship and maintain his grades at a respectable level. He graduated with a degree in graphic design and, best of all, no debt.

If your children have a stake in their college education, they'll be more likely to work hard, so let them earn it through work or a combination of athletic and academic scholarships.

Shrinking Support

A prominent TV personality chatted with us one day after an interview, sharing how he had helped his kids pay for college. He devised a way for them to gradually assume more financial responsibility for their education each year. He fully funded the first year of each child's college education. But each subsequent year, he reduced his support level by 25 percent. The remaining balance became the student's responsibility. One of his three kids found summer jobs to fund his portion. The other two kept their grades up and applied for numerous scholarships. One of them earned a full scholarship by her senior year. Did he handicap his children by "encouraging" them to work? We don't think so.

The Student's Part of Financing College: Why Be Average?

Many believe that student loans are the only way to pay for a college degree. While they may be common (64 percent of students utilize them) and are fairly easy to attain (fewer than 20 percent are declined), they aren't the only, or the best, way. And with 14 percent of student loans ending in default, it isn't best for our economy either. Defaulted student loans must be repaid (with interest and penalties) and are not subject to bankruptcy.

Consider the cumulative effect on an average eighteen-year-old who, with his parents' help, finances a four-year degree. According to CollegeBoard.com (the SAT people), the average annual (retail) cost of attending a public university in 2012 is $25,400. This figure includes tuition, books, room, board, fees, personal expenses, and transportation (the average cost for a commuter student living at home would be $13,600). The price will go up each year, and after four years, the young graduate can expect to pay between $60,000 and $110,000 for a diploma. A study by Nellie Mae, a student loan company, found that the average undergraduate borrower amasses $22,700 in loans by graduation.

While "average" may be considered acceptable, bear with us as we paint a picture of the average post-college life that we've witnessed much too often. Imagine that our average twenty-two-year-old graduate, with an average amount of student debt ($22,700), purchased and financed an average used car (with an outstanding balance of $10,000) while attending school. His total indebtedness is now $32,700.

Romance strikes and our high-flying average student meets the perfect average mate while attending school. After graduation they decide to get married in an average ceremony and combine their households, and their debt. The two lovebirds now owe nearly $66,000, assuming they both have similar college and auto loans. Even if they consolidate all the loans into a 7 percent bundle, they'll be paying their debt for ten years at more than $750 per month.

Next, they decide to buy an average house and finance some average furniture. Those average decisions finally put them over the financial brink, and they'll either file for bankruptcy or divorce within a few years.

If you'd like to see your children avoid being *average*, keep reading.

Get on the College Cash Safari

Discipline and teamwork are the keys to hunting down grants, scholarships, and cash. Here are four things our kids have done to track down school cash for debt-free college educations.

1. Fill Out the FAFSA.

Many private and public scholarships utilize the Free Application for Student Aid (FAFSA) in whole or in part to determine your financial need or eligibility. Your first step is to apply for a Department of Education Personal Identification Number (PIN) so you can electronically sign your FAFSA application. Do this by going to the FAFSA website (www.FAFSA.ed.gov) and following the directions for obtaining a PIN, which will arrive in a couple of days via e-mail. Set aside about three hours to fill out the FAFSA application. You'll need income tax and cash asset information for parents and student. Note: Fill out your FAFSA each year, preferably in February, to be eligible for the most scholarship money.

Your information is automatically sent to the schools you've selected in the application process.

Printed FAFSA applications can be found in most college financial aid offices. Beware of organizations that charge to "assist" in filling out your FAFSA; ask for free help in your financial aid office. Avoid FAFSA.com. It's a private company that charges for FAFSA preparation.

2. Just Say No to Loans.

FAFSA and other applications ask if you are willing to take out loans. The answer is "*No*" (even if you're willing). By checking the "Yes" box, you become a moneymaking prospect for lenders. Some institutions will directly route your form to the loan desk rather than the scholarship office.

3. Hunt Down Scholarship Cash.

Ben Kaplan is a master scholarship safari leader. At age sixteen, he researched and applied for more than thirty scholarships, earning nearly $90,000 of scholarship money in one year. With that money he attended and graduated from Harvard—magna cum laude—and took only six semesters to do it. His website, www.CityOfCollegeDreams.org, is full of useful information, videos, and helpful links to scholarship search tools. He has also authored the best-selling books *How to Go to College Almost for Free* and *The Scholarship Scouting Report*.

There are several different types of scholarships to apply for.

a. Specific college scholarships

These are funded through endowments given to each school's foundation program or specific college. It is incredibly helpful to make friends with someone in the financial aid department because they can give you the inside scoop on the process and let you know of new scholarships or upcoming deadlines. You'll find a variety of scholarships with very specific qualifications regarding gender, ethnicity, grades, major, etc.

b. Privately funded general scholarships

These scholarship funds can be used at any school. Search at your library in *The College Blue Book* or *Foundation Grants to Individuals*, in Ben Kaplan's books, or on one of many websites, including FastWeb.com, FreschInfo.com, Petersons.com, Scholarships101.com, or Zinch.com. You'll find scholarships based on ethnicity, college choice, major, gender, parents' military or public service, employment, grades, writing skills, and opinions.

c. "Unique" scholarships

Not all awards are based on grades—you'd be shocked at what's out there. The Hellenic Society has scholarships for students of Greek descent, the Morgan Horse Association has one, and if you're a great duck caller you could win college money. Do some searching and you'll be amazed.

d. Military service

If your child is physically fit and has the desire, consider joining the Reserve Officer Training Corp (ROTC) in college or enlisting in a branch of the military. Depending on what type of military service selected, they could receive college tuition paid for, college loans paid off after a specific time of service, or tuition paid during or after their service is completed.

Successful hunting requires patience, persistence, teamwork, and a great guide. Here are three examples of teamwork that captured a winning prize.

$100 per Hour or More!

We spent ten hours with John helping him research and fill out scholarship applications. In return, he received $1,000 in scholarships. That was with our first college-bound child. Our hunting skills improved as more of our kids entered the hunt. We did more searching with Becky, and over a three-year period, she was awarded enough scholarship to cover all of her college expenses—now, that's real treasure!

$1,333 per Hour

Brenda and Tim are friends of ours who encouraged all four of their kids to attend college and saved enough money to fully fund their first year and buy them each a car. The kids picked up their parents' frugal habits and each worked diligently to win scholarships to pay for school.

Linda, their third child, attended a state university, which didn't cost her parents a penny. She related her story to us at a graduation party a few years ago. She maintained good grades in high school and graduated in the top 5 percent of her class. Beyond that, she learned how to play the scholarship game. During her senior year of high school, she spent about thirty hours filling out twelve scholarship applications or entering writing contests. Her hard work paid off when she was awarded three scholarships. Two of them renewed each year based on her grades; the third was a onetime award. Her prize for thirty hours of research and writing was $40,000 (about $1,333 per hour).

But she didn't stop. Throughout her college career Linda continued to apply for more scholarships, and won several. No matter how small the award, she always followed up with a handwritten thank-you note.

Joe's Scholarship Bonus

It was a routine e-mail from a homeschooling friend, but in it she listed a $500 scholarship sponsored by the Chartered Property Casualty Underwriters Society to be awarded to an Arizona university student enrolled in a business degree program. Joe followed the instructions and wrote a brief essay about his education and employment goals, then mailed in the packet. It nearly killed us to wait, but an envelope arrived while Joe was traveling on a college baseball trip. The night he returned, we left the envelope on the steering wheel of the car he was going to drive home from school. It was 11:00 p.m. and we were both in bed, but he burst into our room and read the note. "Congratulations," it started, then we gasped as he read, "Additional funds became available . . . your scholarship will be for $1,000!" We cried tears of gratefulness.

This was only one of many "miracle" scholarships that Joe received to fund his education at a small, private university where he's studying business administration and planning on graduating debt-free, of course!

Jump on the scholarship safari, and with a little luck and some keen eyes, you'll be able to bag some "big game."

4. Work Smarter Through College.

While many schools do have work/study programs funded by our tax dollars, we're talking about a different way of capturing dollars for college.

According to a 2010 Bureau of Labor Statistics Survey:

- 32 percent of four-year university students work
- 52 percent of two-year college students work

There's nothing wrong with working while going to school. We have several friends who received some sort of training in a trade prior to entering college and were able to make above-average income while earning a degree.

- Tom worked as a barber while studying engineering.
- Sam worked as a graphic designer while studying music.
- Nathan earned his Licensed Practical Nurse certification and worked in nursing homes while earning his premed degree.
- Brent earned a trade school welding certification and earned his engineering degree while working as a welder.
- Thomas performed several piano concerts at local churches to raise money to attend a public university, where he's studying music.

Help your student take a skill, talent, or passion and turn it into cash. Or your child could find a job on campus or nearby. Most colleges utilize student workers in cafeterias, libraries, a variety of office positions, and even landscaping. With a little discipline, they could work ten to twenty hours a week, keep up with their studies, and earn food and spending money.

Navigating College Choices

Since 1999 we've been committed to learning as much as possible to help our kids successfully navigate college. Each one has encountered different obstacles and challenges. We've discovered many resources to help maximize their time and money. To date, two of our kids have graduated and two others are currently attending. But before you enroll your child, you've got to determine if college is the best place for them.

Is College Worth It?

Many people think that a college or technical school degree guarantees financial security and success. We disagree. In the hands of someone with poor work habits and no enthusiasm for his or her chosen vocation, a degree is merely a worthless piece of paper.

Long before college was even a speck on the horizon for our kids, we taught them to work around the house. A hardworking, responsible, organized young adult will be prepared to tackle life's challenges and be welcomed by most employers. But more importantly, as we've lived and worked with our kids, we've come to know their strengths—and weaknesses. By the time they were ready to enroll in a degree program, we all had a good idea of their talents and passions, and were able to select an educational program that built on their strengths.

As you learn who your children are, you might conclude that college isn't the avenue to pursue, but that a trade school, internship, apprenticeship, or other work-study arrangement would be better. Just because a young adult is more of a "hands-on, less academic, not good with tests" type of person doesn't decrease his or her value as a person. But it may mean that going to a university will not only produce frustration but may cause your child to lose heart, quit, and waste a ton of money. Remember that ethical, hardworking tradesmen such as plumbers, electricians, and air-conditioning specialists provide a necessary service and can make a great living.

Where to Start

If you're pursuing college or tech school, it's important to thoroughly research schools offering programs and degrees that fit your educational goals. Before you settle on an expensive four-year, out-of-state university, you might want to consider the advantages of community colleges.

All five of our kids started taking classes at a community college well before they were eighteen years old. They were allowed to do this through special enrollment for homeschool students. When they graduated high school, each of them had earned about thirty college credits.

Public high school students can also earn college credit by enrolling in Advanced Placement classes (there may be costs involved) taken at their high school or through dual-enrollment at a nearby college. Either way, college credit is earned before graduation—potentially saving thousands of dollars in tuition.

Starting at the community college has been a great option for our family for three reasons, and the first is *not* finances:

1. **Student-teacher ratio.** Class sizes are usually smaller than universities—twenty to thirty students.
2. **Profs.** Most 100- and 200-level classes are taught by full professors, whereas many large universities utilize teacher's assistants (TAs) for some lower level classes.
3. **Cost.** The cost per credit hour at many community colleges is one half to one third that of public universities. Taking a basic core curriculum (English, math, and lab sciences) there, then transferring to a university *can* save a boatload of money.

Visit Schools, Gather Information, and Negotiate

Selecting the right school is an important but massive undertaking. Start looking online to review admission requirements and courses of study. Also talk to their admissions department, course advisors, and financial aid representatives. While establishing a good financial aid package and knowing about your intended major are important, having a face-to-face meeting with an advisor and department chair from your selected major are critical factors also. We did this with both John and Becky at several schools and learned much more than we could have on the phone or from a campus tour.

If your child is entering college with AP credits or transferring from a community college, negotiating the transfer of classes may be necessary. In a perfect world everything would transfer, but we always brought specific course syllabi and college catalogs with us into advisor meetings to help the process be more successful.

The fine skill of negotiation is critical, but unfortunately most kids are inexperienced at it and most advisors are simply looking for easy solutions. Be an advocate for your children. Help them ask the right questions, gather the right information, and get the best education they can.

Get It Right at School

Selecting the best school doesn't guarantee smooth sailing for your children; they'll need a few other skills to successfully complete the trip. Here are five ways to get the best quality for your education buck.

1. Get to the Right Person.

Every large corporation has its politics and, unfortunately, institutions of higher education do also. Helping our kids deal with this aspect of college is much easier at a smaller school. It's less intimidating for them to "climb the ladder" of authority from teacher to department chair to dean of instruction and even up to the president of the college when things just aren't right. Our kids have found that the higher up the ladder they climb, the better their concerns are heard.

We've got to help our kids understand that they are the customers and the instructors and administrators work for *them*—not the other way around.

We've helped our kids negotiate changes in graduation requirements, financial aid problems, lost paperwork, overcharges on tuition bills, and a host of other issues. Teaching them to respectfully question the professionals at school is a critically important skill for anyone involved with a large, powerful, and expensive organization.

2. Get the Right Advice.

Where should your student turn for help in planning schedules and selecting courses and instructors? Other students? College advisors? Most frugal-minded people are dedicated researchers, committed to learning how to get through a system as quickly and painlessly as possible. We encourage parents to learn alongside their college-age kids to help them plan and navigate their course—that is, if the student's desire for independence will allow it. Annette thrives on researching and loves to sit down with our kids at registration time to help them get their schedules as streamlined as possible. She's taught them to review their field of study requirements, consider their work schedules, and manage their courses—resulting in very little wasted time.

Careful planning with trusted advisors can save your student a semester or two of school and thousands of dollars in tuition.

3. Get the Right Classes.

Most courses of study require a certain number of credit hours in math, science, humanities, and behavioral science, and some offer very few options. But if alternate classes are available, help your student select ones that fit with his or her interests, worldview, or moral convictions. For instance, Becky needed a science class with a lab. Because our family conviction is more compatible with intelligent design than with the theory of evolution, Becky chose a class that fit her interests and would also transfer to other schools. Our other kids chose different interesting lab science classes including Plants and Society, and Meteorology. Psychology or sociology can often be exchanged with other social and behavioral science classes such as economics, business, history, or geography. Ask questions, and question every answer.

4. Get the Right Teacher.

Unfortunately, many institutions "sell" their classes as commodities, with instructors simply listed as "Staff." Getting the right instructor *makes* the entire class, so help your kids push the school to get the instructor's name if it isn't listed.

John (at the age of sixteen) had a bad experience with a particular community college English professor and dropped her class. When Steve learned from the department chair that several English instructors had a 60 percent student drop rate, or higher, we helped John set up a meeting with the dean of instruction. Any business that loses 60 percent of its customers has a real problem. We informed the dean of some of the shortcomings we'd observed in the English department in the two classes that John had taken, and he in turn suggested several specific instructors (for English and other classes) who had the highest student retention rates. We weren't looking for easy grades, but great instructors who loved to see students learn. John found a much better instructor, and we held on to that list of excellent professors for our other kids to benefit from.

Another great source we've discovered is RateMyProfessors.com. This is a free website where students comment on their professors' teaching abilities, knowledge of subjects—and their *looks*. There are more than 700,000 professors from 6,000 schools rated on this site. Reading students' opinions of specific professors has helped our kids select better instructors and be better prepared for the instructors' teaching styles.

If your children talk to other students and some trusted instructors, they can avoid wasting time and effort with a less-than-enthusiastic instructor. We can't overemphasize that a great instructor with a positive attitude can ignite the flames of learning and motivate a student to achieve great things.

5. Get Textbooks Cheaper.

The average cost for a semester's worth of books is $500 to $900, totaling more than $7,000 over a four-year period. By doing a little sleuthing, we've found savings as great as 87 percent on textbooks.

The search to save money on textbooks begins a month before the semester starts. Our kids go to the school bookstore (online or in person) and get the exact title, ISBN (International Standard Book Number), author's name, and edition of the book(s) needed. We check various sources to find the best prices on that specific book (always read descriptions, ISBN, and editions carefully). We've had the best luck finding good deals on eBay.com and Half.com, but always check other sources:

a. College bookstores
You can save about 25 percent if you buy used versus new textbooks.

b. CollegeBooksDirect.com
Savings of 25 to 40 percent can be found on this site.

c. CheapestTextBooks.com

This site searches several other websites for the best textbook prices.

d. eBay.com

We've found savings as high as 87 percent with shipping included.

e. Half.com

Save 40 to 80 percent on used books with shipping included.

f. Amazon.com

You can find new and used textbooks on Amazon. If you have a .edu e-mail address, you can receive a free six-month membership in their Prime program, allowing you free shipping of many items. Be sure to read the details carefully so you don't inadvertently get charged a renewal fee.

g. International editions

We recently discovered several listings on eBay and Amazon.com for international editions of textbooks for Joe's classes. The major differences were paperback versus hardback or lesser-quality paper, and some had different page numbers. Joe checked with his professor, who okayed using the book. You can save 60 to 80 percent.

h. Other students

Joe has saved a boodle by purchasing textbooks from friends who have taken the same classes and by posting his textbook needs on a college Facebook group he created. The other student makes more money than the bookstore buy-back price, and Joe gets a great deal. If you try this, make sure the book is the correct edition.

i. Renting

Chegg.com revolutionized the book rental industry, charging about 30 percent below retail. The concept has caught on, and now many campus bookstores offer the same option. When the semester is over, you simply return the book and don't have to worry about whether you will be able to sell it or not.

j. Professors

If we're having trouble finding the required edition at a discount price, our kids will contact their professors (phone or e-mail) and ask if the previous edition of the book will suffice. Many times they say yes.

k. Digital savings

A few college math classes have required a subscription to an online learning website called MyMathLab.com. It was less expensive to purchase a membership directly from the publisher's website rather than the school bookstore. Some schools have gone to digital books, and we haven't found a way to get a discount on that . . . yet.

If you're a diligent sleuth, you can cut your textbook costs considerably and save thousands over four years.

Navigating the college landscape is much easier when you know the way and surround yourself with excellent guides and resources to help you get the right answers.

Managing Money in College

You've selected the right school, applied for the right scholarships, saved the right amount of money, and now you're ready to send your high school graduate off for the education of a lifetime. If you've trained your children from youth to manage money using a cash envelope system or something similar, those habits will be so ingrained that they will continue using them even when away at school. But discussing all of the expenses they'll face is critical.

Covering the Basics

The basic needs of food and shelter must be put into the college money plan. As with any expense, there are multitudes of ways to meet these needs, from inexpensive to extravagant. Find the options that fit with your budget.

Food Options

This is an area where students can waste a lot of money and time, and do themselves physical harm from poor nutritional habits. We knew one gal who went away to an expensive private university she could just barely afford. To cut costs, she basically lived on ramen noodle soup and other inexpensive carbohydrates for months until she started experiencing serious health problems.

Our kids need to have money to eat a balanced diet or their studies will suffer. Most universities have some type of dorm requirement for the first year. College meal plans can range from expensive to exorbitant—but there are options. Usually buying a ten-meal-per-week plan and supplementing with microwavable meals, cereal, and fruit in between cafeteria dining can help to keep the costs down. After their first year, off-campus housing and self-cooking will be less expensive. Arming our kids with some basic nutrition, menu planning, shopping, and cooking skills will keep them healthy and well fed. Our book *Cut Your Grocery Bill in Half* can provide lots of helpful tips.

Shelter

Dorm rooms, fraternities or sororities, and apartments or rental houses are the norms for college students. Getting several similarly focused college students to rent a house or apartment seems to be the least expensive way to live. Sharing cleaning, maintenance, and food costs can really help conserve cash. It is critical to screen roommates carefully and to fully communicate, in writing, the expectations.

Clothing

College-aged kids should be responsible for their own clothing expenses. If they aren't yet, you can pay for some of their clothes when they're home during school breaks or give them a minimal amount for necessities, then let them pay for everything else.

Recreation

Parents shouldn't be responsible for their young adults' recreational expenses. If they want to play, they should pay.

Parental Funding

If you are providing money for living expenses, no matter how responsible your child is, we recommend sending that money on a monthly basis.

Large lump sums of cash can easily be squandered, while managing small amounts faithfully leads to managing larger amounts well. Be sure that you can truly afford to provide what you've promised.

Help Them Set Up a Safe and Realistic System

Cash envelopes are okay, but in a college environment where theft may be more likely, a debit card system, where money is kept in a bank account and tracked on individual account sheets (each one a different category like the cash envelope system), is safer. Transferring a limited amount of "income" to their bank account each month reduces the likelihood of an unexpected spending spree. Kids who are sent to school with a parent's credit card in hand are likely to teach their *parents* the truest reality of the $5,000 stage. Yes, this system does require your involvement, but it also provides monthly opportunities to encourage your student for a job well done!

Prepaid Debit Cards

Loading a prepaid debit card each month with a pre-communicated, limited amount of "income" is another way to help your child manage spending. If you receive a phone call or text in the middle of the month asking for some extra money, you can lovingly but firmly say, "That's all there is for this month, honey. You'll survive, and next month we're sure you'll do a better job of budgeting." Our kids are smart—they'll figure it out! The downside of a prepaid debit card is theft or loss. Kids who are notorious for misplacing things should not use this system.

Online Shared Systems

Technology is truly helpful for managing finances with your student away at school. There are a couple of budgeting websites that you can share access to with your student and work together to manage his or her expenses.

Mint.com is a free website where you link a bank account to their budgeting software. Your child can simply move each expense into a specific, predetermined budget category. Income can be managed in much the same way. The downside of this system is that it doesn't allow you to accumulate cash, for example in a clothing account, from one month to another.

A second option is Mvelopes.com. This is similar to Mint and is linked to a bank account, but it does allow money to be saved in individual "envelope" categories for future spending. We like this program a lot, and recently Mvelopes.com made their basic system available for free.

Either system will allow you to co-monitor and manage the account with your student.

College Is Just the Start

Your children's move toward financial independence takes a huge leap forward during the college years. With careful planning, solid communication, and masterful money management, they can graduate ready to take a stand in the working world. It may seem like a lot of work to get them to this point, but your training and preparation combined with their discipline and diligence will result in a fantastic launch into self-sufficient adulthood.

Dealing with College at Different Stages

$5 Stage and $50 Stage: Ages 0 to 5 and 6 to 11

If you can afford to start saving money in a tax-sheltered savings account for your children, do it. Meet with a trusted accountant or financial planner to make sure that you receive maximum tax advantages while ensuring that your children won't be given all of their money at once. If you can't save the recommended amount for college, don't stress over this; invest in your children's education with your time and enthusiasm. There are plenty of scholarships for motivated, hardworking kids.

$500 Stage: Ages 12 to 17

This stage is the launchpad for college. Involve your teens in character-building activities and those that expose them to careers of interest (see Chapter 11 for ideas). Excellent study habits and good grades should be encouraged to make winning scholarship cash easier.

Junior year: start researching and visiting colleges or trade schools in earnest; also encourage adequate preparation and study time for taking the

PSAT and SAT (or ACT) (see resources in Chapter 4). Discuss how much you expect your children to contribute to their college education. Consider military service as an option.

Senior year: start applying for scholarships, filling out college applications, and completing the FAFSA application process. Your graduating senior should be managing money with a cash envelope or debit card budgeting system before he or she leaves home.

$5,000 Stage: Ages 18 to 23

Communicate your financial limits with your college-bound student and stick to them. A part-time job and summer employment should be required. Throughout the year, your student should continue looking for scholarships, and each February you should fill out an updated FAFSA application.

$50,000 Stage: Ages 24 and Beyond

Graduate schools are expensive, and you'll need to determine your financial involvement carefully. If your young adult earned great grades in his undergraduate years, and you can afford to help out financially, do so. We simply don't recommend that parents take out a loan or drain their retirement accounts to fund graduate school.

If your young adult has spent several years "trying to discover herself" and finally wants to come home and get an education, do a test before investing your money. Let her take a few classes for a semester at an inexpensive school like a community college. If she does well, help her continue and look for scholarships. If she doesn't do well, cut the financial cord quickly and require her to get a full-time job. In the interim, put her to work around your house. Once she gets a job, charge a fair rent amount.

CHAPTER 19

Bailouts: The $50,000 Boomerang

If you've gotten this far reading this book, you know that our goal is to train MoneySmart kids to become financially independent MoneySmart adults. We know that even the most formidable money managers encounter bumps in the financial road of life. How well those bumps are navigated depends on how well the manager has been trained. A well-trained manager won't lose control of his vehicle, but a novice could easily end up spinning out.

This is the $50,000 stage, a time when your grown kids (ages twenty-four and older) might call on you to help them manage some adult-sized problems and expenses. We're talking about bailouts—spending our money or time to repair the damage from a financial spinout. As parents we want to be an emergency safety net or airbag for our kids, but not a continual crutch. An airbag doesn't prevent a crash, but in most cases it minimizes injury. And a safety net for a high-wire performer doesn't prevent the fall or the fear felt with a mistake, but it does prevent death. We don't want to totally insulate our adult kids from the consequences of their choices. We also don't want to create a "welfare situation" where they repeatedly return, looking for more money without making any permanent changes in their habits. We want them to learn from their mistakes, growing wiser and stronger as a result.

231

Bailout Policy

Unlike many governments, we have a limited bailout policy. If our kids dig a hole for themselves, we'll counsel, encourage, and help them find resources, but we won't write a check to have the hole filled for them. There is much value in having to think and work your way out of a problem you created. Albert Einstein agreed when he said, "The significant problems we have cannot be solved at the same level of thinking with which we created them."

If we bail out our adult kids, there is a great likelihood that they won't invest the mental energy to truly solve the root of their financial dilemma. The lesson will be unlearned and the problem repeated, costing even more the next time. Remember, the 5/50/500 rule is the escalating cost of an unlearned lesson. Some of you may say, "Not bailing out your kids is totally uncaring. You're family, and that's what family is for!" We totally disagree. Is it truly loving to continuously enable self-destructive behavior? We'll cover several different bailout scenarios and describe how you can still love your adult kids and help them recover from true emergencies, while not enabling bad habits.

Financial Bailouts: A Thanksgiving Story

Grant and Melody (not their real names, but a real story) raised their son, Peter, in a traditional, faith-based home. When he graduated from college, Peter decided to join an online dating service to assist him in finding a wife. He didn't know how to carefully ask questions of his future bride and ended up in a very difficult marriage to Shannon. When Grant and Melody first met Shannon, they had hopes that Peter's marriage would be successful.

Sometime within the first eighteen months of marriage, Grant and Melody became concerned. The young couple said some things that indicated they were having financial struggles. Every six months they moved to a new apartment, but then suddenly bought a house, so Grant and Melody thought things had worked out. Strangely, though, Peter hadn't consulted with them, relying solely on input from his in-laws during their home purchase.

About a year later Peter and Shannon approached Grant and Melody needing money to make their mortgage payment. Wanting to help, Grant and Melody decided to lend the couple enough money to make the payment, and clearly communicated the repayment terms. They allowed Shannon to work off some of the debt by cleaning their home, deducting a fair wage each time she did. Shannon cleaned their home three times, and then decided that she'd rather not do the work.

Over the next few weeks Shannon and Peter both bought new tattoos, and Shannon purchased a purebred golden retriever puppy for her brother's birthday present. It wasn't long after this that the loan payments stopped and Peter also stopped returning his parents' phone calls.

Three months later Grant and Melody learned that the kids had been evicted by the bank and their home repossessed. By this time, Grant and Melody were fairly certain that they'd never see their money again.

The young couple moved in with Shannon's parents, Bob and Carol. Early on Thanksgiving morning Grant and Melody's doorbell rang. Bob and Peter were standing there wanting to talk. Bob started by lecturing Grant and Melody about the importance of supporting their kids, and then encouraged them to show their love for Peter and Shannon by giving them a financial gift to make this Thanksgiving a time for them to be truly thankful.

Months earlier, Grant had learned some family history about Bob and Carol, which included some serious financial troubles and a home foreclosure. Grant and Melody felt extremely uncomfortable with Bob's request for money, but said that they would consider it.

Grant and Melody decided not to give any more money to their kids, and we encouraged them to stand firm with their decision.

Often gifts of money do nothing but delay the inevitable and often short-circuit the learning process. We reminded them that just like a drowning man could pull his rescuer under water, they could easily become financially compromised if they continued to bail out the kids. They may lose touch with Peter for a while, but we are convinced that eventually the good values they have infused in his life will help to restore the relationship and possibly his good financial sense too.

What Can a Parent Do?

Grant and Melody's story is not uncommon. What can you, as a loving parent, do to truly help your children in a financial crisis, without jeopardizing your own financial security? We recommend moderate actions to help, while measuring your child's commitment to real financial change. If his desire is superficial, you'll soon know and won't have invested thousands of dollars in a failed effort. If his intentions are genuine, your help may be the best encouragement you could give him.

Here are seven effective bailout ideas.

Help without Enabling

EDUCATION Buy him a book on managing finances or debt reduction or pay for him to attend a Crown Ministries or Dave Ramsey's Financial Peace University class.

GROCERIES Buy him a grocery gift card, several bags of groceries, or put together a care package and leave it anonymously on his doorstep. Everyone has to eat, and this can free up money to pay bills. If he continues to struggle for several months, help him locate nearby food banks or apply for food stamps.

Here is a list of helpful items to put in a food survival box to help someone who is struggling financially. Obviously, if there is a particular food he dislikes, don't include it in what you give him. For more helpful ideas visit AmericasCheapestFamily.com/AdultKids.

Beef jerky	Popcorn (microwave)
Breakfast cereal	Powdered milk
Canned pineapple	Pretzels
Canned soup	Raisins
Granola bars	Spaghetti O's
Instant hot cider / hot cocoa	Sunflower seeds
Instant oatmeal	Tuna fish
Jelly	
Macaroni and cheese	
Peanut butter	

UTILITY BILLS Pay a bill or two, directly to the utility company; don't give cash to your child.

CREDIT CARD DEBT Help him sign up with Money Management International to manage his debts, and encourage the destruction of any credit cards.

COUNSELING Pay for several sessions with a counselor to help your child get back on track mentally, physically, or relationally.

MEDICAL BILLS If your child is dealing with a serious medical condition and bills are piling up, contact a hospital social worker or a medical billing advocate (BillAdvocates.com). Consider paying a doctor directly for a past-due bill.

PRACTICAL HELP Rather than giving your child money, visit him (even if he lives out of town) and offer to repair, improve, and organize things around his home.

Things That Won't Help

MONEY Unless there has been evidence of good financial management skills in the past, cash bailouts simply delay the inevitable and create financial dependence, not independence.

LOANS Usually a consolidation loan or another type of borrowing isn't going to solve the problem. But if your child thinks borrowing is the answer, let her go through the process of working with a bank. Bankers are more careful and less emotional than parents. If the banker won't lend her the money, there's probably a good reason why you shouldn't either. If you do decide to lend your child money, write up a contract and stick to it. Keep reading to see how a tough lending policy paid off.

COSIGNING Don't do it unless you're willing and able to pay for the entire item or loan yourself. Once again, if a lender says they need a cosigner, then they probably think the borrower isn't creditworthy.

A Good Lesson—Learned the Hard Way

Do limits and tough communication work with adult children in financial binds? When we asked our Facebook Fans about bailouts for adult children, we received this reminder that love, with limits and accountability, can have a profound impact on financially careless children.

My parents always bailed me out, and I never paid them back, until they had me sign loan documents every time I borrowed from them. I also had to agree not to ask for any money until ninety days after I had paid the balance off. I was never financially responsible because I always had my parents to bail me out. When they made it harder for me to borrow, I finally learned the true value of money. Over a two-year period, I slowly began to watch my expenses. I finally realized that I had no option but to learn to live within my means and do without.

Today, my parents will offer to loan me money, but I never take it. I feel so much better than blowing money I shouldn't be spending.

When I was borrowing money from my parents, I avoided them because I didn't want to have the conversation about when I was going to pay them back. Now that I think about it, I spend more time with my parents and enjoy it even more because there is no guilt.—Kelly

Don't underestimate the pressure that bailouts and loans can put on your relationships. We've seen so many adult children who paid back old debts to their parents enjoy completely restored relationships. We've also seen many parents try to control their adult children's behavior by giving money or things to them or to the grandchildren with strings attached— this is manipulative and not helpful. Please don't do this to your child.

Real Emergencies

Being a safety net means that in the event of a true emergency, you'll get a phone call in the middle of the night. We're talking about medical emergencies, car accidents, abuse, or some other life-threatening, unexpected event. We have an emergency fund: money set aside so we can get on a plane, rent a car, or render help immediately if necessary. It's a limited amount of money (about $3,000), and in thirty years of marriage we've only had to dip into it once, when Steve's mom was dying. If the emergency occurs in your city or nearby, be there; go to the hospital or accident scene to render calm and careful advice. Help your children think through the issues.

If they are in the hospital and are unmarried, stay with them and make sure that they get proper medications and attention. There are too many times when even well-trained medical professionals make mistakes. A lucid, caring family member asking questions and taking notes minimizes risk. It may frustrate medical professionals, but each time we've done it, we've seen their frustration turn into respect.

Real emergencies usually take a long time to fully recover from. When our son John was about twenty-one years old and living on his own, a speeding driver ran him off of the road. His car was totaled, and we helped him work through the insurance process, loaned him a car, and coached him through contesting the cash settlement. The process took about six weeks, but John learned a great deal about working with insurance companies. Medical emergencies, with piles of bills and insurance paperwork deluging mailboxes, can linger for months, even years. Helping our kids deal with these issues is part of being a safety net.

Coming Back Home

You might think your child won't ever move back home, but the statistics are telling a very different story. Whether you call them Boomerangers or Kid-ults, adult children are returning to the roost in record numbers, and we need to be prepared with a plan and gentle, but firm limits.

Common or Rare?

The frequency of adult kids moving back home has ebbed and flowed through history, and we are currently experiencing an increase.

- Social demographer Michael Rosenfeld is quoted in *Time* magazine as saying, "More than 70 percent of singles in their 20s . . . lived with a parent in the 1940s."
- The *New York Times* reported, "In 1980, 11 percent of 25 to 34 year-olds were living in multigenerational households. By 2008, 20 percent were."
- U.S. Census data for 2009 reported that 56 percent of men ages

eighteen to twenty-four and 48 percent of women in the same age group live with their parents.

This issue is not isolated to the United States. In London, the *Daily Telegraph* reported that 28 percent of UK parents are taking drastic measures to support their eighteen-to-thirty-year-old young adults. They're going as far as taking out loans or refinancing their homes to help their kids make ends meet!

What was normal and totally acceptable in the 1940s was rare in the 1980s and has now come back around. Many writers are calling adult kids who are living under their parents' roofs YUCKIES—"young unwitting costly kids"—and calling their parents "baby gloomers." From our perspective this isn't doom and gloom; it could be a real boon, if you have the room. The biggest complaints come from the adult kids saying that living with their parents changes their socialization habits, and from parents who haven't cut the purse strings and are funding their young adult's lifestyle.

The Causes

There are a number of reasons that our adult kids come back home, and some of them simply aren't their fault.

- Poor financial decisions
- High cost of student loans
- Repossessed home
- Divorce
- Depressed job market
- Decreased income or unemployment
- Physical or mental disability
- Parents needing medical or financial assistance

If family is important to you and you're committed to helping your kids become successful, then let's take the stigma away from this scenario and see if we can apply some commonsense thinking, good communication skills, and limits to make it a winning situation for all who are involved. At the same time, we need to be watching for signs of dysfunction or abuse, where kids may be using parents and their parents' money to avoid having to be responsible.

The Agreement

If you didn't put limits on your kids when they were younger, you'll definitely need to set some if they move home. Consider these questions:

- How much rent will they pay? We set a dollar figure and combine it with a certain number of hours of household help each week.
- How much will they contribute to food costs?
- Will they need to cook a meal or two each week?
- What chores will they do?
- Will they pay other household expenses?
- Will you require them to prepare a budget and live on it?
- How long can they stay and what is the exit plan if things don't work out?
- What rules will you set about music, alcohol, movies, and friends (critically important if you have younger children in the home)?
- If your children are unemployed, will you require them to show progress in job hunting?
- If they've been through a divorce, disability, or other traumatic life situation, will you require them to get counseling or coaching to help them recover?

It's important to think through these issues and communicate them in writing. You may need to get input from a third party to help create a fair agreement. Without clear communication, adult children could easily slip back into their adolescent role and let you take care of them. If you still have younger children at home, it's even more important that your adult child sets a good example and supports your house rules. Figures 19.1 and 19.2 are sample rental contracts; names, amounts, and terms can be customized to your situation.

RENT AGREEMENT

As of this date ____ / _____ / ____ , I _____ , agree to pay
                          Date   Renting Child

the sum of $300.00 the first of every month for rent and food expenses. Rent will also

include 16 hours of miscellaneous chores and other house-related projects a month.

Chores will be communicated each week at a family staff meeting.

Rent amount will be in effect for one year and reevaluated each year in January.

_____   _____
      Parent 1   Parent 2

_____
  Renting Child

Figure 19.1 Sample rental agreement 1.

Jack's Rental Agreement

This agreement is in effect from June 15 through December 15, when Jack should have saved enough money for first and last month's rent and a security deposit so he can lease an apartment.

Rent:
Starting with his second paycheck, Jack will pay $400 a month for rent and food.

Utilities:
Beginning with his second paycheck, Jack will also pay $75 for water, gas, electric, Internet, and cable.

Cooking, laundry, and chores:
Jack will be responsible for mowing the lawn on Saturdays and cooking dinner on Wednesdays. He is responsible for the purchase, laundering, and maintenance of his own clothing and any personal items.

Guests and quiet hours:
No overnight guests are allowed without prior notification and agreement. Household quiet hours run from midnight to 6:00 a.m., unless otherwise arranged.

We love you and are glad that we can be a part of helping you get back on your feet financially.

_____	_____
Name	Date
_____	_____
Name	Date

Figure 19.2 Sample rental agreement 2.

Other Bailouts

Rehab

If your adult child has an addictive behavior that has destroyed his life, get professional guidance before becoming involved. If a rehab facility is needed for dealing with addictions—drug, alcohol, pornography, video gaming, eating disorders, or mental illness—and your young adult is willing to truly change, research insurance, state medical aid, welfare, and other options in addition to whatever you can afford. You've got to know your limits. Going into debt or losing your home to help your child won't benefit anyone.

Weddings

Most girls, from their youth, can envision their wedding day, but very few can accurately imagine the cost. As we mentioned in Chapter 17, a wedding is not the time for a bailout or to incur debt, but it is a time for clearly communicated financial limits from loving parents.

Divorce

It takes two to tango, so don't be quick to bail out your child. Recommend counseling and pay for some, if the couple is willing. If your child is involved in a physically or mentally abusive relationship, help him or her have the courage to get out. Research legal assistance if your child needs it, and decide how much you can afford to contribute. You may need to assist in getting an order of protection. We know one woman who had to hide for months from her abusive husband, moving from friend to friend's house until she was finally safe.

Parents need to be extremely careful that they're not bailing out a selfish or dysfunctional child. Let your children bear as much of the cost and work as possible. Emotionally they may be capable of very little, so use your best judgment.

Home

If your child is on the verge of having a home repossessed, don't invest, but do support. Help him set up a budget, plan for the future, get legal counsel, and possibly move. Throwing money at the problem simply won't solve it.

Unemployment

If your child becomes unemployed due to illness, disability, or a downturn in your local economy, help her get services like food stamps and unemployment compensation. You could also aid her in researching new jobs and getting resources from food banks or welfare. Once again, don't do all of the work; young adults need to participate in their own recovery.

Bankruptcy

We don't like the idea of bankruptcy. Anyone who borrows money should abide by their contract, unless the creditor frees them. If your adult child is considering bankruptcy, be very careful about being involved.

If he believes that the bankruptcy is not his fault, and that others caused most of his problems, stay away. So often we've seen the unwillingness to take personal responsibility for bad decisions simply continue until people hit bottom and realize they need real help.

On the other hand, if your child can articulate his mistakes, wants to avoid bankruptcy, but is pushed into it by a creditor, help him get good legal representation and counseling. Pay what you can afford, let him move in with you, but still set limits.

The road of life will contain some financial speed bumps even for MoneySmart families. Responding to our adult child's requests for help with wisdom, grace, and limits will minimize the damage to everyone involved and speed along the recovery in the $50,000 stage.

If you have more ideas about how to deal with adult children in financial need, post your ideas on our website at AmericasCheapestFamily.com /AdultKids.

CHAPTER 20

MoneySmart Grandparents

We've heard many grandparents quip, "If I'd known grandchildren would be so much fun, I'd have had them first!" There is no doubt that after raising your own kids, having young, active, funny, and cuddly children around again can be energizing. But don't forget that you can affect them also. No matter what your physical or financial circumstances, we're hoping that you'll be able to fill that unique role of influence and encouragement in your grandchild's life, as only grandparents can.

Both of us have fond memories of life with our grandparents.

Nanny wanted to help Annette stop biting her nails, so every time Annette would visit, Nanny would give her a dollar to stop the bad habit. It didn't work right away, but Nanny persisted, and five dollars later, the habit was broken. Steve's *yiayia* (Greek for grandmother) would cook him a special breakfast of egg in the hole (a piece of bread with a circle cut out, with a fried egg in the hole) when he slept over and always carried M&M's in her purse to share.

Then there was a time when Annette's grandparents actually moved in with the family while recovering from a medical issue. It was a tight fit, but the memories of spending time playing pool, cards, and board games with her grandparents still brings a smile to Annette's face.

If your adult children are struggling maritally or financially, there are many things you can do, besides a financial bailout, that will be particularly beneficial to your grandchildren and the family as a whole.

As a grandparent, you may have entered this stage of life with great financial resources or with little. If you have been blessed, be careful that you don't indulge your grandchildren with money and things, and handicap them for life. If your financial means are smaller, your time and presence will be the greatest gift you can give—and that is no small thing.

Be Generous but Wise

We've known Nana Jill (not her real name) for twenty years. Her husband died many years ago, leaving her alone but financially sound. She has three children, eleven grandchildren, and many great-grandchildren. All of her children are doing fine financially, but some of the grandchildren are struggling.

Her grandson Nick is thirty-three years old, twice divorced, and the father of two children from his last marriage. He hasn't held a job for more than six months at a time, but he does know how to work a video gaming system. Nana Jill has given financial gifts to many of her grandchildren to help pay for some of their college expenses. Nick approached her to ask if she would pay the $10,000 tuition for a tech school where he could earn five different medical tech certifications in a one-year program. Afterward he would be able to get a great job.

Being a kindhearted woman, Nana Jill gave Nick the money. She was well aware that he had failed at a university, but she hoped that this opportunity would help to turn his life around. The full tuition was paid, but Nick completed only one of the five certifications before the one-year deadline had passed.

Nana Jill didn't compromise her financial situation by trying to help, but she did take a gamble and basically wasted $10,000. The saddest part is that, seemingly, Nick learned nothing from this experience.

We share this story to remind you that giving money isn't always the best or only way to help your grandchildren. In this chapter we want to jump-start your thinking with ways you can help to grow MoneySmart grandkids.

Emotional Encouragement

As grandparents, you can love your grandkids by providing stability if their household is going through adjustment periods due to the addition of a child, separation, divorce, moving, or life's other "hiccups." You can have a profound influence in your grandchildren's life and help their parents by being available for your grandchildren.

- Shuttle kids to school or lessons once each week.
- Share your cooking and baking knowledge with your kids and grandkids.
- If your child is choosing to discipline, educate, or train your grandchildren differently than you did, we know it's hard, but you've got to bite your tongue. Simply love your grandkids every practical way you can.
- Plan special times or outings with your grandkids when they have the day off of school. Consider doing crafts, sewing, or building something together.
- Record audio or video conversations with your grandkids.
- Communicate with them through Facebook or Skype if you live far away. If your budget allows, visit twice each year, even if you must stay in a hotel.
- Support your grandkids by attending their special events: concerts, games, and graduations, etc.

Financial Encouragement

Here are several ways to assist your grandkids with your financial resources. Clearly define your involvement with time and financial limits, like "We'll fund Jack's piano lessons for $100 per month for two years."

Pay for Activities
- Music lessons: instrument or vocal
- Swim lessons
- Sports club team fees

- Club fees: Scouts, 4-H, or other groups
- School activity fees: band, chorus, sports, or others

Tuition

If you have the resources, fund some or all of their tuition for private grade school or high school.

College

If you have money set aside for education, plan carefully how you will distribute it. Set guidelines for earning a "grandparent scholarship," with a minimum GPA (for example 3.25 or better) each year and a requirement to work a part-time job each week for ten hours. If your guidelines are maintained, the scholarship can be renewed each year. Most college scholarships have academic performance requirements; why shouldn't you? Assisting young adults while encouraging responsible study habits and good behavior is smart. Please don't provide your grandchildren with the full amount for their college education all at once. Their life experience and maturity will most likely be inadequate to properly manage it. If you plan carefully, communicate fully, and become involved with your grandchildren, your relationship will blossom and their performance will soar.

Money Management

Teach your grandchildren money management skills by funding the MoneySmart Kids system we've described. If your child is a single parent, this may be the only way for your grandchildren to learn financial management.

Vacations

Fund part or all of a memorable vacation together. Some of our kids' fondest memories have been of when Annette's parents have taken our kids on special trips together or the entire family on vacation for a week (we shared expenses).

Child Care / Babysitting

If your grandchildren are in day care, consider providing one day of child care each week. Your involvement would save the family money and provide you with some terrific bonding time.

Inheritance

When preparing your will or estate plan, keep the financial maturity of your children and grandchildren in mind. Carefully craft your generosity; large lump sums of money or regular trust fund distributions at too young of an age can be a disincentive to productive work. Ask your estate planner about a Family Incentive Trust, where you can set predetermined benchmarks that an heir must achieve before receiving various sums of money. Beyond working with a wise estate-planning attorney, reading the book *Beyond the Grave: The Right Way and the Wrong Way of Leaving Money to Your Children (and Others)* by Gerald and Jeffrey Condon will provide you with lots of excellent examples.

Your role as an encourager to your MoneySmart grandkids is powerful. You can profoundly impact their lives and leave a legacy for generations to come. Remember that the greatest influence is not usually wielded by giving money—it's time, and lots of it.

Because we haven't yet fully experienced this season of life, we'd love to have you post your best MoneySmart grandparents suggestions at AmericasCheapestFamily.com/Grandparents.

CHAPTER 21

The Complete MoneySmart Family

This book has taken us a lifetime to write, and we know we've covered a lot of ground with you. It's easy to feel overwhelmed when so much information is presented, so evaluate where you are right now with your money, your kids, and your lifestyle, and choose one thing to work on at a time: one habit or skill for your kids to work on, one attitude or discipline for you to institute and master in your family.

We've failed, miserably at times, but one thing we haven't done, as much as we've felt like it, is give up. We're stubborn, strong-willed, and the word *quit* simply isn't in our vocabulary. We're slogging through the path of parenthood eagerly searching for ways to do it better. We're constantly looking for tools that will educate and equip us so we, in turn, can train our kids to face the world poised, confident, and prepared.

Diamonds in the Rough

We've had our struggles and dark days, just like you have. Some of our struggles are self-inflicted and the result of bad choices, others come from our past, and still others come from external forces. Regardless of where life's difficulties come from, we're committed to overcoming each and every one, learning the lesson, and putting the "jewel" of a strengthened character on the mantel of our hearts.

One of the most profound and far-reaching good choices we made had to do with children.

Many years ago we made a decision to become foster parents, caring for several foster children along with our two biological kids. The opportunity came along to adopt two little boys (brothers) into our family at a time when Annette was six months pregnant with Abbey. Adding three kids to our family in three months brought with it a myriad of changes and stress.

The boys' birth mother was eighteen years old at the time; her firstborn, Roy, was four years old and her baby, Joe, was twenty-one months. This birth mom had grown up as a foster child, was single, mentally ill, and unprepared to deal with two active sons. The neglect and emotional abuse these little guys experienced deeply impacted their young lives.

At the time we adopted, we didn't know the full extent of the issues we'd be dealing with. These boys faced some enormous developmental and emotional challenges. In the midst of working to stabilize them, we found our lives being turned upside down for several years. We had moments of calm, but there were always issues to deal with, therapists to see, and research to be done. Our marriage was tested to its limits as we came face-to-face with many issues from our own childhoods. We sought answers and healing for every member of our family, and we were totally blessed to have many friends come to our aid.

It was while we were searching for solutions for our kids and ourselves that we developed the final version of our MoneySmart Kids system. It quickly became a stabilizing factor in our family. It provided a tool to give positive reinforcement for habits we wanted the kids to learn and a consistent activity in which everyone could participate. But most importantly, it trained our kids to start thinking, acting, and behaving more maturely and independently.

As we look back at what we experienced, we are amazed that we survived. It was the most stress-filled time in our lives, but at the same time, so rich in memories that we wouldn't trade it for anything. As a result of walking through this crucible, we truly discovered a diamond of incalculable worth.

Every family is going to have struggles, and we're encouraging you that if we can make it through, so can you. Never stop believing that there are answers; never stop believing that there is hope.

Get a Grip on Parenting

There is a tendency in today's culture to be your child's best friend rather than a parent. None of the principles we've shared in this book will work unless someone takes the lead and draws a line in the sand, saying, "This far and no farther." You are the parent, and you need to have a firm grip on the spigot that controls the cash flow between you and your children. Over the course of their childhood, your job is to slowly, steadily, and purposefully diminish the flow by closing your spigot and helping them use their own. It may be hard, especially if you start at an older stage, but truly it is the best thing for you and your child.

The Cost of a MoneySmart Kid

In Chapter 1 we cited how the experts at the USDA expect it to cost $261,000 to raise a child from birth to seventeen years old. Throughout this book we've shared how we raised our five kids, teaching them to work, learn, play, and live as normally as possible. We ran our own calculations to see how accurate the USDA numbers were, compared to what it cost us to raise our kids. We created a spreadsheet based on our current expenses in the categories of Food, Clothes, Utilities, Transportation (car purchases, gas, and maintenance), Gifts, Medical Insurance and Care (including emergency room visits and wisdom teeth extraction), and Housing, and added in the cost of "paying" our kids through our payday system.

The total to raise a MoneySmart kid to the age of seventeen in our household was $103,798. We spent 60 percent less than what the USDA estimated. But then we realized that our calculations included the cost difference between our first smaller home, where we could have continued to live if we didn't have more than two kids, and the larger home we now own. Our home is an appreciating asset, which we can sell and use some of its value for our retirement, so it's unfair to charge one-seventh of it to the cost of raising our kids. With that price tag removed, the real out-of-pocket cost to raise one MoneySmart kid from birth to age seventeen is $58,084—77 percent less than the experts predict.

The truth is we don't have to spend a lot of money to raise kids who turn out right, but we do need to invest lots of time. And once they're grown and living on their own, it's time that you'll never regret investing.

Invest in Family

We've chosen to pour our lives into our kids to equip them for their futures. We've decided that a bigger house, fancier cars, designer clothes, and exotic vacations aren't as important as the relationship we've cultivated with our kids. We're already experiencing the incredible joys of seeing them succeed as they practice the principles they've learned from their youth. There is nothing more rewarding!

As a parent, you're going to invest your time and your money somewhere. Jobs will come and go, investments will rise and fall, but an investment in your family will always bring a positive return. And the deeper and more wholeheartedly you invest, the greater your return.

Whatever age your kids are, start today to combat effects of the 5/50/500 rule. The discipline it takes on your part will produce great results in the life of your family. Choose to invest in your family, not to enable them, but to empower them to walk wisely, to stand firmly, and to live freely as MoneySmart adults.

Join the MoneySmart Family revolution. It's a journey of a lifetime that starts one step, one attitude, one habit, one kid, and one dollar at a time.

Special Online Chapters for Mom and for Dad

We've written two additional chapters that we simply didn't have room for in this book. They are "To the Mom" and "To the Dad," and they're our personal note to you about staying the course as parents and being the best that you can be. You can read them at AmericasCheapestFamily.com/Mom and AmericasCheapestFamily.com/Dad.

Be sure to leave your comments on our website about things you've done to become the best parent you could.

More Ideas for Your Family

We've been collecting stories of how other MoneySmart families have raised MoneySmart kids. If you'd like to read what they're doing, visit our website: AmericasCheapestFamily.com/kids-money.

Acknowledgments

This book has taken a lifetime to write. But it is not the work of only Steve, Annette, and our kids, but of many others who have helped us produce a practical and extremely beneficial resource for raising MoneySmart kids.

To our AmericasCheapestFamily.com family and our Facebook Fans—thank you for buying our books and recommending them to your friends. You inspire us with your frugal tips and success stories.

To Steve Laube—thank you for being our literary agent and believing that every family with kids would want a resource on how to train them to handle their own money.

To the Thomas Nelson staff—thank you for enthusiastically embracing our message of urging kids to be financially responsible and working diligently to produce an awesome book.

To Win Holden—thank you for being such a trusted friend! You're always there for us with sage and practical advice!

To Lyn—our office simply wouldn't run without your part-time help. Thanks for doing whatever is needed at the moment. You're a gem!

To our advisory board and prayer team—we shudder to think of where we'd be without your support, encouragement, and advice.

To our media friends in TV, newspapers, magazines, radio, and online—thank you for allowing us to share our life and message with your audiences.

To all the bookstores that carry our books, whether you are a brick-and-mortar store or an online store—thank you for making our message available to millions. We're grateful!

Index

Other books by Steve and Annette Economides

America's Cheapest Family Gets You Right on the Money
Cut Your Grocery Bill in Half with America's Cheapest Family

Resources available at
www.AmericasCheapestFamily.com

The MoneySmart Kids Financial Training Kit
Teaching Kids about Money Isn't Kids' Stuff—Audio Seminar
Managing Household Finances—Audio Seminar
Stretching Your Grocery Dollars—Audio Seminar

and hundreds of money-, time-, and sanity-saving tips and videos

For information on having Steve and Annette speak at your business, school, library, civic group, or church

Go to www.americascheapestfamily.com/steve-annette-speaking
Or e-mail Speaking@AmericasCheapestFamily.com

Or write to:
Steve and Annette Economides
PO Box 12603
Scottsdale, AZ 85267